W9-CZY-937

19.892

By Richard Bolling
HOUSE OUT OF ORDER
POWER IN THE HOUSE

SBN: 399-50313-7
Library of Congress Catalog Card Number: 68-25779

Printed in the United States of America

Grateful acknowledgment is made for permission to quote
from the following copyright material:

CLAUDE KITCHIN AND THE WILSON WAR POLICIES, by Alex
Matthew Arnett, published by Little, Brown and Company,
1937.

THE COMING OF THE NEW DEAL, by Arthur M. Schlesinger,
Jr., published by Houghton Mifflin Company, 1959.

CONGRESSIONAL CONSERVATISM AND THE NEW DEAL, by
James Patterson, published by the University of Kentucky
Press, 1967.

CONGRESSIONAL GOVERNMENT, by Woodrow Wilson,
published by Houghton Mifflin Company, 1885.

DIARY OF JOHN QUINCY ADAMS, by Allan Nevins, published
by Longmans, Green and Company, Inc., 1928.

FIRSTHAND REPORT: THE STORY OF THE EISENHOWER
ADMINISTRATION, by Sherman Adams, published by Harper &
Brothers, 1961.

GEORGE W. NORRIS: THE MAKING OF A PROGRESSIVE 1861–1912,
by Richard Lowitt, published by the Syracuse University
Press, 1963.

THE HISTORY OF LEGISLATIVE METHODS IN THE PERIOD BEFORE
1825, by Ralph V. Harlow, published by Yale University
Press, 1917.

POWER IN
THE HOUSE

---

*A History of the Leadership
of the House of Representatives*

by RICHARD BOLLING

Capricorn Books: New York

Acknowledgments

It is impossible to acknowledge my debt to the hundreds of people who had some role in the intellectual and political experiences of which this book is a product. Seven persons, however, played a direct role in the writing. To each of them my gratitude is deep. My Washington staff, in addition to their regular duties, typed draft after draft. There would be no book without the heroic efforts of Gladyce Sumida, Judy Campbell, and Dolores Anderson. To Judy fell the bulk of the actual manuscript work, but that meant that the others were doing double duty on the hundreds of tasks that fill a Congressional office each day.

Our friend, Julie Nisonger, who is a talented printmaker, proved to be an extraordinarily perceptive and thorough researcher as we dug for the historical material for the first three parts of the book.

Another friend of long standing, Wes Barthelmes, who was a previous collaborator in *House Out of Order*, did the late evening writing, in contrast to my early morning habits. It is hard to say which words are his and which mine. Once again, there would be no book without Wes.

My wife, Jim Grant, played many roles in the creation of the book, but most important was her seemingly unlimited knowledge of American political and Congressional history and of current events. Her discoveries, evaluations, and interpretations of facts have been invaluable.

Another enormous debt is to my editor, Peggy Brooks. I am certain that after the agony of *House Out of Order*, I would not have braved another effort had it not been for her. I confess I do not know exactly how she did it, but, in a most unobtrusive way, she gave both the necessary personal encouragement and professional advice to make a book possible.

Of course, the opinions, the judgments, the criticisms, the proposed reforms, and all the flaws are mine. I did my writing during those quiet hours which end in full daylight. As my friend, Paul Douglas, the former United States Senator from Illinois, once said of himself, I am blessed with insomnia, and my daily stint would start at any time from two to five A.M. This time I enjoyed it.

Contents

Introduction

This book is the result of my deep conviction that, despite evidence to the contrary, the people of the United States can solve the problems that face them today. The unrest and dismay caused by the civil rights revolution and its white backlash, the rise in crime and violence, serious economic difficulties at home and abroad, the tragedy of the war in Southeast Asia, the shocking revelations of subversion of our own political processes in the Watergate affair, and other events great and small have combined to convince many that the experiment of democracy in America has failed.

It is true that American society has failed to anticipate and to solve some of its major problems. The United States Government has appeared to be unworkable. This failure is, of course, the failure of the society as a whole; the failure of a preoccupied, self-satisfied people, the failure of the elite leadership of the large groups that exercise organized influence—the business, labor, agricultural, education, and information communities. Above all, it is a failure of political leadership. Here I will concentrate on a particular part of that political leadership.

After twenty-five years in the United States Congress, it is my conviction, a heresy in my trade, that with the glaring exception of the outrage of Watergate the primary failures of political leadership at the Federal level are found in the United States

Congress. Such failures occur more often in the House of Representatives, where I serve, than in the United States Senate, with the exception of the one critical field of civil rights. The reason for this, I am convinced, is because the House of Representatives for the past thirty years has failed to organize itself so that it can exercise its share of the political leadership in the effective and responsible manner the American people expect of their Federal Government. What has been needed over these thirty years is a drastic change in the House power structure and major reforms of the House as an institution.

In part, on the basis of the response to my earlier book, *House Out of Order,* which is extremely critical of the current House of Representatives and urges major institutional reforms, I find that the real reason that major reform of the House is not insisted on by the American people and a majority of the members of the House itself, is sheer lack of knowledge of the history of the House of Representatives.

Most members, the public generally, and even sophisticated observers consider the House a static, unchanging institution, which occasionally tinkers with its organization but has basically never changed much since the first Speaker, Frederick A. C. Muhlenberg of Pennsylvania, gaveled it to order in 1789. Quite the opposite is true. The present methods of organizing the House are relatively new and even these have been significantly modified in the past decade. Awareness of these facts must lead, I believe, to the insistence on the part of the American people and the desire of the House members to make any further reforms that are essential to restore the House to its once great role in the Government of the United States.

In the chapters which follow I will prove how different the chaotic and ineffective House, in which John McCormack of Massachusetts long held the title of Speaker, was from the House of 1890, brilliantly reformed and led by Speaker Thomas Brackett Reed of Maine. We will see how, in the Wilson Presidency, Speaker Champ Clark of Missouri and Majority Leader Oscar Underwood of Alabama devised new methods to organize and to exercise the power of the House to replace the tyrannical one-man rule of Speaker Joseph G. Cannon of Illinois.

This history will prove that reform of the House today is as possible as it is necessary. Finally, based on these lessons from the past and my own knowledge of the present, I will detail reforms of the House which are both urgently necessary and possible to achieve in the new Congress which meets in January, 1975.

For twenty-five years I have been observer, student, and participant in nearly all of the great legislative battles that occurred in the House. Those parts of this book dealing with events prior to that date are based on the usual methods of research. My experience has led me to hold strong opinions on a number of subjects and it is only fair that at this point my biases on these subjects be made explicit.

WHAT IS A CONGRESSMAN'S JOB?

No two members of the 435-member United States House of Representatives perform their jobs in exactly the same fashion. Each of us has a different piece of the geography of the United States to represent, and naturally represents a different group of people. The House, of course, is only one-half of the Congress; the other being the Senate, referred to by some as the Upper Body since the Senate sat in a room one floor above the House in the same building when the First Congress was convened. Members of the Senate represent states, whereas members of the House represent Congressional districts within states. The system was devised as a compromise to satisfy both the small population states, which wanted representation by states, and the large population states, which preferred representation based on population. This compromise was a key to the adoption of our Constitution.

For many years the number of members of the House grew along with the country's population, but since 1913 the number has been 435.* Because there are fewer Senators, 100, and because

* The number was temporarily and briefly raised to 437 during the transition of Alaska and Hawaii to statehood. After the 1960 census, under the

they receive more coverage by the press and other media, it is usually considered more important and a greater honor to be a Senator than a member of the House. Members of both bodies receive the same salaries, however. The true equality between the two bodies is proved by the very simple fact that, to become law, a bill must be passed in identical form in both the House and the Senate. Today, an average member of the House represents more than 450,000 people. Thus, he can be in closer touch with his constituency than any Senator, except those few whose states, Alaska, Wyoming, and Vermont, have smaller populations than that figure.

All members of the House have at least three jobs. First, we represent each of our individual constituents, particularly in reference to any problem they may have with any agency of the Federal Government. In this capacity, we are often described as mere errand boys, but the errands can be very important to our constituents. We supply information and see to it that they get a reasonably prompt, carefully considered, and an equitable decision on any problem, for example: the Social Security Administration, the Veterans Administration, or the Internal Revenue Service. Second, we represent all the people in that unique piece of geography, our district. The collective problems of each district differ very much one from another. For an obvious example, one need only think of the problems confronting a man representing a geographically enormous, thinly populated district in a largely rural area, as opposed to those faced by the representative of one of the geographically small, overcrowded districts in an urban ghetto. In addition, the people of one Congressional district differ from the people of another in their politics, religion, occupations, and political views. Third and most important, a member of the House is not only a Representative in Congress from a specific district in a specific state, he is also a United States Congressman. As such, he must help decide the great issues confronting the whole country, whether or not they seem to affect directly his

provisions of current law, the size of the House was returned to 435 and that number apportioned among the 50 states.

particular district and his particular group of the country's population.

Some of those inside and outside the House find a conflict between these various jobs. Many political scientists and a few
members of the House believe that constituent service should be
turned over to a specialist separate from both the executive and
legislative branches but empowered to see to it that wrongs are
righted and equity achieved. Their argument is that constituent
service takes too much of the time of the individual member that
would be better spent on legislative matters. I doubt seriously if
members of Congress will ever give up constituent service. It can
be onerous. Some members devote nearly all their personal energies
to such matters and little or none of their time to legislation beyond answering roll calls. Constituent service can help a member
be reelected, and that is the main reason it will not be handed over
to someone else. There is another reason against shifting this particular job. With it, the constituent has a reasonably direct contact with an elected official who must pay attention to the constituent's problem for no better reason than that he must seek his
vote in the near future. Because a civil servant is more insulated,
more protected, he can be less responsive to the individual than an
elected official. Finally, a member can organize his office, his staff,
and his own time in such a way that, while still seeing that his constituents receive first-class service, he devotes the great majority
of his time to legislation and the legislative process.

Another problem, which is more acute for some members than
for others, is the conflict between the comparatively provincial
interests of a single Congressional district, as opposed to the broad,
national interests of the United States as a whole. Of course, there
is no way of eliminating this conflict. It is built into the system.
The individual member is free to make decisions as to how he
will use his time and whether he will place district or national interest first. Of course, most members are sharply aware that they
are elected for only a two-year term. The two-year term, however, is essential to preserve the people's right to change the
Federal Government frequently. Only the election of every mem-

ber of the House every two years can assure that. The President is elected for four years, the Senate for six years. It is the two-year term of all House members that gives our particular form of representative government the essential capacity for reasonably quick change that plays a key role in a minority's willingness to accept a narrow defeat peacefully.

DEMOCRATS AND REPUBLICANS

To understand the House of Representatives and what it really is, as opposed to what it appears to be, one must understand the difference between the national Democratic party and the national Republican party. In addition, one must know the various kinds of Democrats in the House and also the several kinds of Republicans. For obvious reasons, I will give more time to clarifying differences among Democratic members of the House because the reforms I propose largely depend on action within the Democratic caucus.

Since the early 1930s, the national Democratic party has been less fearful of the intervention of the Federal Government in health, education, welfare, labor, and business matters than has the Republican party. With virtually no exceptions, such interventions are proposed by the Democratic party only after the state, county, or city that previously has had the responsibility has failed or been unable to continue to meet that responsibility. The national Republican party has been consistently less quick and less willing first to acknowledge the other government level's failure to meet the need and second to support Federal intervention in helping to meet the need. Since World War II, the overwhelming majority of Republicans in the House of Representatives has been more conservative than their Presidential nominees in their approach to Federal intervention. Also, nationally, the Democratic party has been less afraid than the Republican party of spending money on Federal domestic programs, and levying taxes to obtain the money to spend on them. The Democratic party has been more internationalist than the Republican party. Since Senator Arthur Vandenburg led the way to a major policy change in his party both nationally and in the Congress, however, foreign policy with regard to collective security has been largely bi-partisan, if never truly nonpartisan.

I have purposely put the fundamental domestic differences between the two parties in relatively unemotional terms. Others would prefer definitions, with which I do not entirely disagree, which describe the differences in terms of contrasting degrees of awareness of the plight of the poor, the uneducated, the unwell, the young, the old, the minorities, indeed all those in our society who are in some way disadvantaged. My reason for choosing the definitions I have used is that motives and verbal claims are less meaningful and much harder to analyze than acts. Fortunately for the democratic process, even the most skilled demagogue in American politics, if elected to office, must at some point in his career act rather than merely promise or say he will act. In the first session of the Ninetieth Congress (1967), for example, there were more than 400 roll calls in the House of Representatives. Many of these were quorum calls merely to show whether a member was present or absent when that particular roll call took place. Many others, although technically votes on motions and bills, were equally insignificant, either because the issue was relatively unimportant, or so noncontroversial that the vote was unanimous, or so near to unanimous that it demonstrated nothing. But in that session, as in every other, there were at least ten votes which constituted acts by members for or against more Federal intervention, for or against the expenditure of more of the taxpayer's money for such purposes.

On domestic issues, a substantial majority of the Democrats in the House usually support their national party's position. These national-party "program" Democrats, as I will call them, include members from every section of the country, including the South. This group includes not only some Southerners but also the moderates, the liberals, and those who pride themselves on being just plain Democrats.

The size of this group varies because the marginal districts in the North, the East, and the West are usually represented by program Democrats, when the Democrats carry such districts in a Democratic election year. In recent years, the number of program Democrats from the South has shrunk. The reasons for this are many, but many Southern program Democrats have been defeated by the civil rights issue—not because they were for civil rights legislation (very few were), but because they were not as strongly against it as their political opponents. Nevertheless, unless the Democrats in the House were reduced in number to fewer than 200, a majority of them would generally support the national party position on the great domestic issues.

There are always a substantial number of Southern Democrats in the House, however, and a few others from outside who wear the party label but usually oppose the position of their national party and the majority of their party in the House. They are, in effect, Republicans with a Southern accent—the conservative Democrats. It is this group which has received extraordinary benefits and advantages from the House seniority system rigidly adhered to by the Democrats until January, 1965. Although their number changes from one issue to another (just as the number of program Democrats supporting proposals made by a Democratic President changes), there have been at least sixty such conservative Democrats voting against their own party on any of the major issues brought before Congress since World War II.

The Republicans in the House are divided too, but on most issues sought and found a remarkable degree of unity under the leadership of Gerald Ford of Michigan (who went on to become Vice-President) and his various lieutenants who came to power in January, 1965. These men deserve much of the credit for the gains their party made in the 1966 elections and for the remarkable stability of their members since then. The variations in party division in the House since the 1966 election have been slight in the last four Congresses with the Ninetieth (1967–1968), the Ninety-first (1969–1970) and the Ninety-third (1973–1974) being nearly identical at about 245 Democrats to 195 Republicans in each case. The Ninety-second (1971–1972) varied only to the extent of 254 Democrats to 181 Republicans. But it is still correct to say that the number of Republicans who often vote against their House leadership on key issues is very small, approximately ten. The rest of the Republicans usually support their House leadership, although as individuals they may have supported anybody from Governor Rockefeller to Governor Reagan for the Presidential nomination in 1968.

POLITICAL LEADERSHIP

Political leadership in a democracy is perhaps the most difficult of human endeavors—to be of high quality, it must combine in one individual or a small group of individuals many different, sometimes seemingly conflicting, qualities. For example, a truly effective political leader must have an ability to foresee problems that will arise in the future. To deal only with the obvious in the present is to be always behind events. Recognizing problems, however, is far from enough. Many of our current urban problems, infinitely complex as they are, have been recognized for years. The analysis which leads to recognition is only the first step. Subsequently, proposals for solutions must be found; their achievement planned; and a majority, both popular and governmental, mustered in support of the plan. Only then can the solutions be implemented.

Thus, the political leader must have a sense of history, awareness of the present, an anticipation of probable and possible future developments within his area of responsibility, and an ability to differentiate between critical and less important problems. He must have the will to face the consequences of decisions to act or not to act, the self-discipline to allocate his time in accordance with those decisions, an ability to keep in touch with public opinion without being fearful of it, and the skill to persuade not only opinion makers and other politicians but also large audiences in both auditorium and living room to go along with him. A political leader must be at home with the essential element of working democracy: compromise.

I find that the process of political compromise is little understood. To some who fancy themselves idealists or purists, compromise is a dirty word. That view demonstrates a real ignorance of how democracy works. Our country and its people are so diverse in every way, their political views so different, that there is bitter conflict over nearly every important new proposal for Federal action in any field of legislation, be it the use of public lands, income taxes, Social Security, highway building, education, health care, or rehabilitation of its poor. The role of the politician is not just to find out what needs to be done in the society but to achieve action by the society on those needs. Without accommodations of conflicting views—that is, compromise—there would never be action in our kind of society. Compromise is absolutely essential to the democratic process. Dictators govern by fiat rather than by marshalling a majority of free men in support of this or that program. Perhaps the most important implicit compromise in the American system is the one by which the results of hard-fought, bitter, and narrowly won elections are accepted by the losers. Richard Nixon lost to John F. Kennedy in 1960 by a tiny margin, but Nixon led no armed revolt. Regardless of whether or not he believed that he had lost by fair means or foul, he knew that the basic compromise to which this country has adhered since the Civil War required as cheerful an acceptance of the results as he could muster.

Compromise is the name of the game in the legislative process. Very few bills, hopefully introduced by sincere and wise authors, become laws and still retain more than 50 to 75 per cent of what their authors originally envisioned as necessary in the public interest. On the other hand, in the legislative process compromise can become tantamount to defeat. There is a point at which supporters of a particular bill must decide whether or not to compromise the bill into ineffectiveness in order to score a nominal victory or to refuse to do so and to suffer obvious defeat, only to return to the task of mustering the public and governmental majority necessary to pass meaningful legislation.

Thus, the political leader must constantly make difficult and fundamental judgments on what best serves his view of the society's needs. Clearly, he must be willing to accept less than 100 per cent, but, if he is convinced that 50 per cent will not solve the problem, he must have the courage to say so and to see his carefully nurtured legislative effort temporarily fail. Thus, the role of the political leader is vastly different from that of the philosopher, political theorist, or anyone who tries to analyze social problems and develop proposed solutions. All of these can and should be purists seeking the ideal solution. The political leader's role is to achieve as promptly as possible an *effective* solution.

In our Federal Government of shared powers but unified total responsibility, this process of achieving solutions to the society's problems is infinitely complicated. It is so complicated that all of the intricate events that lead first to national-problem analysis and finally to national-problem solving are never all known even to the most skilled of its practitioners, the insiders in the executive, legislative, and judicial branches. The millions of interactions among people that must take place before a new solution, a new piece of social legislation, such as Medicare, goes into effect are beyond calculation.

My own analysis of the failure in political leadership at the Federal level to adequately meet the problems of the present decade, would allocate some blame to each of the three branches of the Federal Government. The executive, while more guilty of the governmental failures of today than the judicial, seems to me clearly less culpable than the legislative. This is true in part because the executive branch has greater resources with which to undertake the required analysis and public education than the Congress has been willing to provide for itself. Even more important is the fact that the Federal bureaucracy, despite its inherent inertia, is significantly affected by the policies of *the Executive*, the President of the United States, who has a national constituency and whose failure to solve any major national problem in his Administration may alter drastically the place in history of which he is normally so conscious.

In recent years, the judicial branch of government has played a more constructive role than the legislative branch, as witnessed by the 1954 school civil rights decision and the "one man one vote" decisions of 1962 and 1964. And, as we will see, every Chief Executive in the past forty-two years, including President Eisenhower, in six of his eight years, has been ahead of the Congress in proposing solutions to many of the country's most important problems. Often it has been the Congress, and particularly the House, which has held back change and progress.

In the six years since this book was first published, the membership of the House has become increasingly conscious of the failure of its branch and the urgent need for its reorganization and reform. A number of significant steps have been taken, among which are the passage of the Legislative Reorganization Act of 1970 and the establishment, at the beginning of the Ninety-third Congress in early 1973, of the Select Committee on Committees, which under my Chairmanship is charged with the formidable task of proposing new and better ways to organize and to operate the committee structure of the House through which all legislation is processed.

I

1789-1910:
CZARS, TYRANTS,
AND A REVOLT

I

An Uneven Journey

One can read the history of the United States House of Representatives in the history of its Speakers. This assertion needs qualification, of course. Nevertheless, it expresses the heart of the matter. Strong Speakers have made their own rules—Henry Clay, for example, in the early 1800s; strong Speakers have beneficially changed the rules—Tom Reed, for example, in the late 1800s; strong Speakers have operated under strong rules—"Uncle Joe" Cannon, for example, in the early 1900s; strong Speakers have managed to operate under weak rules—Nick Longworth in the 1920s and Sam Rayburn in the 1940–1960 period, for example. On the other hand, weak Speakers have never productively operated for any appreciable length of time under either strong or weak rules—Warren Keifer in the early 1880s and John W. McCormack in the 1960s, for example.

A strong Speaker is crucial to the House. He is the indispensable man for its legislative and political health, education, and welfare. A Speaker and a football quarterback are kin: each is expected to make that big third-down play. Each should possess a habit of command. No quarterback could tolerate a situation in which he called a pass play but his lineman carried out blocking assignments for a running play. It is important that a Speaker not tolerate an analogous situation in the House.

The House is different from the United States Senate. The

difference can be heard and sensed. Just walk the corridors in the House and Senate office buildings; stand on the floor of the House and the Senate; sit in the public galleries overlooking the chamber of each body.

In the First Congress, convened in March, 1789, the membership ratio between the two branches was 5 to 2: 65 House members to 26 Senate members. In the Congress of today, the ratio is 4 to 1: 435 House members to 100 Senate members.

A Senator is more visible than a Representative. Reporters find the Senate more manageable, easier to cover. The Senate is better mannered and outwardly more genteel. The Senate has been a preferred route for those seeking the Presidency. Thus, the Senate has a function as a "place to pass through" for those who want to build a reputation on their journey toward the White House. Consequently, the Senate has suffered legislatively. Senate snobs to the contrary, House members have generally shown themselves far more knowledgeable than Senators about particular bills during those conferences with Senators to resolve differences between them. George Washington may have been among the first snobs. He envisioned the Senate as a "saucer" in which the hot tea of the House would be cooled. But, in modern times, it has been the "Cotton Ed" Smiths, the Bilbos, the Huey Longs, and the Joe McCarthys, all from the Senate, who have frightened the country.

The House, with its two-year term for members, is more unruly, more gamey, more susceptible to vagrant gusts of opinion, than the Senate with its six-year term, but when effective Speakers have governed, and have not just sat in the big padded Chair on the rostrum, the House has enjoyed as great or greater prestige. From time to time, the House, as the popular assembly, has fulfilled the expectations raised for it as the "depository of democratic principles" and the "grand inquest" of the nation. A few of its Speakers have been among the most powerful public men of their time, such as Henry Clay.

It requires talent to govern a large body of men and women, however. A great sense of organization is needed. The Senate permits the filibuster, open and aboveboard on the floor of the chamber, to impede, block, and delay legislation. Individual Senators have talked for as long as a day in this pursuit. Until 1841, the House also permitted filibustering by speech. Then a one-hour limitation was placed on the amount of time a member might speak on a subject. The House developed an alternative, however, its Rules Committee. The committee seldom made headlines; it operated quietly. Its actions were taken in executive session, sometimes very informally: a handshake here . . . a nod . . . a lack of audible dissent . . . a disapproving gesture . . . scanty records . . . no written rules of procedure . . . secret covenants secretly arrived at. Only a strong Speaker could control the Rules Committee. I know; I've been a member of Rules for the last fourteen years. The Rules Committee, through which most legislation must pass after it is reported favorably from a particular legislative committee and before it is brought to the floor of the House, has become in modern times too often the tail that wags the dog.

The current blighted condition of the House of Representatives is generally analogous to that which existed during the thirty-year period between the beginning of the Civil War and Tom Reed's first Speakership in 1889. George Galloway, a specialist on the Congress, described these three decades in his *History of the House of Representatives:*

It was a period characterized by intense resistances within Congress both to organizational change and to legislation of any sort. The minority became adept in the utilization of the rules to block the will of the majority and the end of the period found an extremely decentralized power within the House.

The majority party could and did have its pocket picked, not by some valiant, righteous minority of high conscience but simply by a few members, exercising obstructing tactics permitted by the cumbersome and outdated rules of procedure of the House. It was minority power of a negative sort. Newspapers, as they do today, complained. "Slowly Doing Nothing," *The Washington Post* said. "Legislative Lunacy," growled *The New*

York Herald. In the fall of 1889, Representative Henry Cabot Lodge of Massachusetts wrote: "the American House of Representatives today is a complete travesty upon representative government, upon popular government, and upon government by the majority."

It was not always thus. This winter of discontent had been preceded by periods when the House basked in the affection of its citizens. The First Congress, sixty-five members in the House and twenty-six in the Senate, enacted a prodigious amount of work. Sixty major pieces of legislation that shaped our Federal system were passed. The first legislative matter discussed in the House was the tariff. Ten amendments to the Constitution, the Bill of Rights, were next adopted by this First Congress. It also appropriated 639,000 dollars to run the new nation for a one-year period. The House performed in public, as opposed to the Senate, which held its legislative meetings privately until the second session of the Third Congress.

John Quincy Adams had just returned home to Braintree from his one-term Presidency when he was asked to run for the House. "No person could be degraded by serving the people as a Representative in Congress," Adams said. Adams was elected in 1830 and served in the House for eighteen years. He died in the House chamber. His diary, containing an entry dated shortly after his first election, states, "My election as President of the United States was not half so gratifying to my inmost soul. No election or appointment conferred upon me ever gave me so much pleasure."

At other times, too, in its 180-year history, the House has correspondingly risen in favor and fallen into disfavor. The House stood in first rank during the Speakerships of Clay and Reed in both procedural and legislative performance. During Cannon's tenure, it was procedurally efficient, although legislatively negative. During the 1911–1915 administration of Speaker Clark and Majority Leader Underwood, the House performed well in both respects. Conversely, the record of the House is spotty prior to the Civil War, as the crisis over the slavery issue grew, and it became more dismal, extraordinarily so at times, during the period between 1860 and the accession of Reed in 1889. In modern times, the institutionalization of the House—growth of customs and usages, thickening of precedents, and fragmentizing of power and responsibility—has impeded its performance, particularly in domestic affairs.

Written histories of the House are qualitatively uneven, incomplete, and even contradictory in respect to its early years. Some developments are untraceable. What follows is a gingerly effort to weave together facts derived both from basic source materials and published histories into a broad brush-stroke account of the evolution of the House of Representatives.

COMMITTEE SYSTEM

The committee system evolved from legislative needs. In the first session of the First Congress, there were no standing (permanent) committees, except for a seven-member Committee on (contested) Elections. At the outset, the procedure was first to discuss the main outlines of a public legislative subject in a "Committee of the Whole House on the State of the Union," a parliamentary device permitting more relaxed procedural rules in an effort to facilitate discussion. A Committee of the Whole on public bills today consists of any one hundred or more House members with the Speaker barred from presiding. Historically, this committee derives from procedures in the House of Commons and the colonial assembly.

In its "disguise" as a Committee of the Whole House, members often agreed to have a specific bill drafted as a result of their discussions. Then members would further agree to establish a select committee, an "impartial board," to do the drafting. This select committee was required to report back such a bill favorably or, important for purposes of leadership control, unfavorably. When it did, this select committee was dissolved. In other words, there was a select committee for each bill. Thus, in the Third Congress, sitting during 1793–1794, approximately 305 select committees were established. In this manner, the House controlled its component committees. There are also indications that the Committee of the Whole itself would sometimes draft specific bills. Congressional literature indicates that Secretary of the Treasury, Alexander Hamilton, the President's man, managed to have financial proposals referred to him for legislative drafting, a procedure hardly conforming to the theory of the "separation of powers" of the legislative, executive, and judicial branches of the national government. This state of affairs was relatively short-lived, however. Additional standing committees were established. Often, the creation of additional standing committees arose out of response to specific situations.

A Ways and Means Committee was established, apparently in angry reaction to Hamilton's bold and continuous interventions in fiscal and monetary legislation. Ways and Means was truly a "grand committee of the House," with substantive legislative jurisdiction over revenue measures, such as tariffs and taxes and, until 1865, over appropriations. Records further indicate, for example, that the Louisiana Territory purchase in 1803 led to the establishment of a Committee on Public Lands and the abolishment of slavery in 1865 to an Education and Labor Committee. The standing committees proliferated after 1816, for they carried out legislative business more efficiently, it was thought. This development coincided with Clay's Speakership. By 1820, there were at least sixteen standing committees; by Cannon's time, ninety years later, there were fifty-eight; and as many as forty-eight in 1946. The 1946 Legislative Reorganization Act reduced these to nineteen. There are now twenty-one, but standing and special subcommittees within these committees have proliferated. There were 141 such subcommittees when the Ninetieth Congress opened in January, 1967.

The growth of committees altered legislative pathways. The Committee of the Whole, as a prior sounding board for legislation, declined in influence. A practice developed of referring bills directly to standing committees each composed of a few members. By 1825, the standing committees had become the primary proving ground for legislation. By this time, Ralph Harlow, a Congressional historian, stated ". . . so far as its organization was concerned, the House of Representatives had assumed its present form." The committees, of course, never functioned as "impartial boards." They reflected political divisions. As the committee system evolved, an effort was made to fill committee seats so as to have all geographical sections of the country represented. Until the 1850s, members of the minority were occasionally given chairmanships. Beginning in 1860, standing committees perpetuated themselves from one Congress to another.

The evolution of the committee system has led to an observation that the Congress, particularly the House, is actually composed of "little legislatures" (committees) that jointly meet from time to time to ratify each other's decisions. Today, it is uncommon for the House to turn back or drastically alter a bill that comes to the floor from a legislative committee. Congress in committee, Woodrow Wilson said, is Congress at work.

LEGISLATIVE-EXECUTIVE RELATIONSHIP

The development of "little legislatures" complicated a President's ability to enact his legislative program. Jefferson, for example, was able to command support in the Congress better than later Presidents because the committee system had not taken root. After Jefferson, the Speaker selected members for committees without advice from a President. One Congressional historian reports that in 1827 the committee system had developed to the point where every committee in the Senate and House was staffed with either a majority or a Chairman opposed to President John Quincy Adams. Later Presidents have been obliged to work for majority support twice over, first within the standing committees when an Administration bill was under consideration, and again when the House met as a body to consider it. The eventual proliferation of subcommittees within the full standing committees added a further complication.

Rows between Jefferson and the Congress provided an early indication of future clashes between these two coordinate branches of the national Government. Each sought to eclipse the other. W. U. Hensel, a biographer of Grover Cleveland, has written:

From the beginning of the history of popular government to the present day, there has gone on ceaseless conflict between the Executive and those whose "advice and consent" was essential to effective administration. Indeed, it is not too much to say that the history of the phrase "advise and consent" is the history of the British Parliament from the Anglo-Saxon Witenagemot, or assembly of wise men, and the Norman Great Council of the Realm. Go back into English history as far as constitutional documents permit, and always, in every period, written in Latin, in French, or in English, appear the words "with the advice and consent."

Jefferson, whom the House had selected as President over Aaron Burr after thirty-six ballots, broadened the ambit of executive action as in the case of the Louisiana Purchase.

On the other hand, the Whig William Henry Harrison took an extremely inert view of his Presidential duties. At his inaugural address, Harrison said soothingly:

I cannot conceive that by a fair construction of any of the provisions (of the Constitution) would be found to constitute the President a part of the legislative power. It cannot be claimed from the power to recommend, since, although enjoined as a duty upon him, it is a privilege which he holds in common with every other citizen; and although there may be something more of confidence in the propriety of the measures recommended in the one case than in the other, in the obligation of ultimate decision there can be no difference. In the language of the Constitution, "all the legislative powers" which it grants "are vested in the Congress of the United States." It would be solecism in language to say that any portion of these is not included in the whole.

Harrison never had an extended opportunity to apply his views. He died a month later. The activist, Jefferson, however, as John Marshall had forecast, managed to "embody himself" within the House. Hamilton had broken ground for Jefferson in this respect. Hamilton, bridging the legislative and executive branches during the Washington Administration, functioned as a shadow floor leader. He and his fellow Federalists ruled the roost. They were frequently physically present on the Hill. "May as well return home what with Hamilton's running things," members grumbled. A Ways and Means Committee, with control over appropriations, tariffs, and taxes, was established toward the end of Washington's second term by Republicans in an effort to restore to the House a measure of autonomy in these legislative areas.

Jefferson continued this intervention during his two terms. House "legislative floor leaders" were the President's agents. In the Seventh Congress, William Giles of Virginia, a floor leader, was referred to as a "prime minister" at least once. Accounts imply there was no one member acting as legislative majority "floor leader" during a session. This seems to have been an interchangeable role depending on dominant personalities and the particular legislation that had priority. Often, the majority floor leader was also chairman of the Ways and Means Committee, because of its broad, substantive legislative jurisdiction. Rules of the House do not provide for such a position, however.

There seems to have been much disharmony. On one occasion, Jefferson sent a Presidential message requesting Congressional response on the belligerency status of European nations. It went to Ways and Means, whose chairman was John Randolph of Virginia, that "Terrible Tempered Mr. Bangs." For four weeks, Ways and Means was unresponsive. Military appropriation bills were delayed. Speaker Macon stepped in and removed the matter from the grasp of Randolph's committee.

Presidents and the Congress continued to fuss at each other. Between the Presidencies of John Adams and Woodrow Wilson, 112 years in all, no President addressed a joint session of the House and Senate. The situation erupted when the House impeached Andrew Johnson, President Lincoln's successor. Up until World War I, senior Senators and House members were angered if the executive branch, without advance consultation, sent up a bill for introduction. Today, most major legislation is drafted within the executive branch. But strong Presidents have dreaded meeting with strong-willed, antagonistic Senators and Representatives. Eisenhower apparently regarded the customary weekly meetings with Congressional leaders as akin to taking castor oil. As one "New Frontiersman" commented, the President and the Congress hold each other "in mutual suspect." The tension is sometimes creative, sometimes not.

LEADERSHIP, FACTIONS, PARTIES, AND THE CAUCUS

President Washington had warned against the establishment of "factions." Yet there are references to party labels during his second Administration. The United States Constitution bears no mention of political parties. In the First Congress, however, differences promptly and understandably arose regarding substantial and devisive issues, such as slavery, internal improvements, the tariff, and currency. Like-minded members soon formed into groups, and from these meetings developed political organizations with attendant tactics and strategies and struggles for leadership. First, there were the Federalists and then the Democrat Republicans, the product of Thomas Jefferson, the party builder. Behind the labels in the beginning were boarding-house factions and then more formal groupings. The initiative in legislation passed to these parties and further reduced the prominence of the Committee of the Whole. The presence of political parties was such in President Madison's Administration that, according to Herbert Agar, Madison of *The Federalist* papers "could write a constitution of divided powers but he could not administer one."

A like-minded group met—that is, it caucused—in order to secure general unanimity and develop harmonious legislative actions and goals. Beginning in 1800, the caucuses of the like-minded nominated their Presidential and Vice-Presidential candidates. By 1809, a member is complaining that "all great political questions are settled somewhere else than on this floor." In 1813, Daniel Webster wrote that ". . . at the proper time the farce of legislating will be exhibited. . . . Before anything is attempted to be done here, it must be arranged elsewhere."

Speaker Clay nurtured the party caucus as an apparatus of legislative leadership. He used it as a technique of discussion, agreement, and discipline. It faded after Clay and after 1832, when the first Presidential nominating conventions were held. Distemper over the perpetuation of slavery further weakened the device of the party caucus. Both Speakers Reed and Cannon, however, refer favorably to it as a party vehicle. The party caucus regained kingly stature on the eve of the 1910 Congressional revolution. In 1909, Democrats voted to endorse Republican insurgents in their efforts to curtail the parliamentary autocracy of Speaker Cannon. This caucus agreed that Democrats who accepted committee assignments made by Republican Cannon were to be punished, unless their leader, Champ Clark of Missouri, permitted their accepting such.

From that time to about 1921, House Democrats regularly used the caucus. Clark gave the impression that during this period each major bill was discussed in Democratic caucus. Since then, the House Democratic leadership has let its caucus atrophy. Republican Speaker Longworth, however, called caucuses of his party to discipline "Progressive Republicans" who had deserted Calvin Coolidge during the 1924 Presidential campaign. Today, the caucus, as Democrats use it, is devoted almost exclusively at the beginning of each new Congress to nominations of party leaders and other organizational work.

As a result, Dixie Democrats—"Republicans with Southern accents," as Hubert Humphrey called them—have been repeatedly reelected under a Democratic party label while voting against, and even campaigning against, their party's Presidential candidate. Then after reelection they vote regularly against their party's legislative program. Only twice in modern times has a Democratic caucus been asked to make substantive disciplinary decisions. In January, 1965, it stripped committee seniority from two Southern Democrats who had refused to support Lyndon Johnson, their party's nominee for President, the previous fall. In 1967, the party caucus separated the errant Adam Clayton Powell from his cherished Chairmanship of Education and Labor. Also, during 1967, the House Democratic leadership, upon demand of restive members, called two caucuses to discuss appropriation problems when Wilbur Mills of Arkansas, the Democratic Chairman of Ways and Means, refused to back the Administration's demand for a 10 per cent tax increase without substantial cuts in domestic spending. These caucuses were indecisive.

With the demise of the caucus, Democratic party leadership in the House was weakened. In 1937, simultaneously with the beginning of Franklin Roosevelt's second Presidential term, coalition governed. Conservative and reactionary Republicans teamed with conservative and reactionary Democrats with a base in the Rules Committee. There, the moderately liberal legislation of the three Democratic Administrations from 1936 to 1948 was mangled and sometimes strangled by the sentinels of the *status quo*. This dismal development undoubtedly is part of any analysis of why the ghettos of America exploded in the summer of 1967.

SENIORITY

The conservative coalition derived its strength from the fact that its members, unlike urban liberals of both parties, were entrenched in safe districts. The more times they were reelected, the greater their *seniority*. Ultimately, they survived long enough to rise to occupy power positions as chairmen of crucial committees and subcommittees.

The first reference to seniority in the House occurred in 1816, according to Joseph Cooper in an unpublished doctoral thesis at Harvard University. Few chairmen or committee members, he points out, in the Twelfth Congress, which sat from 1811 to 1813, held corresponding positions in the next Congress. Cooper states, however, that the reverse was the situation in the Seventeenth, Eighteenth, and Nineteenth Congresses (1821–1827). One hundred years later seniority had developed to the stage that prompted this description from Guy Hardy of Colorado, a five-term Republican:

> Seniority is a powerful influence in the United States Congress. The unwritten law of seniority of service is rarely set aside.
> The preferred office rooms in the House Office Building are assigned the Member of longest service. A Member's rank in

committee is according to seniority and his place at committee table is in order of length of service. The chairman of the committee, while selected by the committee on committees, is almost always the oldest member of his party on the committee.

Conferees who meet with the conferees of the Senate to iron out differences on bills where the two Houses have not agreed are usually the oldest members on the committee which has that particular bill in charge.

The committee on committees is made up for the most part of the Members who have served longest from their respective States. As a rule, Members have to serve some years before they are put on the Appropriations or Ways and Means Committees. The Rules Committee is made up of older Members—no majority member having served for less than 10 years. And the same may be said of the steering committee, there is no one on that committee who has served less than 10 years.

"Fifty-seven Members in all out of the total membership of 435 have served 16 years or more. The Speaker, both party leaders, and 15 chairmanships are held in this group. Those who have served five terms—10 years or more—number only 182. All the key positions, nearly all the chairmanships, almost every Member who is ever a conferee, a large majority of the Ways and Means and Appropriation Committees, all the Rules Committee, all the steering committee, most all of the committee on committees, and minority ranking Members (future possible chairmen) on practically all committees are included in this group.

Actually, seniority has no constitutional sanction. Seniority is not a law. Seniority, strictly speaking, is not a rule of the House. It is specified that a member first named to a committee shall be its chairman unless a majority of committee members elect a chairman. Actually, seniority is custom permitted to become impregnable in recent years. A defensible custom of flexible seniority has now hardened into a characteristic that is harmful to the House and hurtful to the well-being of the nation.

The trend to long service can be illustrated statistically. Until 1901, first-term members in each House composed 30 to 40 per cent of the entire House membership. During most of these fifty-five Congresses, the percentage ranged from 40 to 60 per cent. By contrast, since 1935, the percentage of first termers has ranged between 10 per cent (1957–1959) and 26 per cent (1939–1941). The highest percentage in this century occurred as a result of election to the first New Deal Congress, 1933–1935. Thirty-seven per cent were first termers. The much-discussed Eighty-ninth Congress, product of an anti-Goldwater landslide, found only 21 per cent first termers, an increase of only 5 per cent from the composition of the House in the previous Congress. The Ninetieth has 14 per cent.

Hand in hand with this goes the increase in the mean term of service by incumbents. This mean had never risen above 2.9 terms until 1901 and usually had been below this figure. By the time of the 1963–1965 (Eighty-eighth) Congress, the comparable figure had risen to 5.6 terms. It remained the same in the 1967 (Ninetieth) Congress. Correspondingly, almost without exception, committee chairmen arrive in their positions by outlasting everyone else. The current of Congressional longevity is also illustrated by the fact that John McCormack had served thirty-four years in the House before he became Speaker in January, 1962—longer by far than any other Speaker.

The strong trend to longer service has given contemporary members a different "feel" for the House than its history warrants. The capstone may have been the unprecedented seventeen years plus that Rayburn served as Speaker. Scores of members entered the House during this era; many remain. They knew no other Speaker, except during brief periods when Republicans controlled the House, and Republicans have not controlled it for the last fourteen years. Moreover, no Democrat ran against Rayburn for Speaker. Therefore, it began to become "unthinkable" for *anyone* to do so. Actually, the Speakership was an intraparty competition into the mid-1930s. Now a hushed, almost cathedral-like quality envelops the Speakership. Some of this has rubbed off on the office of majority leader and other party offices. Political differences, whether over issue or office, are usually policy differences. Without policy competitions, political smog sets in. This is a long-standing misfortune of the Democratic party in the House.

Of course, seniority does have its beneficial side. It cannot and should not be discarded. One needs experience in being a United States Representative, just as physicians or computer-data analysts do. Knowledge presumably generates competence and special skills. It is excessive dependence upon seniority for advancement within the House that is indefensible. Today, seniority simply means that a chairmanship is awarded the majority member with the longest uninterrupted service on each committee. The exceptions are few. A committee chairman, in a sense, becomes self-appointing as long as he maintains his seniority intact. Intact seniority is usually a product of a safe district—more bluntly, a politically noncompetitive and politically backwater district. Democratic members representing such districts, mostly in Southern states, are not in sympathy with the majority views of their party. Such a condition obviously works against party harmony. There has developed a situation in which elected party leaders of the Democrats, Speaker and majority leader, are confronted with what is often a set of rival Democratic "leaders," the self-appointing seniors who dominate the committees and often ignore party policies and objectives. Three persuasive comments have been made about seniority as it exists today. Alexander Hehmeyer in *Time for Change* writes:

Congress is probably alone among private or governmental bodies charged with any kind of responsibility which let leadership depend exclusively on the accident of tenure.

George Galloway, in *Congress at the Crossroads*, effectively characterizes the misfortune that ironclad seniority brings to policy:

One of the greatest drawbacks of the seniority system is that it destroys party responsibility or prevents political parties from performing their campaign promises. For if the chairmen of committees owe their places not to their political parties but to the accident of tenure, then they can follow their own inclinations on legislative matters and disregard the platform pledges and legislative program of the party leaders.

Third, the Library of Congress was asked whether any other national legislature in the Western world or any of the fifty state legislatures utilizes seniority as a dominant factor in determining appointments to committees. The library searched and then responded, None.

RULES AND THE RULES COMMITTEE

Seniority, birth of parties, the committee system, executive-legislative relations, and other procedural and legislative developments are elements in the institutional specialization of the House. As the House became legislatively more complex, it became necessary to develop internal procedures to cope.

A legislative body requires intramural mechanisms that relate decision making to procedures, problems, and issues. The House has developed these mechanisms. They include classification of legislation by calendars, agreement by unanimous consent for certain legislation, motions to suspend rules of the House, special orders governing discussion of legislation, and special legislative days for specific category of legislation, such as that affecting the District of Columbia. These facilitate getting legislation to the floor. Most legislation is not deeply controversial. In modern times, the headlined controversies involve in any one session probably at most twenty-five to fifty measures that in some fashion impinge on entrenched economic, social, or political interests. These mechanisms also have helped to manage legislative volume, which grew tremendously as the young nation grew.

Apparently only 142 bills were introduced in the First Congress. Until about 1830, most bills were introduced as products of the Committee of the Whole or the proliferating standing committees. From that time forward, bills were introduced more frequently by individual members. Until 1890, however, a member himself could introduce a bill only with permission of the House and even then only on certain Mondays. During the early 1900s, there were as many as 28,000 bills introduced in a single Congress, some of which were duplications, but with nevertheless a substantial net number. Only about 2 to 3 per cent ever became law, however. In the 1967 session of the Ninetieth Congress, there were 14,593 bills, including duplications. Again, only 3 per cent of these passed the House.

Also the House itself grew: 65 seats in the First Congress; 213 seats thirty years later; 357 in 1890; and 435 since the Sixty-third Congress, according to the 1910 census. The first rules of procedure for the House were simple. They were adopted under four headings in the First Congress: debate and deportment; bill procedure; Speaker's duties; and Committee of the Whole House. Let experience decide when more rules were needed, the eleven-member committee on procedures recommended in its report to the first Speaker, Frederick A. C. Muhlenberg of Pennsylvania. One such addition occurred in 1811. The parliamentary device of "moving the previous question," by which debate may be shut down, was adopted in an effort to muzzle tiresome harangues, particularly Randolph's.

A system of calendars (lists) was devised over the years, beginning in the 1820s. After a legislative committee favorably reported a bill, it was placed, depending on its scope, degree of controversy, and content, on one of five calendars to await action of the full House. When there were a relatively few bills, the House drew directly from the calendars, which included one for appropriation bills, one for private bills, and one for nonappropriation measures. But by the late 1800s, there were hundreds of bills reported from committees. The House could not manage. Therefore, an order of precedence was established to supplement the calendars, so that more important, or favored, bills could get to the floor. Thus, the Rules Committee, originally a select committee solely authorized to report rules for the House, acquired high status. Rules became the place where bills are given precedence and then reported to the floor accompanied by a "special order," more commonly called a *rule*. This rule is a report by the Rules Committee providing for consideration of a measure on the floor. The rule establishes ground rules for the measure, such as the length of time for debate, whether points of order may be raised, and the category of amendments that may be offered. The resolution containing the rule is *first* voted on by the House. If approved by majority vote, the House then takes up the measure itself. If the rule or special order is defeated, as occasionally happens, the effect is to kill the legislation. This happened in a leaderless House in the summer of 1967 to a 40-million-dollar authorization to exterminate rodents.

The Rules Committee grew in influence and in alliance with the Speaker. In 1841, as a result of increasing legislative volume, Rules received special authority to report on legislation to the full House "at all times." At about the same time, Speaker White ruled that a two-thirds majority of the House was no longer necessary to adopt a rule from the Rules Committee; a simple majority would suffice. In 1853, the reports of the five-member Rules Committee were given precedence over other business. Five years later, the Speaker *ex officio* became a member and subsequently Chairman of Rules, making the committee an ever greater power cockpit. Rules became a standing committee in the 1880s. In the early 1890s, Rules was authorized to sit * while the House was in session, a privilege given even today to only two other committees, Government Operations and the Committee on Un-American Activities.

Rules has two other power levers. It is the committee of jurisdiction for changes in the rules of procedure of the House, and it has the privilege of reporting on matters not assigned to it. In 1891, during the term of Speaker Crisp of Georgia, it was decided that a report from Rules may not be interfered with, except for a motion to adjourn.

In 1910 and steadily since 1937, liberals and conservatives envision Rules as agent for representing a majority of the House, both Republicans and Democrats. Liberals tend to hold to the function of Rules as an arm of the majority of the majority party in the House, whose leadership is entitled to release or hold legislation as it wishes. Some contend that this view of Rules with-

---

* In contemporary times, the House customarily meets at noon and may sit until late afternoon or early evening. Committees of the House hold their hearings and transact other legislative business in the morning. The customary meeting time is 10 A.M. Permission may be granted a committee, other than the three mentioned, to meet while the full House is in session. These three committees, however, may meet without advance permission.

holds from the House its constitutionally given right to legislate because experience has shown that many a bill bottled up in Rules would have passed if released to the floor.

The rules of procedure themselves have required overhauling as the House evolved. In 1860, there was limited consolidation and agreement that the rules of one House shall be those of the next unless otherwise amended. This carry-over persisted until the Reed Speakership thirty years later. The first general revision came in 1880. This revision restricted an individual roll call to two callings of a member's name, it authorized "pair" voting, gave preference to revenue and appropriation bills in the Committee of the Whole, dropped the penalty for unauthorized absence, gave precedence to a conference report over other business, created a House calendar on which were placed nonappropriation bills, and made permanent a five-member Rules Committee.

Cannon's misuse of Reed's rules led to substantive alterations in 1911. Today, the book of rules of the House consists of 538 printed pages. Precedents and rulings occupy eleven bound volumes, the last annotated and assembled in 1936. These were compiled first by Asher Hines, Speaker Reed's clerk. Later another Cannon, Clarence of Missouri, who was first Speaker Champ Clark's clerk and then a long-time member and chairman of the House Committee on Appropriations, brought them up to date in 1936. Lewis Deschler, the first man actually to have the title of *parliamentarian* has served in that capacity since 1929. He is a depository of precedents and rulings. The parliamentarian is "the Speaker's man."

OFFICE OF THE SPEAKER

The Constitution provides for a Speaker. Otherwise it is silent as to duties and responsibilities. There is no requirement that the Speaker be a member of the House, although he always has been. At first, he was elected by secret ballot; since 1839 by roll call. Within a relatively few years, the Speaker set a pattern for the performance of the House as it went about exercising its legislative responsibilities, duties, and obligations. Outstanding men in the Speakership consciously strove to enhance the prestige, dignity, and power of that office.

During the first months of the First Congress, House members elected members to committees, unless a committee consisted of three or fewer members. In the latter case, the Speaker appointed. This procedure was short-lived. It caused delays and squabbles over selections. In January, 1790, it was agreed that "all committees shall be appointed by the Speaker unless otherwise specially directed by the House." This power, the greatest source of his authority, remained with the Speaker until a too arbitrary Speaker, Joseph G. Cannon of Illinois, was shorn 120 years later. The authority to name members to committees marked a primary development of the Speaker's office from that of being simply a neutral, nonpolitical presiding officer, as in the case of the Speaker of the British House of Commons. Speaker Dayton in the 1790s operated so forcefully during floor debate that he had to be called to order by the Speaker *pro tem*. The Speaker's power was additionally enhanced because he also both had the authority to select committee chairmen and the Chairman who presided when the House sat as a Committee of the Whole. The House did designate, however, which select committees should be established and how many members each should have.

The power to refer bills to committees is still assigned to the Speaker (although often, with his consent, exercised in fact by the parliamentarian). This discretion has had a major impact upon the shaping of major legislation. A conspicuous instance is the referral of the promising "full employment" bill in early 1945 into the unfriendly hands of the Committee on Expenditures in the Executive Departments, which gutted it, instead of to the more sympathetic Banking and Currency Committee.

In 1858, the designation of the Speaker as a member of the five-member Rules Committee, over which he presided, extended his institutional power still further. He was not only chairman of a committee that controlled the flow of legislation to the floor but also had the authority to appoint and remove the other four members. Thus, the Speaker could bottle up a bill, or he could send it to the floor under a rule that was tailored to his preference—a rule, for example, forbidding any amendments or waiving points of order against the measure. From the chair, too, the Speaker sought to dominate the House. He sought rules that would give him control over the order of business brought to the floor each legislative day. He evolved a strong right to recognize and, perhaps more importantly, not to recognize a member who rose and wanted to speak. Nowadays quite circumscribed, this power of recognition was a powerful tool in the hands of Speakers such as Tom Reed and Joe Cannon. In the 1840s, bedeviled by long-winded speeches that sometimes lasted four, five, and six hours, a rule was established placing a one-hour limitation on speeches. A ruling was also developed that a member usually could speak only once to a subject.

Despite these powers, the House frequently got out of hand. Particularly in the twenty years leading up to the Civil War and in the years afterward, Speakers found themselves hamstrung by agile parliamentary footwork and delaying motions, such as that of *disappearing quorums*. To read transcripts of floor discussions during these years is to encounter page after page of obstructionist, unruly behavior. Committee chairmen were a problem to the leadership. A member, having Randolph in mind, asked his colleagues to approve a resolution

> to prevent in future the most important business of the Nation from being retarded by a Chairman of the Committee of Ways and Means [Randolph] or any other committee by going to Baltimore or elsewhere, without leave of absence . . . to prevent in future the Chairman of the Committee of Ways and Means from keeping for months the estimates for the appropriations necessary for the ensuing year in his pocket, or locked up in his desk . . . and, finally to prevent hereafter bills of importance being brought forward, and forced through the House, near the close of a session, when many members are gone home. . . .

Woodrow Wilson commented that by 1885

the House has as many leaders as there are subjects of legislation; for there are as many standing committees as there are classes of legislation . . . [but] the chairmen of the standing committees do not constitute a co-operative body like a ministry . . . there is no thought of acting in concert. Each committee goes its own way at its own pace.

After the major powers of the Speakership were removed in 1910, the Democrats managed their internal affairs through their party caucus and, when in the majority the organizational affairs of the House as well. For the next ten years, the caucus was a successful instrument under Speaker Clark, primarily because of his able majority leader, Oscar Underwood of Alabama. In the 1920s, the Democrats became a minority party, and the caucus fell into disuse. Authority became fragmented. Democratic Speakers such as Texans John Garner and Sam Rayburn succeeded through the force of their own personalities rather than because of any grant of authority vested in the Speakership. During 1965–1966, the Speakership was given a small amount of additional authority. The twenty-one-day rule, in effect during the Eighty-first Congress, was repealed in 1951 but reinstituted for the 1965–1966 sessions. It enables a bill, pigeonholed in the Rules Committee for more than twenty-one days, to be brought to the floor for action. In this connection, the Speaker was given discretionary authority to recognize a member of a committee for a motion to call up a bill originating in his committee and blocked in Rules. The Speakership was also given wider grant of authority to send a bill to conference.

Regardless of the ebb and flow of the Speakership's powers, its occupant historically assumes three functions: those of presiding officer; legislative leader of his party in the House; and, of course, member of the House with the same rights and privileges as others. As the law of succession was once written, the Speaker was first in line after the Vice President in the event of a President's death.

THE SPEAKERS

Henry Clay made the mold. He was the first "great" Speaker. He was elected in his first year in the House, November 4, 1811. By contrast, Rayburn became Speaker in his twenty-seventh year and McCormack in his thirty-fourth year of service. In Clay's day the House was so much more important as a base of power than the Senate that, on one occasion, Clay resigned from the Senate to return to the House. Hitherto, Speakers had usually been "the President's man." The President, particularly during Jefferson's two terms, was the rider and the House the horse. James Bryce in *American Commonwealth* has observed that in the term of a firm and able Speaker during the nineteenth and early twentieth centuries, a Presidential message had little more impact on Congress than "an article in a prominent party newspaper." With Clay, a period of Congressional assertiveness had begun. His was a splendid Speakership.

Clay, representing the new post-Revolutionary War generation, found the Speakership brick and left it marble. Unlike Speaker Macon, who let the insolent Randolph bully the House, Clay both governed it from the chair and persuaded it from the floor. He never failed to cast his vote on any measure before the House. Internal improvements, the protective tariff of 1824, recognition of the rebellious South American governments, and the Missouri Compromise of 1820 were his issues. He dominated the timorous Madison and fended off the stronger Monroe. As such, he was regarded between 1811 and 1825 as the Number One Powerful Public Man in the Land.

"Our Harry" served intermittently for seven and one-half years as chief officer of the House; the first time occurred when he was thirty-four. Often the House went into Committee of the Whole so that he could express his views from the floor. Clay asserted a valuable prerogative, that a party in placing a member in the Speaker's chair does not lose his services on the floor. Under Clay, the Speaker's parliamentary power was thereby increased hand in hand with personal and legislative influence. Truly, he was the boldest of the Speakers, though he still re-

ceived the pay of a rank-and-file member, 8 dollars a sitting day.*
When he wished to go to war against Great Britain in 1812, the
United States went.

Clay asserted the right of the House to exercise "legislative
oversight," that is, a surveillance as to how the executive branch
administered the programs that the House and the Senate had
passed. This placed a third arrow in the House's quiver, law
making and investigation of wrongdoing in the executive branch
being the others. Investigations were numerous. One Congressional specialist estimates there were 285 investigations by standing and select committees of the House and Senate between 1789
and 1925.

After Clay and before Reed, a period of sixty-five years, there
were few Speakers of competence or who are associated with
formative decisions. James G. Blaine of Maine and John G. Carlisle of Kentucky are two. None carried the whole, hard grain of
greatness, however. Generally, the slavery issue so dominated the
House that members were selected for Speaker for their "dough-
faced" quality, that is, they were not strongly identified as for or
against slavery and its extension. During this interregnum, both
the House and the Speakership decayed. The House needed an
immense reconstruction operation. In 1889, Thomas Brackett
Reed of Maine became Speaker. He also became the director of
reconstruction. Responsibility is like a hot poker; few want to
grab it. Reed did and held on. He fulfilled the definition of a
"great" Speaker; he made the House work. Like all successful
Speakers, before and after him, Reed did what was necessary. If a
chairman of a key committee at a crucial time were particularly
incompetent, then replace him. If a member of his own party
were inexcusably obstructionist, then remove him from his committee assignment. Make those moves in committee and on the
floor that are necessary to achieve one's legislative program.
Anticipate trouble and act to overcome it. This is at the core of
effective leadership, whether in the board rooms of America or in
the corridors of Congressional power. This is acting responsibly.

* The Speaker today receives 43,000 dollars a year as salary, plus 10,000
dollars in expense money. Other members receive 30,000 dollars annually.

In Reed's case, it was both party and legislative responsibility. When fundamental disagreement develops, hard and unyielding to the acceptable thawing of political compromise, then quit. This Reed did in disagreement with a President of his own political party, William McKinley.

Reed had his work cut out for him when he became Speaker in December, 1889, at the opening of the Fifty-first Congress, in the first year of the Benjamin Harrison Presidency, but Reed had resolved, while serving in the minority, not to be, as were Speakers before him, as Gulliver in bondage to Lilliputians. For the most part, the Speakership of his immediate predecessor, the able and talented Carlisle, had been a disaster, although he had further developed the right of recognition of a member. Other pre-Reed Speakers had fared even less well. The House chamber, indeed, had been a most disorderly place. Randolph had brought his unruly hound dogs onto the floor. There had been canings, fistfights, shootings, and other unnerving assaults and intimidations among members. Procedural rules were made and repeatedly broken. In the 1850s, Speaker Banks put across a resolution to revise the rules of the House. The committee of jurisdiction never reported back.

On the threshhold of the Civil War, a riotous scene preceded the election of Pennington of New Jersey as Speaker by one vote. Perhaps with these disorders in mind, Woodrow Wilson wrote in 1885:

> Outside of Congress the organization of the national parties is exceedingly well-defined and tangible . . . but within Congress it is obscure and intangible. Our parties marshall their adherents with the strictest possible discipline for the purpose of carrying elections, but their discipline is very slack and indefinite in dealing with legislation. At least there is within Congress no visible, and therefore no controllable party organization. The only bond of cohesion is the caucus, which occasionally whips a party together for cooperative action against the time for casting its vote upon some critical question.

Reed had character, intellect, wit, and wisdom, a high order of integrity, and a "raw and ready honesty" at a time when Americans were running in the money-making street. He never mistook popularity for political prestige. The political courage of the 6 foot, 3 inch, 275-pound Reed was as large as his girth. Champ Clark compared him to a "great three-decker in a surging sea." He knew how to count correctly in advance the votes for and against any bill. He knew the rules of the House. He once recalled that while doing Navy duty on a gunboat on the Mississippi River during the Civil War, "I knew all the regulations and the rest of them didn't. I had all my rights and most of theirs." He came to the House in 1876 to replace Blaine, who had moved into the Senate. By his second term, he was recognized as a walking treasure trove of parliamentary knowledge. He did not sit silently as the House machinery creaked, when it ran at all. It may be astonishing to elected public officials that, during Reed's time, it was not uncommon for a House member, for example, to write critically about his colleagues and his party. Reed wrote indignant, scathing critiques for *The Saturday Evening Post*, the *North American Review*, and *Century Magazine*, among others. He did this while minority leader of his party in the House. He wrote in one magazine article that the House led "a gelatinous existence—the scorn of all vertebrate animals." Henry Cabot Lodge, then serving with Reed, also wrote critically of the House. There is no rule that says a member of Congress should be deprived of his freedom of speech and pen.

James Cox, later a Democratic Presidential candidate, served with Reed. He pronounced the judgment that Reed, rather than the vastly inferior McKinley, might have been President "but for a sarcastic turn of mind and a sharpness of tongue." Reed's frankness was irrepressible. At one session, he told his colleagues that, as for the Civil War, he was "weary of discussion of the great and fine traits of generals who deserted their country in its hour of peril." Once a member rose and, by way of introduction, referred disarmingly to his "modesty." Reed, from the Speaker's chair, suggested the member "had much to be modest about." The epigram that a statesman is a dead politician is attributed to Reed. When it was suggested he die, Reed declined: "death is the last infirmity of noble minds." When opponents gibed that the

Fifty-first Congress, in which he was Speaker, was the first "billion-dollar Congress," Reed replied, "It's a billion dollar country." Once from the Speaker's chair he addressed a member: "Hicks, you weren't in school yesterday. Did you bring an excuse from your Mother?" Confronted with long-winded members, he remarked, "Better a pound of fact than a shipload of language." Would he run for the Presidency, actually a long-held desire? "They [his Party] might do worse and I think they will." Yes, he once acknowledged, "One, with God, is always a majority, but many a martyr has been burned at the stake while the votes were being counted."

Reed differed fundamentally with leaders in the opposing Democratic party, such as Crisp, a future Speaker. He correctly viewed the rules of the House as being designed to effectively promote the legislative operations of the House. Crisp took the position that the rules were basically designed to protect minority rights. There was, as it turned out, no bridging this philosophical chasm.

Reed's first Speakership was auspicious for the Republican party as well. It marked the first time in fourteen years that it had controlled the House, the Senate, and the Presidency. Reed vowed some changes would be made. He took aim at the two-pronged obstructionist technique that, in effect, generated the filibuster. It consisted of *the dilatory motion* (motions designed to waste time and impede legislative business) and the *disappearing quorum*. On one occasion, eighty-six roll calls had been taken when opponents sought to defeat a measure concerning sharing revenues with the states. On another, James Baird Weaver of Iowa had employed dilatory motions to keep the House tied up in an effort to obtain consideration of enabling legislation for a territory of Oklahoma. Reed first focused on the disappearing quorum, a kind of parliamentary hemorrhage. The disappearing quorum was at best annoying; at worst, which was customary, it was a bone in the throat of an issue-oriented, serious-minded Speaker, determined to make the House work.

With typical gift of phrase, Reed described the disappearing quorum as that system of metaphysics whereby a man could be present and absent at the same time. A member, Reed said, like any other particle of matter, could not be in two places at once. The disappearing quorum appears to have begun with John Quincy Adams. Beginning in 1832, he continually violated a rule of the House that required those present to vote. This violation spread to other members. Eventually, it became practice, sustained by Speakers, that for a bill to be approved or disapproved a quorum must not only be present during roll call but must actually vote. The House of Commons had long ago solved that one by setting a quorum at 40. The House of Representatives set its quorum at 165. This created an opportunity for an obstructionist minority to sit silently in their seats during roll calls and cause major bills to be left drifting for a lack of a quorum. For without a quorum, the House under its rules could only adjourn or order a call of the House as a continued effort to muster a quorum. It was absurd, although Reed himself during his very early years in the House opposed an effort in 1880 to outlaw it.

On January 29, 1890, a contested elections resolution, recommending seating of a Republican candidate in a West Virginia Congressional election, was brought before the House for approval. Democrats sought of course, to block the resolution. After discussion and a voice vote, a roll call was ordered. The result was announced: 162 yeas; 3 nays; and 163 not voting. Those voting totaled 165, meeting the then requirement for a quorum. Immediately, members asked to withdraw their votes. Two did. This made a recapitulated tally of 161 yeas and 2 nays, two short of a quorum. More than one hundred members were present but silent. Democrat Crisp snapped loudly, "No quorum."

Reed then spoke seventeen revolutionary words: "The Chair directs the Clerk to record the following names of members present and refusing to vote." Reed then ticked off the names of thirty-eight members he sighted on the floor amid, the *Congressional Record* reported, "hisses . . . cries of 'order' . . . applause [Republican] . . . cries [Democratic] of 'revolutionary' and 'unconstitutional.' . . ."

McCreary of Kentucky protested amid the uproar, "I deny the right of the Speaker to count me present."

Reed from the rostrum retorted, "The Chair is making a statement of the fact that the gentleman from Kentucky is present. Does he deny it?"

Laughter and applause from the Republican side. In explanation, Reed told the House:

> The Clerk announced the members voting in the affirmative as 161 and 2 who voted in the negative. The Chair thereupon having seen the members present, having heard their names called in their presence, directed the call to be repeated. And, gentlemen not answering when thus called, the Chair directed a record of their names to be made showing the fact of their presence as bearing upon the question which has been raised, namely, whether there is a quorum of this House present to do business or not, according to the Constitution of the United States.

The uproar continued into January 31, two days later. Quotations of constitutional precedents at all levels of government were gravely quoted by both sides. Reed repeated his quorum ruling during this period and met with similar noisy reaction. Reed remained firm; the opposition expended itself, and the ruling stuck.

The New York Times in its news stories let its feeling be known. One set of headlines read, "On the Volcano's Brink . . . The Republicans Defying All Decency . . . Speaker Reed's Revolutionary Ruling Precipitates a Contest, In Which His Party is Not Fair." The paper quite correctly pointed out that Reed had facilitated his strangling of the disappearing quorum by first postponing adoption of rules for the House in the Fifty-first Congress until after his act. The House had convened several weeks before his quorum ruling but Reed did not call up proposed rules for discussion until mid-February.

Reed, that Republican Cromwell, took aim at the rules of the House on February 12, 1890. Since 1860, rules of the House in one Congress had been binding upon the next unless amended.

Long before that, cumbersome and complex rules had been adopted. Reed knew why.

"Ever since the slavery question came to trouble the peace of the country," Reed said, "the rules of the House have been framed with the view of rendering legislation difficult. The South was anxious that there should be ample means at its disposal to stop any measure detrimental to its cherished institution."

Henry Cabot Lodge noted that the rules, as in the case of many other matters, started properly enough. "Rules devised originally to facilitate business and to give reasonable protection to the rights of the minority, which under the old and less crowded conditions were both suitable and unabused, had gradually been perverted until public business was at a standstill and the power to arrest all action had passed to an irresponsible minority—a contradiction of the first principles of free government." The House had become, said Lodge, then a House member and Reed's fellow Republican, a "helpless inanity." Of course, a disordered and ineffective majority compounded the process. A dispatch in *The New York Herald Tribune* characterized the cumbersome rules as the work of "brooding Buddhas in seclusion of their committee rooms who designed them to retard rather than promote business." A majority of the majority party in the House should be permitted to operate.

On February 14, after two days of debate, Reed secured adoption of new rules by a vote of 161 to 144—a 17-vote margin in a House in which his Republican party held a 16-vote majority. Robert La Follette of Wisconsin was one of those supporting the rules changes. It marked the first general revision since 1880. The substantive changes in rules involved four elements: uprooting of dilatory motions; establishing of 100 as a quorum in Committee of the Whole; changes in the order-of-business scheduling; and formalization of Reed's ruling as to disappearing quorums. Another time-wasting procedure was eliminated by permitting bills to be considered introduced when filed, rather than having them read during a House session.

When the Fifty-first Congress adjourned in 1891, the House members did not offer their customary "thank you" to the

Speaker. Reed, a newspaper correspondent reported, walked from the chamber of the House to his office, sat down, put his head on his desk and cried. Deserved recognition did eventually come to Reed. The Supreme Court upheld the constitutionality of a rule that those present may be counted for purposes of determining a quorum. An observer came to write that since Reed had been Speaker, it would never again be worthwhile for another member to fill the office. Sir Henry Irving, the great English actor, commented that a portrait of Reed looked like the Stratford bust of Shakespeare. Fifty years later, Speaker Bankhead of Alabama commented on the earlier strong men of the Speakership. "We must necessarily admire the grip they had on their parties and their firm determination to rule this House in large measure according to their view of their public and party duties. . . ."

In the Fifty-second Congress, Democrats held control of the House by a heavy margin. The Reed rules were not adopted. They were adopted in the Fifty-third Congress, however, when Democratic control had heavily shrunk. Then, in the Fifty-fourth Congress (1895–1897), the Republicans regained control of the House by a 135-seat plurality; Reed was again Speaker, and his rules took precedence. Reed waxed; minority obstructionists waned. Reed identified his procedural reforms with a period in which

> party responsibility has begun, and with it also the responsibility of the people, for they can no longer elect a Democratic House and hope the minority will neutralize their action or a Republican House without being sure that it will keep its pledges.
>
> If we have broken the precedents of a hundred years, we have set the precedents of another hundred years nobler than the last, wherein the people, with full knowledge that their servants can act, will choose those who will worthily carry out their will.

Reed's expectations, unfortunately, were only temporarily fulfilled.

Reed ruled his party and the House with fine, iron-handed

impartiality. He transferred obstructionist members of both parties from their committee assignments. He struck down with darts of epigram members who dared face up to him from the floor. He taunted the two minority Members of the five-member Rules Committee. "We've decided to perpetrate the following outrage and of which we will desire you to have due notice," Reed would tell the two Democrats. Nevertheless, he was not tyrannical, as Cannon became. Members regarded Reed with deep, if distant, respect. Under Reed's Speakership, the House capably performed its obligations. It passed the Sherman Anti-Trust Act, the McKinley Tariff Act, a veterans' pension bill, as well as bankruptcy and meat-inspection legislation.

Reed was not, however, invincible. Like other public men, Presidential ambition took him by the arm. His was an unsuccessful, erratic effort to secure the Republican Presidential nomination at the 1896 convention in St. Louis. Cabot Lodge nominated him, but his stiff-necked attitude toward soliciting delegate support assured failure. He received eighty-five votes. William McKinley, who had served under Reed in the House and for whom Reed had a minimum high regard, became the nominee and the next President. Political associates believe Reed returned to the House and the Speakership in 1897 in a weakened position.

The "Manifest Destiny" of the Mahans, Theodore Roosevelts, and Beveridges became his undoing. Reed opposed the national fervor for expansion and war with Spain. He opposed annexation of the Hawaiian Islands and the Philippines. Referring to the Philippines, Reed said the United States would be acquiring "the last colonial curse of Spain." He spoke out little, however, in the face of rising enthusiasm for expansion, whipped along by the Hearst newspapers. In explanation, Reed told a story about the Kansas pup barking futilely at a cyclone; better "face the breeze but close your jaws." In 1898, Cannon, then chairman of Appropriations, drafted a 50-million-dollar defense appropriation bill at President McKinley's request. Reed, though Speaker, was not consulted. Subsequently, Reed stepped down as Speaker and as a member at the close of the Fifty-fifth Congress in March, 1899.

He had not stood for reelection. He left Washington, D.C., to practice law in New York City and died three years later during a visit to Washington, his political home.

Clay had rescued the House from Presidential domination. Reed rescued the House from the tyranny of an obstructionist minority. In each instance, the House prospered. So did the country, when the House was in order.

2

The Man from Illinois

Speaker Cannon, the happy autocrat, ran a tight ship—too tight, as it turned out. In the last phase of his eight-year Speakership, Cannon had crossed the line separating strong leadership and absolutism. Nevertheless, one political writer, George Rothwell Brown, suggests that Cannon "was the emory wheel against which Americans sharpened their understanding of their own political problems." Cannon, physically as small as Reed was large, acquired the habit of command as one of the triumvirate that ran the House during Reed's first Speakership.

Both Cannon and McKinley had unsuccessfully run against Reed for Speaker in 1889. Afterward, Reed appointed McKinley Chairman of Ways and Means, which has jurisdiction over tariffs, the major continuing issue in American politics in the nineteenth century, as is often forgotten. At that period, the Ways and Means chairman was also majority floor leader. Reed appointed Cannon Chairman of Appropriations. He then appointed both men to the five-member Rules Committee which he chaired. Thus, Reed, McKinley, and Cannon among them held all necessary power levers in their roles as Speaker, Chairman of the Rules, Ways and Means, and Appropriations Committees, and as floor leader.

Cannon, like Reed, believed that party discipline was indispensable in a House growing in size with each decennial census. At this time, the House had 391 members. His strong control, similar to that of Reed's, was enhanced by the power of the Speaker to recognize a member out of order. To this day, the Speaker's power of recognition is a major device. It can be exercised negatively, that is, simply refusing to acknowledge a member who stands on the floor and asks to speak; or a Speaker can ask the standing member the purpose of his request. Under precedents of the House, this does not constitute an act of recognition by the Speaker. This enables the Speaker to deny a member the floor if he disapproves of the member's purpose. Furthermore, there is no appeal from a Speaker on a question of recognition, nor is the Speaker's exercise of the power of recognition subject to a point of order. During the Speakership of Cannon, the most reliable, really the only reliable way for a member to get recognized was first to develop a record of support for the Speaker's position, drop by his office, and request to be recognized on a specific day. If Cannon approved, requesting members' names went on a list of recognitions Cannon carried with him to the Speaker's chair.

In Cannon's hands, ultimately this power became such that a member might as well remain in his lodging if he were at odds with Cannon. His every opportunity to rise to influence was controlled by the Speaker's power to appoint committees. Wearing his hat as Rules Chairman, Cannon dictated which bills the House would consider.

In his first term, he was highly influential but not invincible. Bills he opposed did pass, but by his third term as Speaker, Cannon, the "Iron Duke," had gathered tightly the reins of House power. Aside from his right to recognize, or not to recognize, a member, Cannon used the unanimous-consent calendar as a reward to keep members in line. If they did as he told them, their bills got on the calendar. He also manipulated calendars in order to avoid floor action on a bill he opposed. Ah, said one discontented member, the calendar should be renamed a "cemetery . . . therein lie the whitening bones of legislative hopes."

Another power rein was that of pending bills. There was the device of special rules issued by the Rules Committee. These were used to change existing rules. For example, when Democrats refused unanimous consent, Cannon, as Chairman of Rules, brought out a special rule permitting suspension of rules by majority vote instead of the customary two-thirds majority vote. This cleared the way for a bill to be passed by a majority vote. Special rules could also be employed to fend off unwanted amendments. On one occasion, in spite of protests, Cannon ordered a third calling of the roll of the House while stalling for time in which a sufficient number of his supporters could get to the House chamber.

As had Reed before him, Cannon transferred members from committee to committee in order to achieve policy objectives. During seven Congresses, spanning the period 1897–1910, according to Robert Luce of Massachusetts, Speakers reappointed 65 per cent of the committee chairmen. Twenty-three per cent of the remaining committee chairmanships were filled by appointing members already on these committees, although not the most senior, and the remaining 12 per cent of the chairmanships were filled by appointing members who had not been on the committees they were appointed to head. One specific example of Speaker Cannon's manipulation occurred in 1903, when a four-term member, Jesse Overstreet of Indiana, was jumped to Chairman of Post Office and Post Roads over two more senior members, one with sixteen terms' experience and the other with eight. In the Sixtieth Congress, Cannon removed from the Agriculture Committee a member who had defied him. Also, in that Congress, James Tawney of Minnesota, was removed from Ways and Means because, from the point of view of Cannon, he was regarded as unreliable on the tariff question over which his committee had jurisdiction. Tawney was placed on Appropriations as Chairman, over the heads of two more senior members, because there he was considered "regular." Cannon made Sinclair Weeks of Massachusetts chairman of a committee Weeks had never previously served on. In 1909, James R. Mann of Illinois was transferred to Interstate and Foreign Commerce as Chairman, in order to protect a favored bill involving railroad regulation.

Gilbert Nelson Haugen of Iowa once described Cannon's atti-

tude toward offending members who had supported President
Theodore Roosevelt instead of him on meat-inspection legislation:

> I believe nine members of that committee [on Agriculture]
> stood by the President. The other members of the Committee
> were against the legislation as outlined by the President, and so
> was the Speaker. What Happened?
> In the next Congress when the time came for making up
> committees the names of seven of the nine members who had
> stood for the Roosevelt proposition did not appear on that
> Committee. The Chairman of that Committee on the morning
> after election found his political carcass outside of the breast-
> works. A new Chairman was appointed.

During his Speakership, which spanned eight years, Cannon
made forty-one transfers of members from one committee to
another on ten major committees, according to one study. This
would indicate that Cannon used his power of committee appointment sparingly. There are indications that growing schisms
within his party, as well as legislative objectives, played a role in
his transfers. In addition to these forty-one, Cannon filled ninety-
nine vacancies caused by resignation, death, or defeat. The remaining committee vacancies seemed to have been filled by a
seniority system modified by party standing, fitness (as leadership
views it), and geographical and economic-interest factors.

Cannon used the party caucus to bind balky members of his
own party to legislative positions. "Wisdom resides in caucus
rather than in an individual," he remarked. Cannon explained his
maneuvering on grounds that members of his party whom he had
removed or demoted had "failed to enter and abide by a Republican caucus, and this being a government through parties, for
that as well as for other sufficient reason. . . ." His advice to
party strays was, "It's a damned good thing to remember in
politics to stick to your party and never attempt to buy the favor
of your enemies at the expense of your friends."

In institutional terms, therefore, Cannon, like Reed and Clay,
believed that power and responsibility were different sides of the

same coin. A blurring of one affects the value of the overall piece. Cannon thought it unpardonable error not to use the authority of the Speakership to the fullest. Both Cannon and Reed scorned the "Sunday-school Speaker who patted the good boys on the cheek and turned the other cheek to the bad ones." Cannon admired Clay and Reed for organizing the House so that legislation of the majority could be acted upon. He would not tolerate the delay of a much desired bill, as has happened in the modern era when, for example, the Democratic leadership stood by and let Wilbur Mills of Arkansas, Chairman of the Ways and Means Committee and, of course, a Democrat, sit on a much needed Medicare bill for six years.

It should not be imagined that there existed an absolute condition of "push-button" Speakership. There were curbs in the form of customs, usages, and precedents. Furthermore, in his memoirs, Republican James Watson of Indiana states that he had persuaded Cannon to let John Sharp Williams of Mississippi, Democratic floor leader between 1903 and 1908, select Democrats for committee assignments, although such selections were the Speaker's prerogative. On the floor in 1912, Cannon once said that he and Williams had an understanding for three of Cannon's four terms as Speaker that Williams "should have his way about minority appointments, and as I recollect now there were not to exceed four cases where the minority leader did not have his way. . . ."

Luce once suggested that the leadership actually was like a shadow commission. The Speaker was the most visible member, of course, but he was advised by the legislative majority floor leader and the Chairmen of Rules and Appropriations. That the Members had such an impression is reflected, for example, in the discussion in February, 1908, when the House was considering a resolution authorizing the distribution of a Presidential message. The *Congressional Record* carried this account:

> Mr. Hughes of New Jersey: I desire to offer the following amendment [i.e., to the resolution]
> The Clerk read as follows:
> Add the following words: "So much as related to new legis-

lation [i.e., in the Presidential message] be referred to the 'big five' of the House."

(Laughter)

Mr. Payne: Mr. Chairman, I am afraid I shall have to raise the point of order on that.

Mr. Williams: Upon what ground does the gentleman from New York raise the point of order—that is, new legislation or a new rule?

Mr. Payne: Because there is no such committee in the House except as it exists in the exuberant imagination of my friend . . . (Laughter)

Nevertheless, Mary Parker Follett in her authoritative history, *The Speaker of the House of Representatives*, expressed the larger and correct view that the history of the House is really the history of the Speakers, and she was perplexed by the view that the Speaker should be simply a presiding officer, "the political Speaker is the ordinary, historical Speaker." She discussed at length our ambivalence toward power:

> People were formally told that the Speaker was a powerful man who even appoints the committees. It was as though the country should suddenly be informed that the President nominates his Cabinet. Yet, it was necessary then to point out the Speaker's position, and it is hardly less essential now. Until the great weight of the office is thoroughly understood, the Speaker will not be held by the people to the strict accountability which is the proper adjunct of power.
>
> That authority and responsibility should never be separated has become an axiom; yet in the government of the United States they are separated in the Speakership. No assembly can be efficient without a recognized leader: this is a point upon which we should no longer deceive ourselves. The theory of the House is still that it is an assembly of equal factors. But the fact is that it is a hierarchy of private members, chairmen of committees, members of the committee on Rules and above them all a Speaker. His status as the leader of the House of Representatives should be looked squarely in the face. That once accepted, there should be no delay in uniting power and responsibility. . . . if he [the Speaker] becomes a recognized legislative leader responsible for the legislation of the United States, his office will be a prize little less valued than the Presidency.

This was the case in the Administrations of Clay, Reed, and Cannon. They put iron into the institution of the Speakership. They did not come into the House of Representatives from their home districts to preside idly. The character and purpose they had shown in the House were qualities they had brought with them.

Joseph Gurney Cannon was born of bare-bones poor Quaker parents in North Carolina. He studied law in Ohio and moved to southern Illinois, settling first in Shelbyville. In despair at his lack of professional progress, he once tore up his law diploma and stomped on it. Like Reed, he was candid and spoke shirt-sleeved English; he was called a "gymnastic" speaker. As Chairman of the Appropriations Committee, he often stripped off his coat, waistcoat, tie, and even collar when really warmed up to the matter he was discussing on the floor. Unlike Reed, he was a narrow and parochial man. Clay, Reed, and Cannon had a vision of the House. Clay's was a vision of a growing new nation; Reed's was one of a peerless institution charged with carrying out a maturing nation's business; Cannon's would be an equally clear but negatively charged vision. All three combined technical ability with a conscious advocacy of issues. All three represented an illustration of a person in authority who wanted to get something done.

As a young man in his twenties, Cannon had met Abraham Lincoln. He admired and supported Lincoln, which was not an opinion easily held in southern Illinois. The region had a goodly share of Copperheads, Southern sympathizers. In 1864, seven unarmed Union soldiers were murdered at the courthouse at Charleston, Illinois. Cannon, state's attorney for the district in which the foul deed took place, was the prosecutor at the ensuing trial. Later Cannon prosecuted still another Copperhead accused of killing a Union soldier. The defendant was found not guilty. The next day the acquitted, drunk and armed with a handgun, accosted Cannon and threatened to kill him. Cannon, with help of a friend, boldly bluffed him, just as later he would invite from the Speaker's chair a motion to depose him in March, 1910. In each situation the bluff succeeded.

In his memoirs, Cannon tells a story about the arrest of Abraham Lincoln's stepmother, Sara Bush Johnston Lincoln, on the charge of shoplifting in Charleston, Illinois. Cannon was still state's attorney and investigated. Mrs. Lincoln had taken a small piece of calico from a drygoods store to match with some material at home. It was a "careless inadvertence." Cannon had the charge secretly erased and attributed the arrest to a Copperhead scheme to embarrass the President. "There are times when a judicial officer may take some liberties with the strict letter of the law in the interests of justice, and certainly this was a time," Cannon wrote. This was the man who was first elected to the House in 1872. In all, he would serve twenty-three terms, four as Speaker. When Cannon retired at eighty-seven in 1923, he was sixth-ranking Republican on the Appropriations Committee. Today, his hometown of Danville is represented in correspondingly rock-ribbed Republican fashion by Leslie Arends, minority whip.

Cannon would be called today, in political terms, a standpatter at best. Ironically for a Speaker who ruled his roost, Cannon believed that a government is best that governs least and that in so doing its legislative branch is an unequivocal coordinate of the executive. Cannon thought America "a hell of a success," as one newspaper worded it. This attitude in a troubled America, both enriched and beset by industrialization, helped toward his undoing. He was a high-tariff man when Republican manufacturers in New England sought lower tariffs on such materials as hides. Cannon disdained organized labor, while at the same time the brutalizing thrust of industrialization and Western expansion had provoked strong demands for legislative remedies from labor unions and granges, among others. Sordid and hurtful industrial conditions created lively, powerful reform movements that captured the loyalty of large numbers of the population. In 1899, Horatio Alger had died, but the myth continued to persuade. Fortunes were made, while resources were plundered, cities sullied, rivers defiled, and a working force mistreated. It wasn't that the industrial giants were bad men, someone observed, but there's "nothing like distance to disinfect dividends."

Between 1899 and 1905, there appeared Lincoln Steffens's

The Shame of the Cities, spotlighting political corruption; Frank Norris's *The Octopus,* spotlighting the life-and-death power of railroads and trusts over farm areas; John Dewey's influential book, *The School and Society;* The Socialist Eugene Debs; the International Ladies Garment Workers Union; the first direct primary; the National Child Labor Commission; Charles Evans Hughes's investigation of insurance company scandals; the International Workers of the World (IWW); demands for legislation to protect child labor, natural resources, and consumer-protection legislation. In the states and in the cities, political parties were themselves under attack. The direct primary, first adopted in Wisconsin in 1903, made the *initiative* and the *recall* the weapons in the fight.* The tide of political insurgency, in which reformist Republicans and Democrats joined, soon lapped at the Speaker's chair. Cannon made Canute-like statements on such occasions: "When we abandon political parties representing policies in which the people believe—we fly to anarchy or despotism or both."

Cannon's approaching time of troubles was aggravated by other matters. He had incurred the opposition of the Anti-Saloon League because of his position on an interstate liquor bill. The bankers' panic of 1907 had raised the tenor of discontent among farmers and workers and also revealed weaknesses in banking functions and operations. Furthermore, Cannon and the Republican President Theodore Roosevelt, Mark Hanna's "Damned Cowboy," were politically at odds. Roosevelt viewed the White House as that "bully pulpit" from which to preach his activist views of the remedies for the nation's unmet needs and its social failures. He even held a Speaker's Dinner in an effort to get along with Cannon. Cannon scornfully referred to Roosevelt supporters among House Republicans as being "tainted with Teddyism." The incoming President, William Howard Taft, gave indications that he would encourage an insurgent move to dump Cannon. Cannon liked Taft no better than Roosevelt. Taft raged in pri-

---

* The *initiative* is a procedure whereby a specified number of voters may propose a law by means of petition. When the required number of signatures are obtained the proposal is either submitted directly to all voters of a jurisdiction or to the state legislature for approval. The *recall* is a procedure by which an official may be removed by vote of the people on petition.

vate correspondence against what he regarded as the crudities and cynicism of Cannon. The Speaker disliked Taft for his support of revisions in the high tariff Dingley Act of 1897. Insurgents, perhaps a hard core of twenty-five in the House, cried "sell-out" when they heard that among the first great personages the equivocal Taft had received following his inauguration were Cannon and Senator Aldrich. Taft had made his choice between his party's regulars and its insurgents. Accounts of the day reflect the same sense of outrage that liberal Republicans vented when two other Republicans of different hues, Senator Robert Taft and General Eisenhower, met following the latter's Presidential nomination in 1952. Republican insurgents became as anti-William Howard Taft as they were anti-Cannon. This devisiveness within the Republican party placed a Democrat, Woodrow Wilson, in the White House in 1913.

Inside the House, Cannon had been sporadically under fire during his Speakership. A two-minute demonstration on the House floor in 1904 urging his nomination for President had temporarily disguised a troubled atmosphere. The House had been restless during the Speakership of his immediate predecessor, David Henderson of Iowa. There was so much unrest that the revolt against the Speaker's powers might have come years earlier than it ultimately did. Instead, however, Henderson did not stand for reelection to the House, and the domineering Cannon became Speaker in 1903.

In 1908, insurgent Republicans rebelled in the House chamber. John Nelson of Wisconsin, a supporter of Theodore Roosevelt, complained that the President "has been trying to cultivate oranges for many years in the frigid climate of the Committee of Rules, but what has he gotten but the proverbial lemons?" During this time there were proposals regarding the Speaker's appointive powers that would variously limit the number of appointments a Speaker could make to one-third, two-thirds, two-fifths of the total committee assignments. Other proposals were aimed at calendars, his position on Rules, and his right of recognition. Nothing happened however.

In January, 1909, an episode occurred that heaped additional hot coals upon Cannon. The House refused to accept a Presidential message sent it by Theodore Roosevelt on a controversial subject. Roosevelt wanted the jurisdiction of the Secret Service officially expanded beyond that of thwarting counterfeiting to the protection of the President and his family, an outgrowth of McKinley's assassination. The refusal was rare, perhaps the first since the Presidency of Andrew Jackson. Muckraking magazines and newspapers denounced Cannon and Cannonism. In part, their position was based on opposition to one man's tyranny; in part, on his political standpatism; and, in part, on his fiercely held high-tariff views that conflicted with the publishing industry's desire for lower duties on the importation of printing paper. Cannonism became an omen of darkness.

In 1909, at the opening of the Sixty-first Congress, a strong effort was made to change the rules of the House and oust Cannon. Rep. Ken Hechler of West Virginia in his book *Insurgency* relates a fascinating story of how tariffs, Tammany, and traders frustrated the effort and left Democratic minority leader Champ Clark publicly in tears. It failed in large measure apparently because of a Democrat, John Joseph Fitzgerald of New York City.

Opponents of Cannonism prepared to fight another day. Champ Clark in his political autobiography said that a substantial amount of support for clipping Cannonism resulted from the aggressive hatred of two Democratic members from Missouri for a third Democrat, John Sharp Williams of Mississippi. They erroneously had expected that Williams, minority leader preceding Clark, would become Speaker the next time the Democrats controlled the House. Then in January, 1910, a brush fire broke out. Members were discussing a proposal for a twelve-member, joint House-Senate investigation of the Interior Department. The Speaker would appoint the six House members. George Norris of Nebraska, an insurgent Republican, introduced an amendment that would have had the House itself elect the six members instead. It was adopted; Speaker Cannon had suffered a rebuke. Then on March 15, the week of the successful big revolt, Democrats and defecting Republicans succeeded in knocking out funds for an automobile for the Speaker. Cannon's effort to recoup failed. The sound of the political tumbril could be heard.

The decisive confrontation began the next day, March 16, 1910, Calendar Wednesday.

3

Revolt

Calendar Wednesday was designed to provide each committee with the opportunity to bring to the floor nonprivileged legislation that was blocked in the Rules Committee. On Wednesdays, except during the last two weeks of a session, names of committees are called alphabetically. When named, a committee may then call up certain types of bills previously reported by it.

Calendar Wednesday, adopted in 1909 by a five-vote margin, represented a concession by Speaker Cannon to discontented members. He envisioned it as a safety valve to mollify insurgents. Because of procedural restrictions surrounding its use, Norris called it "the most comical parliamentary joke that ever came down the legislative pike . . . a homeopathic dose of nothingness." On the surface, it did seem to be only a minor dilution of the Speaker's powers. It became a springboard from which the final assault on Cannonism was launched, however.

Cannon himself was wary about Calendar Wednesday. During the first session of the Sixty-first Congress, he had been able to avoid having one, either by adjourning the House from Tuesday to Thursday or by making certain his lieutenants brought up such privileged matters as tariffs on Wednesday, but on that fateful Wednesday, March 16, in the second session, Cannon could not postpone a test. At the time, Cannon's party held a forty-four-seat margin. This figure is misleading, because there were many Republican insurgents, forerunners of the La Follette Progressives, ready to bolt their party if the issue was promising. In fact, the discontent among the insurgents was so pervasive that many withheld their vote from Cannon when he was renominated for Speaker at the beginning of the Sixty-first Congress a year earlier. Cannon was elected by only twenty-six votes.

As in the past, Cannon confidently set out to postpone another Calendar Wednesday on that March 16. A lieutenant, Edgar Dean Crumpacker of Indiana, moved that the House consider an amendment to a joint resolution dealing with the thirteenth decennial census. Cannon ruled the proposal privileged because it dealt with a matter, the census, that the Constitution required the Congress to have made every ten years. As privileged, it would supplant Calendar Wednesday in the order of business for the day. A point of order was raised against Cannon's ruling, however. Cannon overruled it. In turn, this was appealed on grounds that not even privileged business could be brought before the House this day without first obtaining agreement by two-thirds of the members to scrub Calendar Wednesday. The battle had begun. When it finished four days later, the Speakership would never again be as powerful.

There are many members associated with the ensuing battle. The most prominent is George Norris of Nebraska, an insurgent Republican, but Norris has been assigned a fuller measure of influence than a reading of those momentous days warrants. He was a leader but late to the cause. In 1904, Norris was pleased that Cannon came to Nebraska to campaign on his behalf, but two years later Norris became unhappy with Cannon when the latter did not give Norris an assignment to Ways and Means. Subsequently, Norris discovered that Cannonism evoked a warm antagonism among his constituents. He frequently denounced the Cannon system during his reelection campaign in 1908, which he won by only twenty-two votes.

Oscar Underwood of Alabama and James Beauchamp (Champ) Clark of Missouri, both Democrats, actually gained the victory over Cannon. Underwood, for example, provided much of the intellectual timber for the argument against the Speaker's administration. Clark, writing later, said the issue was Reed's rules brutally administered by Cannon. Champ Clark was to seek his party's Presidential nomination in 1912 on the strength of his role in the Cannon fight.

The issue was most clearly drawn in the form of a verbal duel between Underwood and Crumpacker. Underwood, the most promising legislator in the House in terms of ability and political knowhow, first noted the background of Calendar Wednesday. The Speaker's ruling endangered both its promise and intention, he pointed out.

> The reason you could not do business under the old rule on the call of the calendar was that the chairmen of committees, under direction of The Speaker or the Rules Committee, could inject between the House and the calendar other business that they denominate as privileged business, and your calendar was gone. Now, the House in its wisdom in adopting the rule for Calendar Wednesday, said that this Calendar Wednesday should not be interfered with except by a two-thirds vote of this House. That does not mean a ruling of the Speaker; that does not mean a decision of the Speaker as to whether a matter is privileged or is not privileged.
>
> It means a vote of two-thirds of the Members of this House. If the gentleman from Indiana [Crumpacker] had brought this bill into the House on some other day besides Calendar Wednesday, could not the House have rejected the consideration of his bill by a majority vote? Then, if the House can refuse to consider a question of taking the census or relating to the taking of the census on any day of the week, why can not it by its rule say it shall not be in order to consider it on one day in the week? If it is in order because it is privileged to consider this bill because it relates to the taking of the census, it is equally in order to consider today a bill raising revenue. Does not the Constitution of the United States fix the duty on Congress and on this House to consider all revenue bills? Is a bill to take the census of any more vital import to the people of the United States than a bill to raise revenue to support the government? Is it of any greater privilege in the history of this House? Not at all. And therefore if this House today votes to sustain the Speaker and recognize the bill of the gentleman from Indiana as privileged, and thereby set aside Calendar Wednesday, you open the door to inject between you and the

call of the calendar an appropriation bill, a revenue bill, and
other matters of privilege that will destroy the rule you
adopted in the last session of Congress for the benefit of this
House.

Therefore, I say it is of the utmost importance that the
Membership of this House shall, when the roll is called today,
declare whether they stand for the House to attend to the
business that the House thinks should be considered, or
whether they intend to go back to the old system and allow
the Rules Committee to say to you what business shall be trans-
acted in this House.

Crumpacker rose in rebuttal:

If this resolution is not privileged today, it has no privilege at
all. I want the membership to bear that proposition in mind. If
this resolution does not go through today, it can not go
through, because if it has any privilege at all, it is not under the
Rules of the House but in spite of them. If it has any privilege
at all it is under the Constitution; and if the rules are higher
than the Constitution today, they will be tomorrow, and every
other day of this session of Congress. There is no use in quib-
bling about this proposition.

Just prior to the voting, Cannon summed up his position:

The Chair in ruling that this is a privileged question follows
a uniform line of precedents wherever the matter has been
ruled upon in the history of Congress.

Now, in order that Calendar Wednesday may be protected,
gentlemen say that the Chair should be overruled and a precedent established that no business of any kind can come up for
consideration on Calendar Wednesday. "But," says somebody,
"what harm can it do?" So far as the Chair is personally concerned, whatever might perhaps be in the mind of one or more
Members, seemingly to rebuke the Chair, through pique or
otherwise, the Chair cares nothing about a proposition of that
kind. If the House sees proper to overrule the precedents and
to make this precedent that may come to plague the House in
the future, well and good. The House has the power to do it
and the Chair has no feeling of pride or vanity in the premises.
"But," says somebody, "is the House bound to consider this
question when it is before the House?" No. There is no pos-

sible question that can come before the House that it is bound
to consider. On the question of consideration, if the point of
order had been made upon this joint resolution, the House
could have refused to consider it. That is one way in which
the House could have gone on with Calendar Wednesday.

Having said this much, if the Chair has succeeded in placing
the House in possession of the reasons which caused him to
make the ruling he did make, he is quite content, as the Chair
must be, with what the majority of the House may do. If the
Chair was four inches wide and one thousandth of an inch
thick, the Chair would feel some gratification if the House
should see proper to overrule the Chair upon the point of order
that the action of the majority of the House, under its rules, in
reversing the present Speaker, would make it plain that he has
no more and no less authority than any Speaker who has preceded him, and would set at rest the question whether the
Speaker "doth, like Colossus, bestride the world."

Cannon then put the question. By yeas and nays the decision of
the chair was overruled: 112 yeas to 163 nays. Thirteen were
recorded as "present" and 100 not voting. The margin was fifty-
one votes, in a House Cannon's Republicans held by a forty-four-
seat margin. The fall of the House of Cannon was underway.

George Rothwell Brown, a newspaperman, noted, in *The
Leadership of Congress*, that the significance was not that a
Speaker's ruling had been overturned by the House. The signifi-
cance of the vote was rather that

the oligarchy had been met in parliamentary battle to the
death, and that it had gone down to defeat on an issue which
lay at the root of the greatest question then agitating the national mind. The effort of the organized leadership with its vast
powers to thwart the will of the liberals and balk them of the
fruits of the first victory they had won [in establishing Calendar Wednesday, that is] had failed. If Mr. Cannon had been
psychic he might have read the handwriting on the wall, but he
was not, not even then.

It was now Norris's cue to enter the drama. On the next day,
March 17, St. Patrick's Day, Norris rose. After two unsuccessful
tries he was recognized and offered a resolution. Its content was

privileged under the Constitution, Norris said, by virtue of Cannon's logic in ruling the previous day on the census resolution. In fact, Norris conceded he did not believe the disputatious census resolution was, in fact, privileged under the Constitution and had so voted, but, if it were, as Cannon had ruled, then his, Norris's resolution, was too.

Accounts of the episode state that the Norris resolution, when read, caused a great commotion. Actually, it was the same resolution Norris had introduced in May, 1908, and which Cannon pigeonholed in the Rules Committee. Even if Norris's timing on St. Patrick's Day was a surprise the general insurgency movement was not. It had surfaced before, usually futilely, from time to time. Cannon had been aware of the unrest for years, but, perhaps, as he had remarked on another occasion, "rain doesn't always follow the thunder."

The Norris resolution would have abolished the existing five-member Rules Committee, whose chairman was Speaker Cannon. In its place a fifteen-member Rules Committee would be established, nine of whom would be members of the majority party. Membership would be fairly apportioned geographically. All fifteen would be elected by the full House, instead of being named by the Speaker. Moreover, the Speaker was specifically barred from being a Member. The elected Rules members would select a chairman from among themselves. The Rules Committee would also appoint members of other standing committees, another major diminution of the Speaker's power.

Why was the resolution privileged? Norris's argument, of course, was that analogous to the census matter, the Constitution also specified that the House "may determine the rules of its proceedings." Cannon supporters pointed to the "may" as permissive language, not mandatory. They noted that the House during the Fifty-first Congress had functioned for a time without specific rules. A Cannon chieftain, John Dalzell of Pennsylvania, raised a point of order against Norris's resolution on the grounds it was not privileged.

Memoirs and other written accounts indicate that insurgent Republicans felt queasy at this point. It was their "moment of truth." The price of the parliamentary reforms they advocated in the privacy of their homes and offices meant, in the cold, exposed atmosphere of the House chamber, a necessary alliance with the minority party, the Democrats. However, they could take heart from a comment by Sir John Harrington during one of England's violent periods: "Treason doth never prosper; for if it doth prosper then None dare call it Treason."

Champ Clark, Minority Leader and a future four-term Speaker, spoke:

> I remember hearing the Speaker say one day that this House could pass an elephant through the House if it wanted to, and that seems to me to be "going some"—to use a slang phrase. Well, now, if we can change the Speaker, why can not we change the rules? Suppose that a majority of the Members of this House had made up their minds to change these rules. How are you going to do it? If it is not a matter of privilege and you can not get it up that way, how are you going to accomplish it? Suppose some gentleman here offers an amendment to the rule or a new set of rules or a new rule. He puts it in the basket. It is referred to the Committee on Rules [the committee of jurisdiction] and it might as well be referred to the sleepers in the catacombs. I violate no secret when I tell you the Committee is made up of three very distinguished Republicans and two ornamental Democrats. They have a majority of one, but a majority of one in a committee of five is as big as a majority of forty-seven is in this House, and my own opinion is, both from observation and experience, that there never would be a rule reported out of that committee that the Speaker and his two Republican colleagues do not want reported. It is an impossibility in nature.

Reform of the rules was a House Democratic party position taken in caucus when the Sixty-first Congress opened in 1909. At that time they agreed to support any insurgent Republican effort in this direction. John Nelson, an insurgent Republican, decided to endorse an alliance with Democrats.

> The gentleman well knows we are not seeking self-interest. We are fighting for the right of free, fair and full representation in this body for our respective constituencies. . . . The 200,000 or more citizens of Wisconsin have some rights of

representation here under our Constitution. But what is that right under the despotic rules of this body? Merely the privilege to approve the will of a Representative Connor from another state invested with despotic power under artificial, unfair and self-made rules of procedure. . . . We are fighting with our Democratic brethren for the common right of equal representation in this House, and for the right of progressive legislation in Congress.

Nelson's last eight words constitute the heart of the matter. Cannon and his supporters were told that they were faced with Congressional revolution under color of law. Champ Clark said as much: "We made up our minds months ago to try to work this particular revolution that we are working here today, because, not to mince words, it is a revolution." This frank statement may have run off some Southern Democrats on grounds that, as one writer of the period put it, it smacked too much "like Mexican political reforms and they resented it." To Cannonites, party allegiance was the higher law in the House.

In the thirteenth hour of the debate, Mann took the most advanced position on behalf of Cannon:

> . . . on the whole, the rules of the House are probably the best considered, most scientifically constructed and finely adjusted rules governing any parliamentary body on Earth. . . . No such scenes and no such arbitrary action can take place in the House as I have often witnessed in the City Council of Chicago and the legislature of my State.
>
> But there never has been and there never will be any set of rules devised by which each one of four hundred Members of the House can at any time bring each one of 30,000 bills before the House for immediate consideration and disposal.

Cannon took the floor. He made a few telling points as to why some House members were moved about on the committees. The reasons were not always as the aggrieved members or their associates had stated. In general, Cannon explained his moves in this way:

> They failed to enter and abide by a Republican caucus, and this being a government through parties, for that as well as for other sufficient reasons [that Cannon never explained], the

Speaker of the House, being responsible to the House and the country, made the appointment with respect to these gentlemen as he conceived to be his duty in the execution of the trust reposed in him.

Opponents thought Cannon had cast his net too far. They saw little to sustain the view that the Speaker, any Speaker, is constitutionally responsible to the country or has a mandate from the country. A Speaker may be many things, they argued, but he gets there usually because he is elected by members of his own political party in the House.

The battle continued on and off the floor. In its thirteenth hour, a motion to recess was defeated by seven votes. Off the floor, calls went out to bring absent Cannon supporters back to Washington. Only 275 had voted on March 16th in connection with the census matter. As the battle mounted in fierceness, returning members would raise the total to more than 350. Sixty-five-year-old David Hollingsworth of Ohio, a first termer, was raising the devil on the floor because an agent of the sergeant-at-arms had routed him from his bed in a downtown hotel and ordered him to the House floor at 5 A.M. to help fill a quorum. Sometimes, Cannon was in his office—to sleep, to eat, to talk with his lieutenants. Sometimes, he would appear on the floor and listen smilingly to fiery denunciations about Cannonism. Norris, in keeping with other insurgents, said he was "fighting a system," not the Speaker. Cannon's agents negotiated with the party mutineers but mostly with the Democratic opposition leaders. Cannon men indicated an agreement could be reached on a change in the Rules Committee both as to size and means of appointment. Nevertheless, they wanted deleted any specific prohibition against the Speaker's service as a member of Rules. In the late stages of negotiation, there was an indication that the Speaker might be willing not to be a member, if he were not specifically barred. This was unacceptable, however, to both Democratic and insurgent Republican leaders of the mutiny.

At 4:50 P.M., Friday afternoon, March 18, the House managed to adjourn. It had been in continuous session for twenty-six hours. It agreed to reconvene at noon on Saturday, the following day. Newspapers in large, front-page headlines were predicting Cannon's defeat. The press and public galleries were jammed. About twenty enthralled Senators, Robert La Follette among them, were visitors on the House floor.

As promised, Cannon immediately ruled on the point of order made against the Norris resolution by his chief lieutenant, Dalzell, two days earlier. Expectedly, Cannon ruled to sustain the point of order. A wrangle, including two procedural roll calls, occurred, after which the House voted 162 to 182 not to uphold Cannon's ruling. Seven were recorded as present and thirty-seven not voting. It was 1:45 P.M.*

The Norris reform resolution was now the pending order of business. Norris then offered a substitute. It resembled the original one only in that it struck down the existing Rules Committee; otherwise, it was quite different. It instructed the House to establish within ten days a ten-member Rules Committee, of which six would be members of the majority party and four the minority. Also dropped was a geographical element contained in the original resolution. Each party caucus would select its members, but they would be subject to election by the House itself, and, as in the original resolution, the Speaker was prohibited from being a member.

Clark, addressing himself to the substitute resolution, asked its passage.

---

* Writing years later about the occasion, Clark conceded that "technically speaking, under the rules of the House, he [Cannon] ruled correctly in the Norris resolution. The Democrats and insurgents never claimed the contrary. But we boldly and candidly asserted that what we were doing was a revolution in parliamentary procedure for the good of the House and of the country. The only way we could accomplish it was to overrule the Speaker, which we did. . . ."

Underwood agreed. Clark's observation was borne out in January, 1911, less than a year after the revolt against Cannon. Charles Fuller of Illinois, a Republican, made a motion to change the rules of the House. As had Norris, he claimed his proposal was privileged under the constitutional provision authorizing the House to determine the rules of its proceedings. Mann made a point of order that the Fuller resolution was not privileged. Cannon agreed with Mann's contention. This time, however, the House, composed of the same members who had upset Cannon's similar ruling against the Norris resolution, upheld him on this occasion by a vote of 235 to 53! Only 26 Democratic votes were among the 53 votes.

. . . This is a fight against a system. . . . It does not make any difference to me that it is sanctified by time. . . . There has never been any progress in this world except to overthrow precedents and take new positions. There never will be. . . . We are fighting to rehabilitate the House of Representatives and to restore it to its ancient place of honor and prestige in our system of government.

The House adopted the Norris substitute by a vote of 191 to 156. Five were carried as present and, again, thirty-seven not voting. Victory was fashioned out of 149 Democrats and 42 defecting Republicans. The losing 156 votes were all cast by Republicans. On various other roll calls that day as many as forty-three Republicans bolted to join the Democrats.

"Proud to say that men of Illinois take their politics like a Kentuckian takes his whiskey, straight," Cannon remarked. "God bless the insurgents, for, as far as I am concerned, only He can bless them."

Speaker Cannon had been bludgeoned to his knees, but he had not lost his wits. He sensed that most insurgent Republicans did not want to pursue their course to the point where he would be unseated as Speaker. Other insurgents wanted Cannon removed but first wanted Cannonism prolonged as a popular issue until their reelection campaigns, eight months away. Thus, Norris moved to adjourn. The atmosphere in the House was one of jostling, pushing, shouting, near fights, clogged aisles, and a general milling about. Cannon acknowledging that Norris's adjournment resolution was privileged, asked him to yield. It was 4:33 P.M.; Norris did. Cannon made a few remarks in which he said he had interpreted the voting as reflecting "no coherent Republican majority in the House." His remarks may have been prepared in anticipation of just such a moment. Watson, a Cannon aide and later a Senator, wrote later that he had helped Cannon prepare just such a speech while the debate raged. Cannon's private thoughts, as set down later by L. W. Busbey, his secretary, were to the effect that he refused to resign and "become responsible for creating a worse condition than existed."

Cannon, gambling, asked for a motion to depose him. Albert

Burleson of Texas, a Democrat, obliged. There were calls for adjournment. The *Congressional Record* noted at this point in the transcript: "Great Confusion in the House." Cannon called for a vote on the Burleson resolution. It lost 155 to 192, with 8 present and 33 not voting. Underwood and Clark voted to declare the Speakership vacant. Insurgent Norris voted to retain Cannon. In fact, all except nine insurgent Republicans did.

Cannon was still Speaker when the House adjourned at 5:30 P.M. He had lost his shirt, but saved his chair.

II

1911-1930:
A STUDY
IN CONTRASTS

I

Woodrow Wilson: The New Freedom and W.W.

Cannonism as an issue remained politically potent. It helped propel Democrats into control of the House after the 1910 Congressional elections, which came eight months after the Cannon revolt.

During the campaign, the Democrats had coupled Cannonism and the high-duty Payne-Aldrich Tariff Act into one decisive issue. They claimed credit for the House upheaval. This claim found warm response among voters. The resulting political harvest was a bountiful one. A forty-four-seat Republican plurality in the Cannon House was converted into a sixty-five-seat Democratic plurality in the new Sixty-second Congress. For the first time since 1893, the Democrats controlled the House.

Conversely, it was an election disaster for many of the Republican Old Guard. Before the election, Nicholas Longworth of Ohio, a future Speaker and a Republican regular, had publicly stated that he would no longer support Cannon for leader. He further had predicted that, if the Republicans were returned as majority party and all Republicans attended their organizing meeting, "Mr. Cannon can not again be elected Speaker." Cannon survived the election. Returned to the House, Cannon was assigned to the Appropriations Committee he had chaired before becoming Speaker. Only this time he was placed last among Republicans on the Committee. Six of his committee chairmen from the last Congress went to the political scaffold in their campaigns for reelection. The six included Tawney, Appropriations Chairman.

In the spring of 1911, the Democratic caucus nominated Champ Clark, minority leader in the last Cannon House, for Speaker in the Sixty-second Congress. His selection was unanimous. Of course, Clark's nomination was the equivalent of election in the Democratically controlled House. The caucus selected Oscar Underwood of Alabama as both majority floor leader and chairman of the Ways and Means Committee, positions which Polk, Fillmore, and McKinley each had occupied before becoming President.

In organizing the House, Democrats set out to redeem a plank of their 1908 national platform. At that time, they had pledged support for adoption of "such rules and regulations to govern the House of Representatives as will enable a majority of its members to direct its deliberations and control legislation." This pledge was not made out of some abstract inclination toward democratic parliamentary procedure. It was a means of getting the country moving again. The Democratic party supported statehood for Arizona and New Mexico, popular election of Senators, publication of campaign expenses, and altering the existing protective tariff to one for revenue only and at rates that "will not destroy fair and honest competition in the home market." The Democratic party in the House performed radical structural surgery through the party caucus, an apparatus also effectively used earlier by Republican Aldrich of Rhode Island to regulate his party's affairs in the Senate.

The change took place through the party caucus, where confronted by Southern sectional strength, policy could be adopted only by a two-thirds vote. The Democratic caucus met in executive session, but its proceedings were entered in a public journal. Democrats, as the majority party in the House, voted to strip the Speakership of its power to appoint members of both majority and minority parties to most committees and to name the chairmen. With exceptions, the power of appointment had been a tightly held and cherished one ever since the First Congress more than 120 years before. The Speaker, under the newly adopted plan, did retain authority to name members to select committees and to appoint a chairman when the House sat as a Committee of the Whole House. The Democrats' new method of appointment vaguely resembled one suggested by Godlove S. Orth of Indiana thirty years earlier. The immediate proposal, however, was apparently the work of four Democratic members, Representatives Shackleford of Missouri, Hughes of New Jersey, Hay of Virginia, and Cordell Hull of Tennessee.

The new design worked this way. The Democratic members of the Ways and Means Committee would serve as a committee on Committees. They themselves would have been previously elected to Ways and Means at the party caucus. The committee on Committees, in turn, would make nominations for assignment to other standing committees, including Rules. These nominations would be submitted to the party caucus for approval and ratification. After that, the Democratic nominations would be brought to the floor, along with the Republican ones made under a different procedure. There the House members, Democrats and Republicans, would vote for the nominees of both parties and select the committee chairmen. Of course, such an election was a bit of a farce. When the Democratic party was the majority party, for example, its members would supply the necessary votes on the House floor to elect the nominees of their own party "and they would not interfere with the nominations of the minority." As it developed, the Speaker, when a Democrat, was not excluded from consultations about standing committee appointments.

An analysis made of the first post-Cannon Congress, the Sixty-second, shows a reshuffling of Democratic committee assignments with seniority often ignored, as well as many of the Republican members who had been favored in the previous Congress. There were at least forty transfers of Democrats from previously held assignments on seventeen major committees. In the Sixty-third Congress, there were at least fifty-eight such transfers. Thirty-nine of fifty-six committees were chaired by Southerners. Despite the new method of appointment, ranking on committees included the factors of experience, ability, geographical equity, as well as length of service.

A glimpse of the effort behind the transfers is given by a future Secretary of State, Cordell Hull of Tennessee. Hull in his memoirs writes about the work of the Democratic Committee on Committees, which consisted of fourteen Democrats, including Hull.

> We were determined to strip each committee of every possible vestige of special privilege and so to mold such committees as those on Agriculture, Labor and the Judiciary that they would join in securing maximum recognition by legislative actions for classes of American citizens who had been long neglected or discriminated against by numerous policies of the government. . . .
>
> If we had the least doubt about a prospective member's attitude we sent for him beforehand, cross-examined him and pledged him unequivocally to do teamwork. We turned down William Sulzer as chairman of the Military Affairs Committee because he was extravagant. Edward Pou of North Carolina was removed from the Ways and Means Committee and Claude Kitchin, from the same state, substituted for the reason Pou had once voted for a tariff on lumber [Pou recovered to become Chairman of Rules in 1917 and 1931-1934]. All this was a tremendous job, but we accomplished it in good time, and thus made up the committees of the House. The result was an effectively working organization along progressive lines.

In sum, it had been decided that a majority of the majority party, in this case, the Democrats, should be allowed to govern. It was a paramount policy decision. Republican committee assignments were also reshuffled by the new appointing authority, Minority Leader Mann.

In the new Sixty-second Congress, the House Rules Committee was enlarged by one to eleven members, seven from the majority and four from the minority. In keeping with the Norris reform, the Speaker was deprived of a seat on Rules, a privilege he had held for more than fifty years. Furthermore, his power of recognition was circumscribed. As the majority party, the Democrats were able to get their new committee plan, the revised rules of procedure, and alterations in the Rules Committee adopted by the full House. In addition, Calendar Wednesday was changed and made a more reliable protective device against a domineering Speaker. The unanimous-consent calendar, established two years earlier, was retained. This provided two days a month when bills, minor in scope but often important to individual members, could be called up for floor action without the sponsoring members having to obtain recognition by the Speaker.

A parliamentary bypass in the form of a *discharge petition* was established to enable a public bill to be brought to the House floor for discussion and a vote if it were being blocked in committee. A committee was to be discharged from jurisdiction over the bill if a specified number of members signed a petition. Today, 218 signatures are required. At other times, far fewer have been required. Procedures under which the full House acts on the discharged bill, however, are cumbersome. Furthermore, many members hesitate to sign a discharge petition because this offends powerful committee chairmen in whose eyes the device is considered a vote of "no confidence" in themselves. Therefore, the hopes for the discharge petition have been unfulfilled. Since its establishment in 1910, more than 820 petitions have been filed, but only twenty-three bills have been consequently discharged, and, of these, only two have become law: the 1938 Fair Labor Standards Act; and a 1960 pay-raise bill for Federal employees. Occasionally, however, a bill has suddenly been moved from its pigeonhole as the tally of signatures neared the required number.

The Clark-Underwood rebels with a cause had created a new power base in the House. At the top, stood the quietly strong Oscar Underwood of Alabama, a leader in the fight against Cannonism. Underwood's base rested upon three pillars—he was Chairman of the Ways and Means Committee, Chairman of the Committee on Committees, and legislative floor leader for his party. It had become customary for the Chairman of either Ways and Means or Appropriations also to be majority floor leader. For example, Thaddeus Stevens of Pennsylvania and Cannon each had served as majority floor leader, as well as Chairman of Appropriations. As late as the 1930s, a majority floor leader, Democrat Henry T. Rainey of Illinois, also held an active major committee assignment, though not the chairmanship. In recent years, this practice of wearing two hats has been abandoned, with occasional exceptions. One such occurred in 1967 when Majority Leader Carl Albert of Oklahoma took a troubleshooter assignment on the Education and Labor Committee because its combative Democratic members were badly divided.

Underwood, not the Speaker, was the most influential man in the House. An observer of the period thought Underwood now held a "semi-ministerial" position, drawn from British parliamentary life. Underwood himself had incorrectly predicted that, under the new arrangement, the chairman of the altered Rules Committee would become majority leader. During Underwood's period of House leadership, six future Speakers were sitting in the House: Republicans Frederick Gillett of Massachusetts and Nicholas Longworth of Ohio; and Democrats Henry Rainey of Illinois, Joseph Byrns of Tennessee, and two Texans, John Nance Garner and Sam Rayburn.

Despite the competition, Underwood may have been the best Democratic legislative leader in this century. He combined, Claude Bowers wrote appreciatively,

> conciliatory leadership . . . [and] unflinching courage. When the powerful industrial forces in Birmingham [Alabama] protested against his proposed reduction in the tariff schedules, he met them courteously but firmly with a simple reiteration of his principles; and when a great plant of the United States Steel Corporation was in process of construction in his home city and work was suspended, the implied threat was disregarded, and soon the officials of the corporation were busy with explanations and apologies.

Similarly, Underwood fought the Ku Klux Klan and legislation prohibiting the manufacture and sale of alcoholic beverages. Underwood was also his own man. Both he and Clark opposed repeal of a treaty clause that exempted coast-to-coast domestic shipping which used the Panama Canal from paying tolls. Wilson, under pressure from Great Britain, had proposed it.

Underwood gave life to his authority. The House, with its revised committee assignments, combined with a comfortable

Democratic margin, must be ranked as one of high accomplishment. Inexplicably, *The New York Times*, under C. R. Miller, then a conservative paper, called the Sixty-second Congress a "fussy, excited and confused body." A successful constitutional amendment was proposed to the states for the direct election of Senators. A parcel post system was established. A measure was approved to implement the soon to be adopted Sixteenth Amendment to the Constitution authorizing a Federal income tax—a net income of 100,000 dollars incurred a tax of slightly more than 2,260 dollars. Also enacted were improvements in pure-food laws and the establishment of an eight-hour working day for those employed under government contract. New Mexico and Arizona were admitted to the Union as the forty-seventh and forty-eighth states. A separate Department of Labor was established. The Interstate Commerce Commission was given authority to make fiscal valuation of railroad properties, a step toward determination of equity of fares. It was a productive performance.

Underwood held his own even when an activist President of the same political party entered the White House in 1913. Woodrow Wilson didn't like Speaker Champ Clark anyway. They had taken each other's measure while competing for the Democratic Presidential nomination the year before. Wilson thought the House Speaker "a sort of elephantine smart-aleck." Clark reciprocated.

Wilson, the first Democratic President in this century, believed in Presidential leadership. His supporters expected his New Freedom program of domestic improvements to curb concentrations of wealth, dissolve economic injustice, and improve social conditions. Their expectations were partially fulfilled. Their children would grow into the voters that supported the New Deal in a later harsh time.

Wilson, twenty-eighth President of the United States, addressed a joint session of Congress in April, 1913, the first to do so since John Adams. He favored such House allies as Underwood, whom he respected. The feeling was mutual. They were good legislative collaborators. The accomplishments of the House illustrate this: the historic Underwood-Simmons Tariff Act, the first general revision in the direction of lower duties since 1846; the Clayton Anti-Trust Act; the Federal Reserve Act; and the establishment of the Federal Trade Commission.

An impressive aspect of the Wilson legislative program was the promptness with which Administration requests were acted upon, and this occurred at a time when the House had just been increased to its present size, 435 members.

In 1913, the Federal Reserve legislation was introduced in June and signed into law that December, six months later. The tariff bill was proposed to the Sixty-third Congress in March, reported from the Ways and Means Committee in April, cleared the House in May, and was signed into law in early October, seven months later, an astoundingly brief span of time considering the historically controversial nature of tariffs. The proposal for an eight-hour work day for railroad employees was sent to the Congress in a special message on August 16, 1913. It became law seventeen days later.

In mid-January, 1914, Wilson proposed legislation in the area of monopolies and trusts. Within ten months, Wilson had before him the Federal Trade Commission Act and the Clayton Anti-Trust Act, both of which he signed. All these were disputatious measures that affected major economic interests, but Wilson's legislative leaders moved them promptly through the Congress.

One reason for the swift-moving progress was a temporary revitalization of the Democratic caucus. The Democratic caucus rules, adopted in 1909, had emphasized unity in matters of "party faith or party policy. . . ." Any Democrat not abiding by the caucus rules "shall automatically cease to be a member of the Caucus." On party matters, members were bound to abide if a policy of legislative position was assumed by a two-thirds vote, if that vote represented a majority of all Democrats in the House. There were escape hatches. A member was not bound if he had "made contrary pledges" to his constituents prior to his most recent election or if the matter involved "a construction of the Constitution," or he had contrary instructions from the party organization in his district.

In April, 1911, the Democratic caucus adopted a position by

which members "endorse the bills presented by the Ways and Means Committee . . . pledge ourselves to support said bills in the House . . . with our votes, and to vote against all amendments, except formal committee amendment, to said bills and motions to recommit, changing their text from the language agreed upon in this caucus." The party caucus journal records show that the Democratic caucus also instructed the Rules Committee as to content of the special orders it issued.

George Galloway in his *History of the House of Representatives* describes the period from 1911 to 1920 as one where "King Caucus supersedes Czar Cannon." In support of this characterization, the 1911 *Caucus Journal of the Democratic Party* carries an entry about an adopted resolution offered by Underwood. It states that the committees, Democratically controlled, "are directed not to report to the House during the first session of the 62nd Congress, unless hereafter directed by this caucus, any legislation except with reference to the following matters."

Wilson approved the revitalized caucus:

> The Caucus is meant as an antidote to the Committees. It is designed to supply the cohesive principle which the multiplicity and mutual independence of the Committees so powerfully tend to destroy. . . . The caucus is the drilling-ground of the party. There its discipline is renewed and strengthened, its uniformity of step and gesture regained.

This has not been the case in recent times, where flaccid leadership and autonomous committee chairmen control the House Democrats.

In 1915, Underwood moved to the Senate, where he eventually also became Democratic floor leader. His successor in the House was Kitchin, who also was both majority leader and Ways and Means Chairman.

During the 1915–1917 sitting, there were additional legislative gains for the Wilson Administration: a child labor law; establishment of the Tariff Commission; rural credits; greater autonomy for the Philippines; and additional naval expenditures. Kitchin, however, articulate and alert, grew to oppose publicly Wilson's foreign policy exercises in respect to the warring European powers. President Wilson tried to convince Kitchin personally; he did not succeed. For example, Kitchin fought the naval building program proposed by Wilson. Kitchin believed it would lead to further involvement in European rivalries. Consequently, defense bills were handled by Rainey of Ways and Means, rather than by Kitchin. Criticism of the antiwar majority leader grew. Demands mounted for his resignation after he had made a well-tailored midnight speech on the floor of the House against our formal entry into World War I on the side of France and Great Britain:

> . . . Let me at once remind the House that it takes neither moral nor physical courage to declare a war for others to fight . . . and I have made up my mind to walk it, if I go barefooted and alone. . . . Half the civilized world is now a slaughterhouse for human beings. This Nation is the last hope of peace on earth, good will toward men. I am unwilling for my country by statutory command to pull up the last anchor of peace in the world. . . .

A few hours later, at about 3 A.M. on April 6, 1917, the House approved by a vote of 373 to 50 a declaration of war resolution. Kitchin was one of 50 members voting nay. Yet the following month Kitchin energetically advanced a revenue bill, including a controversial increase in second-class mailing rates to finance the war he opposed. On several occasions, he felt himself obliged to chide members who had voted for the war resolution but balked at approving heavier imposts for funding the war.

Kitchin weathered the heavy storm, including a steady drumbeat of newspaper criticism. An admiring biographer, Alex M. Arnett, makes a reference to Kitchin's "turning of the floor leadership over to some other member when differences between him and the President reached a crisis." Kitchin had raised the point with himself as to the wisdom of the official party leader in the House leading opposition to a President of the same party. Records of the period however, indicate no formal abdication of his leadership position. Nevertheless, during America's direct participation in the war, Wilson took a greater degree of control as the party's legislative leader in the Congress. He often dealt directly with committee chairmen of both House and Senate. Wilson also maintained a liaison with Garner, a rising Democrat whom he respected. Clark continued as Speaker. He, too, had his legislative troubles with the President; for example, Clark opposed the military draft—"nearest to a convict's life," he labeled it.

In 1919, Democratic loyalists, calling themselves "the reorganization committee," sought to punish Clark for differing with Administration programs. Their efforts to remove Clark from party leadership fizzled, however.

Meanwhile, the Republican party in the House continued in a disorganized condition, although Theodore Roosevelt gave it continual pep talks from as far away as Africa. The 1916 Congressional elections seemed to give Republicans a thin edge: 213 Republicans, 212 Democrats, and 7 members of minority parties. Despite the plurality of one, however, the Republicans did not organize the Sixty-fifth Congress when it opened in April, 1917. Thomas Schall, a blind member from Minnesota and a Progressive, made an emotional speech in which he urged that a Democratic President should have a Democratic House and Senate. Until that time, there had been nine other occasions since the Civil War when there was "divided government," that is, one party controlled the Congress and another the Presidency. In the balloting five of the seven "others," including Schall, supported Clark for Speaker. The vote was 217 for Clark; 205 for Republican Mann, a brusque, capable figure; 2 for Republican Gillett, who would become Speaker two years later; and 2 for Republican Progressive Irvin Luther Lenroot of Wisconsin. Two members voted present.

During this period, House Republicans appeared to be of two minds in respect to the caucus, or *conference*, as they called it. Norris, for example, regarded the caucus as an evil. A biographer, Richard Lowitt, states that Norris looked forward to the time "when the progressive, patriotic sentiment of the American people will drive the caucus and the political boss and the political machine out of business." Norris, Lowitt continued, wanted Republican members free to offer amendments on the floor without being bound by a caucus position. Their party caucus decisions were made not binding.

Shortly before the opening of the Sixty-fifth Congress in 1917, the House Republican caucus established a seventeen-member Committee on Committees to make assignments. Since 1911, committee assignments had been made by party officer Minority Leader Mann. He became chairman. Currently, this Committee on Committees, unlike that of the Democrats, is composed of a member from each state that has a Republican in the House. Each committee member casts as many votes as there are Republicans in his state delegation. In addition, in 1917, a five-member *advisory committee* was established, with Mann also as its chairman. As nearly as can be determined, it had party housekeeping responsibilities and made policy suggestions. Apparently, the Republican Steering Committee evolved from the advisory committee.

Between 1919 and 1925, House Republicans maintained a policy that their Steering Committee should not include any ranking member of a major committee and that no ranking member should be placed on the Rules Committee. Later, the Steering Committee became a "policy committee" that included party officers. The Steering Committee may have met daily in the Sixty-fifth Congress. At these meetings, the committee members would summon Republicans on the legislative committees to discuss the strengths and weaknesses of legislation from the viewpoint of the overall position of the well-being of the party. Sometimes, the Chairman of Rules was invited to sit in when the Republicans were the majority party. Coordination, however, was less than ideal, at least on one occasion, when, during a Republican administration, Rules approved a rule covering one Republican's resolution to investigate an executive branch department. The Republican Speaker Gillett was not then a member of Rules. At the outset he was not even a member of either the Committee on Committees or the Steering Committee of his own party. Later, he did attend sessions of the Steering Committee. Thus, the Republican structure of party leadership reached as diffused a condition as that of the Democratic one.

Republicans quarreled. Mann was unpopular within his own party. In 1919, with Republicans now in the majority, he sought to be his party's candidate for Speaker in place of Gillett. This antagonized Longworth and other Republicans. As a result, they sought to oust him as chairman of the Republican Committee on Committees. They failed; however, Mann, minority leader since 1911, did not step up to majority leader in the Republican House. Instead, Frank Mondell of Wyoming, schooled in the Cannon style of leadership, was elected. Two years later, in 1921, Mondell also became Chairman of the Steering Committee and the Committee on Committees.

Changes in the structure of each party were widely discussed. The altered method of committee appointment attracted comment. In 1937, Norris, then a Senator, expressed a view that overall changes to the party structures were beneficial because these changes had made the parties more responsive to voters.

This view, however, was not unanimously shared. Both during and after the 1910 revolt, some House members and interested observers were dubious about the new improvements. Regardless of party affiliation, they sensed that, under the new order, power would ultimately be dispersed so widely that there would not be a sufficiently integrated institution, the House, to make the policy effective. Others felt that there had simply been a trade-in of a Speaker-dominated, five-member Rules Committee for a ten-member committee dominated by six members of the majority party. They noted that two of the five members on the discarded Rules Committee were renamed as members of the revised committee and that no insurgent Republicans were named to it. *La Follette's Weekly* commented that basically it meant little except "the temporary humiliation of an old man of bad eminence."

On the other hand, Victor Murdock of Kansas, insurgent Republican, favored even more decentralization. Murdock was one

of the nine insurgent Republicans who had supported the Burleson motion to depose Cannon. He wrote in the September 22,
1910, *Independent:*

> Popular disbelief in the adequacy of major laws, popular
> doubt of the willingness of Congress to pass effective law, has
> naturally bred a conviction among many that Congress is natu-
> rally not responsive to public opinion, and that, consequently,
> any major action by Congress must be forced not merely by
> means of agitation, but by prolonged and mayhap threatening
> agitation.

The executive branch, Murdock continued, reaped the benefit.
The Presidents "veer away from the constitutional function of
advising with Congress, and advance, at the opening of a new
Congress, with a legislative program which an aroused and sympathetic public opinion demands shall be carried out."

Murdock thought additional changes beyond the Clark-
Underwood alterations should be made in order that (1) Congress might become a more responsive representative body; (2)
Congress might regain its status as one of three coordinate
branches of the Federal government; and (3) "a new type of
Congressman" might develop, "one who insists upon effective legislative action and assumes individual responsibility for legislation." This point dovetailed with the insurgents' philosophy. In
one sense, they tended to be antiparty. They believed, in
Cooper's words, that the "party has no claim which exceeded the
conviction of individual members since the party rightfully only
existed to the extent that agreement existed." Nevertheless, many
persons were quite certain the 1910 business, carried to an extreme of decentralization as Murdock and other Progressives
seemed to desire, would breed ill.

A Republican House leader, John Dalzell of Pennsylvania, a
supporter of Cannon, chided the Democrats: "Gentlemen of the
Majority you are on the back track. Your reforms are all shams
and fraud. You have taken the power away from the Speaker.
But you put it all in the Chairman of the Ways and Means Committee. Instead of Cannonism and Reedism and Crispism, you
have today, Underwoodism."

George Rothwell Brown in *The Leadership of Congress,* sensed the problems that would arise to plague the political parties and the House because of the new internal machinery:

An analysis of the fundamental spiritual difference between the old system and the new is essential to an intelligent understanding of the difference in the manner of operation of the two systems.

Despite all the faults inherent in the system which Reed had inherited from Colfax and Blaine and from Henry Clay, and had improved, and had passed on to his successors, and which Cannon had made into a perfect piece of political mechanism, it at least had this to commend it to the people, that it had the courage of its convictions, was honest and stood four-square, and was at all times in the open, exposed to the pitiless glare of publicity. Every action it committed was instantly known throughout the country. The oligarchy demanded power commensurate with its responsibility, but the people could always hold it to that responsibility. The names of those who constituted the oligarchy were matters of public record. [Brown reported it difficult and sometimes impossible, for example, to know the names of members of the Republican Steering Committee and the Republican Committee on Committees. The existence of the Steering Committee, he said, was even denied for a time.] The name of the Speaker was known, and it was known to everyone that he stood at the head of the House, the creator of the committees, having the power of appointment and of removal, that therefore if a committee refused to report a bill which the country demanded the Speaker as the master of that committee was responsible. The names of the members of the Committee on Rules were known. Aside from the Speaker, the chairman, there were only two of the majority party, and in Mr. Speaker Cannon's time, and in Mr. Reed's time, their names were household words. With the exception of the committee chairmen, who were the Speaker's lieutenants, and the Floor Leader, who was the chairman of the Committee on Ways and Means, there were few other members of the inner circle. Not only were these responsible leaders of the House up to the 62nd Congress [when Clark's Speakership began, that is] thus indicated in public documents, but they took pride in distinguishing themselves among their fellows by a peculiar badge which they wore. This was a red carnation, and that small flower in the button-hole meant that men served as leaders of the House unafraid and unashamed. It was a touch of grim sentiment.

The new order became a system of secret government in the House of Representatives, and in this lies its chief weakness and greatest menace. It does not operate in the open, but under cover. It does not stand four-square to all the winds that blow, nor does it court publicity. It avoids the light and suppresses all mention of itself. The names of the gentlemen constituting this system are nowhere of public record except with respect to the Speaker, the chairmen of committees of the House, and where they appear in the list of Representatives. The Floor Leader is known simply by that title and by none other.

The members constituting the committee on Committees and the Steering Committee are not a part of the organization of the House, but of the caucus; they are not responsible to the House itself, or to the American people, but to the caucus [Democratic] or conference [Republican, as it is styled]. Not being responsible they can not be held to accountability. Under the old system if a bill in which the people were interested could not pass for the reason that it could not be brought before the House the Speaker and his Committee on Rules could be arraigned at the bar of public opinion. Under the new system if a bill in which the people are interested can not obtain consideration nobody can be held responsible for the reason that nobody knows that anybody is responsible. The Speaker can not be thus held, since it is notorious that the Speaker has no power, and the Floor Leader cannot be held to account, since the House openly has clothed him with no power.

Obviously, there is a responsible power somewhere in the House, for the country from time to time has evidence that certain bills are put forward, and that others are held back. Where then has gone the power that Reed and Cannon used to wield? That is a question of vital concern. . . . Previously the country could see the wheels go around. Now it can not.

Brown's viewpoint is not an isolated one. Luce, discussing his House experience, wrote:

The reformers believed they had put an end to dictatorship. Yet that some few men continued to guide is not to be questioned. What was really accomplished was to lessen the public knowledge of who those men were. Congressmen might know, but since 1910 the public generally has not known who should be rewarded or punished. Irresponsibility has been increased . . . the benefits of the change have not been conspicuous enough to impress anybody as important.

Other Congressional scholars agree. W. F. Willoughby of the Brookings Institution suggested that the primary objections to the discarded leadership system was that the powers were concentrated in the hands of one individual, not that the concentration was in one location. He therefore suggested objections could have been met by enlarging the Rules Committee or by a caucus committee.

As it turned out, the faults in the newly developed structure of the Democratic party were not particularly grievous during the Administrations of the strong-willed Wilson. The *laissez-faire* mood of the 1920s further postponed the crisis. The blighted condition of the House and the fragmented House Democratic party made their bruising impact only when political leaders of a nation beaten to the ground by severe economic depression during the 1930s, sought to meet the neglected agenda of unmet national needs.

It is a political truth easily defined that an elected majority should be permitted to govern until the voters speak again. This truth has been violated so often in the House it has been forgotten. Edmund Burke has written:

For my part, I find it impossible to conceive that any one believes in his own politics, or thinks them of any weight, who refuses to adopt the means of having them reduced into practice. It is the business of the speculative philosopher to mark the proper ends of government. It is the business of the politician, who is the philosopher in action, to find out proper means toward those ends, and to employ them with effect.

2

Harding, Coolidge, Hoover, and Normalcy

The 1920s was a period of dreary conservatism. The Presidents and the Congress generated homilies such as "less government in business and more business in government." Republicans controlled the White House, the Senate, and the House between 1919 and 1931, a dozen years that drifted into the Depression. The Democratic party turned its back on the New Freedom program of its last President, Woodrow Wilson, and thereby deserved its defeats, for its program was virtually indistinguishable from that of the Republican party. Only the yeasty, insurgent Progressive Republicans provided an alternative. In 1924, their candidate, Robert La Follette, received 4.8 million votes for President, 16 per cent of the total. In this election, the Democrats had nominated John W. Davis of West Virginia, their second most conservative Presidential candidate in this century. Davis received 29 per cent of the vote against Coolidge, the smallest percentage ever tallied for a Democratic nominee.

In social terms, the period is represented by the automobile, the radio, the motion picture, professional sports, the Ku Klux Klan, Sinclair Lewis's George Babbitt, and the Scopes trial. In political terms, by the prohibition disaster, protectionist tariff disasters, liquidation of wartime controls, Teapot Dome, and generous tax reductions for the wealthy.

A social historian has described the 1920s as the "Indian Sum-

mer of the Old Order." During this period, the American people,
by wide margins, successively elected as their Presidents a
commonplace, handsome child-man, a "Puritan in Babylon," and
an outdated, rigid Manchester liberal. Harding called a national
conference on unemployment in 1921, when there were 5.7 million unemployed, representing nearly 12 per cent of the total
labor force. The conference concluded, in effect, that unemployment was not a Federal responsibility. The tart-tongued Alice
Roosevelt Longworth observed that Harding's nomination came
at a convention "wormy with politicians—riddled with intrigue."
It seemed somehow natural that Coolidge (who took on a jungle
war of his own when he sent the Marines to Nicaragua in 1927)
returned to Northampton, Massachusetts, to occupy a 36-dollar-a-
month rented duplex. In the summer of 1928, Hoover accepted
his party's nomination in a speech in which he held out the vision
that America was "nearer to the final triumph over poverty than
ever before in the history of our land."

If this were indeed the condition of the country, the news had
not reached the farmers of America, for example. The farmlands
were blighted and in some areas disaster ridden. By 1933, cotton
would be selling for an horrendous average of 5.6 cents a pound,
and wheat would tumble to 33 cents a bushel from an early 1920s
price of 2 dollars 15 cents. Between 1920 and 1932, aggregate
farm income was to decline nearly 66 per cent, from 15.5 billion
to 5.5 billion dollars. The farmer's share of national income
would fall from 15 per cent in 1920 to 7 per cent in 1933. Twice,
in 1927 and again in 1928, Congress passed McNary-Haugen Acts
for farm relief. Coolidge, who had inherited Harding's collection
of plunderers in August, 1923, vetoed each one. In the industrial
sector, productivity increased 40 per cent between 1919 and
1928, but real wage earnings only 26 per cent. Consequently,
neither the farmers nor the urban working men and women were
dancing the gay Charleston until dawn or otherwise sharing in
the heady wine of Scott Fitzgerald's Jazz Age.

During this time of "passive" Presidents, Harding, Coolidge,
and Hoover, the Congress, particularly the House, stood dominant. The House consolidated its "power of the purse." In 1920,

authority shorn from the Appropriations Committee thirty-five years earlier was restored.

In 1885, during Carlisle's Speakership, jurisdiction over appropriations had been apportioned among nine committees. This meant, for example, that standing legislative committees, such as Agriculture and Military Affairs, would also issue appropriation bills to finance the departments, agencies, and bureaus they legislated for. Cannon said this dispersal was undertaken because the strong-willed Chairman of the Appropriations Committee, Samuel Randall, a former Speaker and a Democrat, had strayed from the low-tariff party line. Cannon thought, too, that department heads encouraged dispersed appropriations authority on grounds that each department would fare better in terms of appropriations. Thoughtful House members disliked the dispersed system. They believed it had led to domination of the Congressional appropriations process by the executive branch.

As a result, a remedial effort was begun under Appropriations Chairman Swager Sherley of Kentucky at the conclusion of World War I. After weeks of animated hearings, the Committee set in motion a successful resolution to recapture for the Treasury 15.4 billion dollars in unexpended wartime appropriations and unexecuted wartime contract authorizations. Sherley's successor, James Good of Iowa, cosponsored a bill that became law in 1921 to establish a vastly improved budget system for the executive branch, including establishment of the General Accounting Office under a Presidentially appointed comptroller general and the Budget Bureau, now the fiscal arm of the President. It was Good's resolution that restored to the Appropriations Committee exclusive jurisdiction over general appropriation measures in the summer of 1920. Majority Leader Mondell provided the votes.

Once again, this is an illustration of a major change brought about by resolute leadership. Many Republican legislative committee chairmen stood to lose influence because of this change. Therefore, Mondell was going against the wishes of the powerful members of his own Republican party, but he acted. Also, Mondell ignored strict seniority when he decided upon a chairman for the revitalized Appropriations Committee. He chose Martin Madden of Illinois, who was regarded as the strongest chairman since Thaddeus Stevens, its first chairman fifty-five years before.

In 1927, a related development occurred. At the time, each of eleven committees had authority to inquire into the expenditures of one or more departments of the executive branch. These functions were combined and placed under one committee, the Committee on Expenditures in the Executive Departments, now known as the Committee on Government Operations.

Legislatively, the Republican Congresses of the 1920s often stood against Republican Presidents, particularly Coolidge, though the House was headed, ironically, by Speaker Frederick Gillett of Massachusetts, who was Coolidge's Congressman, for his district included Coolidge's home town, Northampton. Gillett, a party elder, became Speaker at sixty-eight and served, unassertively, from 1919 to 1925. His floor leaders, Mondell and Longworth, surpassed him both in power and influence. Rayburn once said Gillett liked being Speaker because it made him "feel fine to go in first to dinner. Gillett didn't really enjoy the power."

There are three footnotes to his uninspired administration. First, the House repeatedly denied an elected Socialist, Victor Berger of Wisconsin, his seat. Berger spoke and wrote in opposition to participation of the United States in World War I. As a result, he was convicted and sentenced to twenty years in jail by Federal Judge Kenesaw Landis. On appeal, the Supreme Court reversed the conviction, and Berger was seated and served three terms. Secondly, Alice Robertson of Oklahoma is credited, by one account, of being the first woman to preside over the House. Third, the Rules Committee received added authority when Speaker Gillett ruled that it is the executive organ of the majority of the House, whichever political party controls, and, therefore, it could originate a resolution to consider a bill whether or not the subject matter had been referred to it.

Nationalism walked hand-in-hand with "normalcy." At the outset of the first Republican House in eight years, Mondell set the tone. It would be "the era of reconstruction and return of old policies," he said. House Republicans had the votes to turn back the clock. Their pluralities during the 1920s ranged as high as 165 seats.

There was a rush to liquidate wartime regulations and most war-created agencies. The maritime shipping industry received protectionist wrapping in the form of the Jones Act. The same was done for manufacturers in the form of the Fordney-McCumber Tariff of 1922. The Interstate Commerce Commission, originally established to protect the public interest, was given a new responsibility of protecting the railroads' rate of return. On the plus side during Harding's Administration, the Federal Power Commission was established and an agriculture credits program enacted. Despite a stingy President, the Congressmen raised their annual salary from 7,500 to 10,000 dollars in 1923. The House also passed a soldiers' bonus bill over Coolidge's veto. They turned down as well his proposal that the United States affiliate with the Permanent International Court of Justice [World Court] at The Hague and added unwanted Japanese exclusion and national origins features to a 1924 immigration bill.

Congressional Republicans, although in the majority during the 1920s, were not without problems. Until 1923, Mondell as floor leader rode the two horses of orthodoxy and insurgency. In 1923, with Mondell no longer in the House, the tandem parted. That fall, insurgent Republicans, calling themselves Progressives, decided to nominate Henry Cooper of Wisconsin against Speaker Gillett, who sought renomination when the narrowly Republican Sixty-eighth Congress convened in December, 1923. They refused to help organize the House for their party unless the rules of the House were changed to their satisfaction. This resulted in a two-day deadlock, during which Republican Gillett and Democrat Finis Garrett of Tennessee matched each other vote for vote for election as Speaker. Finally, Majority Leader Longworth met with the unruly political truants, Nelson of Wisconsin, Woodruff of Michigan, and LaGuardia of New York. Out of this came an agreement to put the rules of the last Congress temporarily in effect while the Rules Committee itself developed suggested changes. This cleared the way for Gillett to be reelected Speaker.

The Rules Committee held open hearings at which members were invited to give their views. In mid-January, 1923, Rules reported to the full House. Then followed a five-day floor fight about the rules. Every member had an opportunity to speak. Rules of the House were altered as follows:

The discharge and consent calendars were made more workable; the Chairman of the Rules Committee was prevented from exercising a pocket veto, as had been the habit of Philip Campbell of Kansas; a rule could not be voted on the same day it was issued by the Rules Committee, except during the last three days of a session, without agreement by a two-thirds vote of the House; and more prompt action on contested elections was ordered. Democrats and insurgent Republicans also succeeded, by a vote of 208 to 177 over the conservative Republican leadership, in deleting from the House rules a provision that amendments to a revenue bill must be germane to the provisions of the bill—the so-called *Underwood rule*. Democrats, looking ahead to the fight over a Mellon tax bill, led the fight for the change. A crush of servicemen's bonus bills led to a successful effort to lower the required number of signatures to discharge a bill from any legislative committee from a majority, 218, to 150.

In December, 1925, Nicholas Longworth, fifty-eight-year-old Republican from Ohio, became Speaker, succeeding Gillett who had been elected Senator. Longworth was the most regular of the regulars without being moss backed. It was Longworth's party regularity that gave him an advantage over John Tilson of Connecticut, whose seniority and longtime prominence in the party leadership should have provided him with a stronger claim. While floor leader and Chairman of Ways and Means, Longworth supported high tariffs and opposed United States membership in the League of Nations. He held to party orthodoxy, although he had married a daughter of Theodore Roosevelt. Longworth had not supported his father-in-law's candidacy for President in 1912 on the Bull Moose ticket, though Longworth's wife, Alice, did. Longworth supported Taft and campaigned for him. Taft lost; so did Longworth. A Bull Moose Congressional candidate for his Cincinnati district seat had split the vote. Two years later, however, Longworth ran again, this time successfully. He remained in the House until his death in 1931. Longworth had a clear view of the Speakership: strong leadership; insistence on rules that enable a majority of the majority party to function effectively, a condition that does not exist in the House today; and fairness.

Robert Kintner and Joseph Alsop, who covered the Hill, described Longworth's interesting combination of qualities as: "toughness, urbanity and finesse." They were often invited to his private office off the Rotunda for a chat. During Prohibition years, the records are discreet as to whether they had a "touch." Refreshments were certainly available when later Speakers Garner and Rayburn carried on Longworth's innovation. It grew into a valuable "Board of Education," composed of the Speaker, a few highly favored members, and a few highly favored newspapermen.

Longworth's first major political act as Speaker sprang from his views on party orthodoxy. He resolved that punishment should be applied to a baker's dozen of defecting Republican Progressives, ten of them from Wisconsin. They had bolted their party's nominee, Coolidge, and, instead, had supported La Follette in the 1924 Presidential campaign. They had also supported Cooper against Longworth for Speaker. They had refused to support a party position that 218 signatures be required to set in motion a discharge petition.

Characteristically, the Progressive Republicans in both the House and Senate acted throughout the 1920s as though they were a party apart from the regular Republican party. In 1923, they had actually drafted their own legislative program, which was a harbinger of New Deal proposals, ranging from protections for labor unions to farm relief and restrictions on employment of children. They even held their own caucus. "I'd rather be right than regular," Fiorello LaGuardia said.

Longworth said they were neither right nor regular. For these defiances, two of the Progressives were ousted from their seats on

Ways and Means and the Rules committees. The others were denied participation in the party caucuses, stripped of their committee seniority but not transferred to other committees. In the next Congress, the Seventieth, they were readmitted to the caucus. LaGuardia, a prominent, lonely Eastern Progressive, sought a seat on Judiciary. He was assigned to the Alcoholic Beverage Traffic Committee.

Longworth took this position in respect to the defectors:

> I want to most emphatically disavow any feeling of enmity or hostility toward any member of the Wisconsin delegation, or any one in this House who supported the La Follette-Wheeler ticket in the last campaign. On the contrary, I have only feelings of the greatest respect and friendship for them all. Nor do I think that they committed any crime. On the contrary, they only exercised the right any American has, to support the cause that he believes for the best interests of the country. They believed evidently that the election of President Coolidge and the carrying forward of the Republican program and of Republican principles were injurious to the country, and they, therefore, supported Senator La Follette for President and did all they could to defeat President Coolidge and to elect him, and in a large number of cases to defeat at the same time Republican candidates for Congress.
>
> They had a perfect right to do this. They did it with the utmost deliberation. But while they expected and hoped for victory, they must at the same time have been prepared to take the consequences of defeat.
>
> Surely no sane man could have believed that the consequences of defeat could have involved anything less than divorcement, temporarily at least, from any of the advantages to be gained by membership in the victorious Republican Party. . . .
>
> These gentlemen showed their true colors in the last election. They repudiated the Republican platform; they had a Presidential candidate of their own; they opposed the election of President Coolidge even more vigorously than they did that of Mr. Davis [Democratic candidate]. While they had no hope of electing their candidate, they avowedly hoped to elect a group in Congress sufficiently large, as one of their leaders said in the campaign, "to hamstring the administration of President Coolidge."

At the election, the people repudiated this sort of thing by a huge majority, but owing to peculiar conditions in their states, these gentlemen were returned to Congress. They have asked, notwithstanding their bitter opposition in the last election, to be treated as members of the Republican Party, and to hold their positions on the committees. The Republican Party has a substantial majority with or without them [247 to 183]. Ought we to have acceded to their request? To my mind such a course would have been a deliberate violation of the mandate imposed upon us by the electorate. By the mandate we are instructed to do certain things which they demand. We had to meet the situation, and we have met it by excluding them from participation in our party counsels and from representation on the important key committees. We have no ill-will toward them. What we have done was not in any sense by way of punishment.

We have left the door open for their return to our party, and will welcome them back upon their return, but until they do so we propose to proceed according to the American system of responsible party government.

To Longworth, party loyalty did not entail supineness toward a President of one's own political party. As Speaker, Longworth successfully took to the floor to urge the House to override Coolidge's veto of a naval building bill. "I agree with you as to the efficiency of the Bureau of the Budget and I believe in following them whenever I can," Longworth told the House. "But, mind you, the Bureau of the Budget is not responsible to the people of the United States, and we are." As Speaker, he also helped override Hoover's veto of a veterans' benefit bill. He believed a Speaker, occupying an office reduced in power, could nevertheless manage the House and an appreciable share of national legislation by means of energy, firmness, vision, and determination. His efforts in those directions, of course, were made easier by an aloof, usually indifferent Coolidge in the White House one mile away from the Capitol. One newspaper editor observed, "A Republican Congress has devoted itself to bloodying the President's nose, boxing his ears and otherwise maltreating him."

Nick Longworth once told the House:

I believe it to be the duty of the Speaker, standing squarely on the platform of his party, to assist, insofar as he properly can, the enactment of legislation in accordance with the declared principles and policies of his party, and by the same token to resist the enactment of legislation in violation thereof.

"I believe in responsible party government . . . Just as I stand for this, the American custom of responsible party government, I am against the European system of bloc government. I have observed its workings abroad at first hand. It works badly enough over there where legislation is generally a matter of bluster and trafficking between groups, and where governments fall overnight. Here it won't work at all, because it is un-American.

In keeping with this view, Longworth restored to the Republican caucus a requirement that members be bound by its decisions. Then, as now, the House Republicans used their party caucus as a means of achieving legislative cohesion. George Galloway has estimated that the House Republicans caucused more than forty times during the eight Eisenhower Presidential years.

What of the Democrats during the twelve-year period of Republican domination in the House extending from 1919 to 1931? During that period, its Southern wing *was* the Democratic party. In 1921, for example, 99 out of 134 Democrats, or 74 per cent, were Southerners; the following year, 109 of 207; in 1929, 101 of 190; and in 1933, a total of 109 out of 219, or 45 per cent. Not surprisingly, therefore, three out of four ranking Democrats on the committees in 1924 were Southerners, and in 1933, 28 of 47 permanent committee chairmen were Southerners. In 1937, the percentage was 30 per cent; in 1943, almost half, 47 per cent. By comparison, when the Ninetieth Congress opened in 1967, 87 of the 247 Democrats were Southerners, or 35 per cent. Southern Democrats, however, continued to chair a majority of the committees, 11 out of 21. Furthermore, a Northerner has never chaired the Democratic Committee on Committees, which nominates Democrats to the standing legislative committees. Until very recently, Southern Democrats on this committee have equaled or outnumbered Democrats from other regions. Rarely has a Northern Democrat risen to be senior man of his party on Appropriations, discounting Clarence Cannon, a rural Missourian. Eleven Democrats have served as Speaker since the Civil War. Six of these have been Southern men.

As one raised in Alabama, I am thoroughly familiar with the many courageous, extremely able and fine members of the House from the South. The fact remains, however, that on certain key social issues the Southerner, with all these fine qualities, is unable to extricate himself from the segregationist flypaper. When Oscar De Priest, a Negro Republican from Illinois, first entered the House in 1929, he encountered a number of deliberate harassments. Members protested they did not even want him assigned to a suite next to theirs in the House Office Building. Fiorello LaGuardia, however, said he'd be pleased to have him as a neighbor. Later that year, Southern state legislatures in the South passed formal condemnatory resolutions when De Priest's wife was invited by Mrs. Hoover to a tea at the White House. At the 1936 Presidential convention, a delegate, Senator "Cotton Ed" Smith of South Carolina, a lace-curtain Ku Kluxer, walked out on the proceedings because a Negro minister gave a blessing and a Negro delegate was present on the floor.

Northern Democrats, including those from the city political machines, are more responsive to critical domestic problems. It is a pragmatic reaction. More of the Northerners' constituents vote, and the Northerner, therefore, runs a greater political risk of not being returned to Congress if he does not respond.

The predominance of Southern Democratic members with seniority may be explained by a passage from Samuel P. Huntington's *Revised Theory of American Politics* that reflects conditions in the 1920s:

> In any rural area there is usually only one dominant economic interest. Economic life of the area is dependent upon his industry and both parties reflect it, making little difference in the parties. Party choice is determined by noneconomic, historical and traditional factors, which, once determined, there is no reason for change. Rural north Republican; rural South Demo-

cratic. A second party loses its important characteristic of opposition. Rural politics is based largely on personalities . . . friends and neighbors pattern.

Huntington is describing the anatomy of a "safe" district. It survives political landslides, such as the one in 1946 when Republicans captured the House while the Democrats lost fifty-four seats. Only two of these losses occurred in Southern Congressional districts, and both of these were in Kentucky. Southern House members were able to climb further up the lucrative seniority ladder as they replaced more senior, defeated Northern and Western Democrats.

The Southern dominance of the Democratic party, extending into the 1930s, meant that most Democratic Members shared certain assumptions about government and society.

Perhaps this is a reason the caucus was seldom used for legislative purposes. This dominance meant that the House Democrats were presented with few mavericks and, therefore, had no occasion to flick the lash of party discipline as the Republican regulars were forced to do. Perhaps this ingrained condition partially accounts for the unwillingness of later Democratic leaders to invoke discipline when the party took on liberal coloration in the 1930s. As the party's positions became more liberal, a set of dissenters developed, some in leadership positions. Unlike the former Republican dissenters, however, who were liberals, the Democratic dissenters were deeply conservative, and, unlike the Republican leadership, the Democratic leadership permitted their dissenters repeatedly to turn their backs on both party platforms and Presidential candidates without punishing them.

Both Republican insurgents and liberal elements within the Democratic party were encouraged by the Congressional elections in 1930. The elections proved liberals correct in their complaints about Congressional inaction in the face of neglected domestic problems, compounded by an economic depression of growing severity. The stock market had crashed in October, 1929. There was noticeable grumbling among normally conservative but alarmed Republicans about Longworth's excessive conservatism, especially among his Cincinnati constituents. Long-worth barely survived reelection in November, 1930. Forty-nine other Republicans lost. The Democrats were emerging from their twelve-year political eclipse in the House. The seeds of change, represented by the New Deal, were sprouting.

III

1931–1945:
DEPRESSION
AND WAR

I

Roosevelt, the New Deal, and the House

Disaster racked the country, especially the city and the farm. The Depression seemed to have no bottom. The farm sector of the economy was in ruins. The bankruptcy rate per 1,000 farms had increased, for example, from 0.21 in 1920 to 1.20 in 1926. Tens of thousands of farmers lost their farms. During a nine-year period carrying into 1929, farm mortgage indebtedness had been increased by 2 billion dollars. Agricultural land values had tumbled from 79 billion dollars in 1920 to 44 billion dollars twelve years later. Total farm income stood at 5.2 billion dollars in 1932, only about one-third of the 1920 figure.

Matters were no better in the industrial sector. Approximately 60 per cent of American families in 1929 had incomes under 2,000 dollars a year, a sum established by a prestigious Brookings Institution study as the amount sufficient to provide only basic necessities. In 1932, national income totaled 41 billion dollars, one-half the total in 1929. Per capita income, adjusted for changes in cost of living, fell from 681 dollars in 1929 to 495 dollars in 1933. Business inventories rose in face of falling demand. Manufacturing production in the middle portion of 1932 stood at less than one-half of the maximum level of output in 1929. In 1932, total wages amounted to about 40 per cent of the 1929 figure and

salaries 60 per cent. For those with a morbid interest in charting
the misfortunes of the stock market, between 1929 and 1932, General Motors had declined from 72¾ to 7⅞; United States Steel
from 261¾ to 21¼. Between 1929 and 1932, exports declined
from 5.2 billion to 1.6 billion dollars and imports from 4.4 to 1.3
billion dollars.

During 1932, approximately 273,000 homeowners lost their
properties by foreclosure. Approximately 4,300 national and
state banks had failed in the past three years, 1930 through 1932,
more than 500 in the one month of October, 1931. The permit
value of residential construction dropped 92 per cent during
1928–1933.

Efforts were made to relieve the situation. President Hoover,
an intelligent and highly capable civil engineer, seemed unable to
adjust his theory of the market place to the actual, dreadful economic condition. Hoover "had a sense of purpose so precise as to
be stultifying," a student of the executive branch, Richard Neustadt, has written.

There was a Federal Farm Board authorized in 1929 to buy
"glut" commodities from farmers. A one-year moratorium on
war debts and reparations was put into effect in 1931. Yet both
were offset by the 1930 Smoot-Hawley tariff legislation which
raised duties on our imports at a time when we were a great
creditor nation with overseas private investment of nearly 14
billion dollars. Approximately 1,000 professional economists
warned of its grave consequences: curtailed commerce; cost-of-
living increases; and harm to overseas investments. They peti-
tioned Hoover to veto it. Instead, he signed it.

Hoover ultimately became convinced of a need for a 45-
million-dollar relief measure for livestock in Arkansas, but, as one
historian commented, he opposed a 25-million-dollar appropriation to feed the families who owned the livestock. In 1932, the
Reconstruction Finance Corporation was established to make tide-
over loans to banks, businesses, and industries. It was a dole to
business organizations but not to individual, suffering businessmen. Hoover was opposed to direct relief, which he insisted was
a local or, at most, a state problem. Direct relief from the Federal

Government to individuals is bad for the checks and balances devised by the constitutional fathers, he reasoned. In the spring of 1932, an army of bedraggled "bonus marchers," ultimately to number 20,000 moved into Washington. Hundreds stood on the Capitol steps, while inside the Senate voted down a soldiers' bonus. In late summer, the stricken marchers were driven from their squatters' settlements on the Anacostia Flats with the help of Federal bayonets and Federal tear gas. Tens of thousands hit the road. The Missouri Pacific Railroad noted 186,000 migrants on its lines in 1931, nearly fourteen times as many as two years earlier.

There were millions needing relief. In October, 1930, there were 4.3 million jobless, or about 8 per cent of the national labor force; one year later, there were 8 million, or 16 per cent; 12 million, or 24 per cent, in the fall of 1932; and perhaps 13 million, nearly 25 per cent, in early 1933. Wage cutting had started in earnest in 1931. The 45- and 35-dollar-a-week stenographer of 1929 had become a 16-dollar one three years later. Americans were starving. Mayor Curley of Boston acknowledged that, on one April day in 1930, there were thirteen bodies in the city morgue as a result of either starvation or financial desperation. A. J. Liebling, the newspaper historian, has written that the daily newspapers seemed to share or acquiesce in Hoover's continuous assurances that the good ship Lollipop would right itself. Instead, the wolves were having litters at the cabin doors. It was a credibility gap that the newspapers themselves had created. It is possible to read leading newspapers of that period for day after day without encountering any attempt to "tell it like it is."

Franklin D. Roosevelt defeated Hoover by 7 million votes. Walter Lippmann, in another of his astounding misjudgments on men and issues (over a period of fifty years), dismissed Roosevelt as a "pleasant man, who, without any important qualifications for office, would very much like to be President." Amid the poverty and despair, President Roosevelt received lots of advice and a warning. An eminent economist, John Maynard Keynes, informed him by means of a letter published in *The New York Times:*

You have made yourself the trustee for those in every country who seek to mend the evils of our condition by reasoned experiment within the framework of the existing social system. If you fail, rational change will be gravely prejudiced throughout the world, leaving orthodoxy and revolution to fight it out.

Democracy, as Herbert Croly has written, was no self-fulfilling prophecy.

Reasoned experiment was needed, and reasoned, and sometimes unreasoned, self-contradictory experiment Roosevelt gave the country after that bitterly cold day in March, 1933, when he became President. He enjoyed a sympathetic majority at the opening of the Seventy-third Congress; Democrats held 71 per cent of 435 House seats and 62 per cent of 96 Senate seats. Richard Hofstadter has called the New Deal "A temperament," not a philosophy. Roosevelt acted upon a condition, not a theory. Unlike Harding and Coolidge, he was not a reluctant President. He rewrote the rules by which the American economy had been operating.

The most pressing tangible problem was unemployment, the most intangible problem, confidence in self and country, Roosevelt told an attentive nation in his first "fireside chat" broadcast. There is discussion today as to whether the Federal Government ought to be designated as "employer of last resort" in stubborn pockets of severe unemployment, particularly among Negroes. For approximately six years following 1933, the Federal Government did become the employer of last resort for millions of destitute men and women, a major portion of them white-collar workers. Undisciplined private enterprise had collapsed on them; sweet, private charity had been inadequate. Roosevelt promised to put the millions back to work.

The Seventy-third Congress, convening March 9, cooperated on both unnerved sides of the aisle. Republican Minority Leader Bertrand H. Snell of New York told the House: "The house is burning down and the President of the United States says this is the way to put out the fire." The 1936 Republican Presidential candidate, Alfred Landon, certainly didn't sound like one in 1933. "Even the iron hand of a national dictator," Landon said, "is in

preference to a paralytic stroke. . . . I now enlist for the duration of the war." Another Republican, Senator Vandenberg of
Michigan, agreeing, said the country needed a dictator "who
dictates."

Prior to the legislative successes, however, came a fierce leadership struggle among House Democrats. Garner as Vice President
elect had tried to select his successor as Speaker, but his attempt
failed at the party caucus March 2, 1933. "The little band of
conservatives whom Speaker Garner relied upon to carry on his
leadership in the next [Seventy-third] Congress was unhorsed at
the Democratic caucus . . .", one newspaper dispatch reported
the next day. Garner supported John McDuffie of Alabama, the
party whip. Rainey campaigned in part on grounds that it was
about time a Northern man became Speaker. Rainey at seventy-
two was the oldest man ever to become Speaker; he defeated
McDuffie by a vote of 166 to 112. A third candidate, John Rankin
of Mississippi, received twenty votes. Subsequently, McDuffie,
whose supporters included William Bankhead and Rayburn and
Massachusetts members, found himself stripped of his position as
whip. A Northerner, Patrick Boland of Pennsylvania, was elected
in his place.

Rainey had become Speaker as a result of a three-cornered
deal. Joseph Byrns' forces agreed to aid the contending Rainey.
In return, the Rainey forces agreed to support Byrns for majority leader. Another contender for Speaker, Thomas Cullen of
New York, a Tammany type, it was agreed, should become "assistant" majority leader. Texas votes were lured to the Rainey-
Byrns-Cullen "ticket" out of an understanding that one of their
delegation, James Paul Buchanan, would become chairman of
Appropriations, a position then held by Byrns of Tennessee.
Byrns became majority leader by a vote of 151 to 140. It all had
fallen into place as agreed. At one point during the party caucus,
it appeared that candidates for renomination as clerk, doorkeeper,
and postmaster might be swept out also. There was even a hot
race for Chaplain of the House. New Democrats, unsuccessful in
the challenge, said the House Chaplain should be one of them, not
a Republican.

The new majority leader, Byrns, made it clear that his election was a result of policy differences with the conservative Garner men. The new leadership accepted a larger role for government in efforts to end the depression. "Failures in the last Congress," he said, "have been due to the fact that the determination of policies has come entirely from the Speaker's Chair; it will now come from the Party. We will put over Mr. Roosevelt's program."

The new Speaker, Rainey, announced that for the first time House Democrats would have a Steering Committee led by a chairman. It consisted of twelve members selected by the Chairman of the House Democratic caucus. Each represented a different geographical area. Other members were the Speaker, majority leader, caucus chairman, and whip. Rainey envisioned the Steering Committee, which most Southerners, including Rayburn, profoundly distrusted, as a place to resolve party differences and to bring legislation to the floor, but only when "it is known that there are enough Democratic votes to assure the legislation." It represented, Rainey said, "a long step forward, and it takes from the Speaker powers and gives it [sic] back to the House."

The leadership under Rainey responded promptly and with verve to the country's needs. Speaker Rainey and Majority Leader Byrns, with the assistance of the panicked "opposition," guided a generous batch of remedial legislation to passage. The country, apart from Union-League types, approved.

The House on the first day of the first session of the Seventy-third Congress passed the emergency banking bill without copies being available to individual members. Two days later, however, Democrats, led by Wright Patman of Texas and Fred Vinson of Kentucky, refused in caucus by a 174 to 108 vote to be bound to support F.D.R.'s bill for a one-year reduction in veterans' pensions and government salaries. The bill did pass a few hours later by 266 to 138. Democrats had supplied 92 of the nay votes. Therefore, although uncommonly cooperative, the first New Deal Congress was not a rubber stamp. Speaker Rainey even drafted his own fiscal program and urged it on Roosevelt. More give-and-take occurred than is generally known, according to Raymond Moley, a Roosevelt adviser.

Successive New Deal Congresses authorized three job programs: emergency work relief, by means of the Civil Works Administration; long-standing public works, such as the Tennessee Valley Authority complex through the Public Works Administration; and work, such as reforestation through the Civilian Conservation Corps, which would be noncompetitive with private industry. A long list of other measures held out further promise. Battered businessmen, for example, through the National Industrial Recovery Act (NRA) received permission for price and production quota agreements in return for promising to improve wage levels. Impoverished farmers were given assistance in the form of the Agricultural Adjustment Act. In the form of NRA's Section 7a, harassed labor unions received limited protection against employer harassment and intimidation. It helped, because, between mid-1933, when its members represented less than 6 per cent of the labor force, and mid-1936, the American Federation of Labor increased its membership by 75 per cent. The United Mine Workers of John Lewis doubled its rolls during a three-year period.

Banks were closed, wrung out, and reopened. The Federal Deposit Insurance Corporation was established. The gold standard was formally abandoned. The Home Owners Loan Corporation was set up in 1934. Tariff walls were breached the same year with the Reciprocal Trade Agreement Act. Other legislative accomplishments included the Security and Exchange Act and the Tydings-McDuffie Act for Philippine independence.

A national system of social insurance, covering 26 million Americans, was established. Today, nearly that number are receiving benefits and approximately eighty-nine million in their working years are covered by Old Age and Survivors Insurance. The Federal Communications Commission and the Federal Housing Administration came into existence. A housing program of modest dimensions was established. The crime-splattered prohibition amendment to the Constitution was repealed. The rural electrification and the soil conservation programs were innovations for the farmers. A cotton control program attempted to establish tenant farmers and share croppers as independent farmers.

During this period of high achievement, the Rules Committee operated as an arm of the House leadership. In the Seventy-third Congress, it operated most of the time under the chairmanship of Bankhead. He envisioned Rules as "the political and policy vehicle of the House of Representatives to effectuate the party program and the party policy." Consequently, Rules reported a dozen closed rules (no amendments permitted) to protect key legislation of the New Deal during those first two years. The House accepted all but one.

The Democratically controlled Seventy-fourth Congress opened in January, 1935, with a mammoth Democratic margin in the House, 322 seats to 102 Republican seats, with 10 held by Farmer-Labor and Progressives. The margin apparently disconcerted the Democratic leadership who worried about the unorthodox views the newcomers might have. As a result, the leadership put through a change in the discharge petition to require 218 instead of 145 signatures. *The New York Times* reported that Republicans looked on in "considerable merriment," because, only four years before, House Democrats had succeeded in having it lowered to 145 from 218.

By the end of March, moreover, the Seventy-fourth Congress was moving less promptly at Roosevelt's urging. Three months into the session, the legislative program of the President hadn't budged. For example, there was a 4-billion-dollar emergency relief appropriation, which didn't clear the Congress until April. This contrasted with the far more prompt actions in the 1933–1934 Congressional session. Although programs finally were approved, they pleased few. Organized labor complained because the emergency relief measure did not contain a prevailing wage provision designed to prevent relief wages from depressing wage rates of private industry in specific localities. Labor was further disenchanted with Roosevelt because of his ambiguous attitude toward Senator Wagner's labor bill to encourage collective bargaining. Originally, it had not been a New Deal measure, although popular history has stamped the entire legislative product of those years with Roosevelt's *imprimatur*.

Roosevelt was feeling pressure from political evangelists. He was kept mildly left of center by such plans as Dr. Townsend's for 200-dollar-a-month pensions for Americans over sixty and by the share-the-wealth orations of Senator Huey Long of Louisiana. As a consequence, Roosevelt adopted the Wagner bill. He would also send to the Congress tax legislation, not for revenue, but ostensibly to make for more equitable distribution of wealth.

There was thunder on the right, too. Southern Democrats had fallen promptly in a line during the first half of Roosevelt's first term. The Southern states had been desperately stricken by the Depression, but as raw poverty eased somewhat among their white constituents, the states'-rights syndrome, so much a part of this breed of politician, emerged again. Their allies included Northern machine Democrats in the House, many of whom were intensely parochial, city types, whose political support for the New Deal did not extend beyond a few "bread-and-butter" remedial measures. One such was John O'Connor of New York, who fought the New Deal from his decisive position as Rules Committee Chairman. Within the committee, O'Connor had support from rural Midwestern Republicans. This strangely assorted group comprised a political alliance that dominated the House for the next quarter century.

They slowed the flow of legislation. Beginning in 1935, votes became more difficult to round up and keep rounded up. As the severest depression pains were eased, Republicans regained their courage and Southern Democrats theirs. Dismaying evidence emerged indicating that the Senate and House were disengaging from the economic battle long before the country had been economically restored to health.

The story of the conservative headlock clamped on the New Deal is persuasively documented by James T. Patterson in a recent book, *Congressional Conservatism and the New Deal*. From the beginning of the New Deal, about 25 of 35 Republican Senators opposed the New Deal and about 110 of 117 Republican House members. This opposition wasn't meaningful until Southern conservative Democrats, dominant voices in the party in the 1920s, joined in after the severest social tremors of the Depression had ended.

> Opposed to heavy government spending, fearful of the spread of Federal bureaucracy, loud in defense of states' rights and individual liberty, these men composed the earliest conservative force in Congress under Roosevelt's administrations. . . .
>
> Some simply resented Roosevelt's tardy distribution of patronage, and though they held their tongues and their adverse votes until the pork rolled into their districts, they remained embittered. Others, chiefly rural Republicans, had nothing to gain in the way of patronage and felt secure enough in their home districts to attack Roosevelt for partisan or factional reasons. And a handful of others, closely allied to reactionary financial interest, came to oppose the New Deal because they feared for their pocketbooks or their jobs. . . .
>
> A more important source of irritation resulted from Roosevelt's very success with Congress: the more adeptly he handled congressmen, the angrier some of them became. . . .

The quarrel began during the long, hot legislative summer of 1935. It involved two ferociously fought-over measures. One, regulating private utilities, contained a so-called "death-sentence" clause governing utility holding companies. The second was Roosevelt's tax bill, including provisions for a graduated corporations' tax, surcharge on individual income taxes, and an increase in inheritance-tax schedules. Both bills were enacted, but relations between the Congress and the President were strained raw in the process. Moley judged that the "split in the Democratic Party began" on the day the tax legislation was introduced.

The utility regulatory bill, ultimately to be one of Rayburn's major legislative achievements, arrived in the Congress as an aftermath of the exposure of Samuel Insull and others of his ilk. It struck at an important, highly conservative sector of the business community. Its "death-sentence" title authorized the new Securities and Exchange Commission to dissolve utility holding companies within five years. Politically disparate members, such as O'Connor and Senator Matthew Neely of West Virginia, were aligned with Wendell Willkie against the bill. Passed by the Sen-

ate, the bill was diluted in the Interstate and Foreign Commerce
Committee. Rayburn, as committee chairman, tried unsuccessfully to have the Administration version retained. His committee
wouldn't agree. The Administration sought to recoup. Accordingly, Rayburn asked that Rules report the bill with a rule requiring a roll-call vote on an amendment to restore the "death sentence." It was thought that members would not dare vote publicly against such an amendment. O'Connor, Rules Chairman, refused. Denied a roll-call vote, the leadership obtained a teller
vote, where numbers, not names, are recorded. The "death-
sentence" amendment was voted down. An effort was made to
substitute the Senate version, but it failed by more than 110
votes. The diluted House version was then passed. Finally, a modified "death-sentence" provision, satisfactory to Roosevelt, was
adopted in House-Senate conference. In late August, 1935, the
House and Senate accepted the conference version.

The tax bill was a product of pressure from the political left
which believed the momentum behind the New Deal was dissi-
pating. The tax bill was designed less to raise revenue than as a
gesture toward those favoring redistribution of wealth. Democratic Congressional leaders felt they had not been consulted
about it. Those who had long felt Roosevelt was a "traitor to his
class" now had a new handle to beat him with. Even those inclined to support such a measure noted that Roosevelt asked for
such a tax program but had left it to Ways and Means to draft
the legislation. Democratic floor leaders in both House and Senate
were annoyed. A bill did pass the House and Senate that August,
however, and was signed into law the same month.

The deep economic crisis continued unabated into 1936. The
agenda of unmet national needs was still lengthy. The Supreme
Court had declared unconstitutional certain major New Deal
building blocks, such as the National Industrial Recovery Act
(NRA), the Guffey Coal Act (a sort of "little NRA" for coal), a
bankruptcy act, the Agricultural Adjustment Act, and a "hot-oil"
law in the petroleum industry. Programs that did pass were often
patchwork policies and heavily logrolled. Congratulations were
due for the Social Security Act, although a similar national sys-

tem of old-age insurance had been established in Germany under Bismarck long ago. Despite the recommendation of his Presidential committee on economic security, however, Roosevelt declined to recommend a system of national health insurance to the Congress. Even our present national, Federally assisted program of health care for the elderly was not to be enacted for another thirty years.

The brutal condition of the Negro wasn't even touched on. In fact, the new housing and farm programs were flagrantly discriminatory. White America was taking care of its own. The country was still ill housed, ill fed, and ill clothed. As the 1936 election approached, Lippmann, once again wrongheaded, asked for a moratorium on additional New Deal legislation: "As the forces of recovery grow stronger, the people . . . will be interested in quiet government, in solid and steadfast leaders, in the deflation of public activity."

Landon, who a few years earlier had pledged his support to Roosevelt, became the Republican Presidential candidate. Roosevelt was renominated, at a party convention that for the first time in one hundred years nominated its candidate without a Southern-imposed requirement of a two-thirds majority vote of the delegates. He defeated Landon by an 11.1-million-vote margin. Landon had only the eight electoral votes of Maine and Vermont as consolation.

In January, 1937, Rayburn and O'Connor, representing the east side of Manhattan, contested for majority leader on the eve of the opening of the Seventy-fifth Congress. Fred Vinson of Kentucky, later United States Chief Justice, was Rayburn's campaign manager in the bitter contest. Powerful Carl Vinson of Georgia supported Rayburn. To O'Connor's dismay, Rayburn also won support from within the New York City delegation. Thomas Cullen of Brooklyn, ranking Ways and Means member, led a bolt of eight House Democrats to Rayburn. Edward Flynn's Bronx delegation supported Rayburn. E. E. (Gene) Cox of Georgia, fiery anti-New Dealer on Rules, supported Rayburn.

Presumably Rayburn also enjoyed White House support. After all, he had stage-managed the New Deal programs for the reform of financial and commodity markets and he had been in the forefront of the battle to abolish utility holding companies. He won the contest in party caucus, 184 votes to 127. This was the third time O'Connor had been thwarted. He had sought to be Speaker in 1933; Rainey was chosen. In 1936, he had wished to succeed Byrns. Now this. A few days after the contest, Krock of *The New York Times* noted that "the House leadership isn't much these days." He noted that O'Connor remained as Chairman of Rules "where he can give trouble to his leader any time he feels like it." O'Connor did.

The Washington Post commented editorially: ". . . the group now holding the reins of the House is more likely to exercise independent judgment upon New Deal legislation than some of the challenging factions. . . ." *The New York Post* added up the number of Southerners in important positions and commented that it was "not a good augury for a harmonious session." The forecast was correct, although the Democrats enjoyed a seemingly crushing preponderance of House seats, 333 to 89 Republican.

The new Seventy-fifth Congress opened amid labor unrest, sit-down strikes inside the automobile plants in Michigan. Ten strikers against Republic Steel Corporation had been killed the previous Memorial Day in a battle with police. Trade unions despaired of getting what they regarded as protective legislation. Section 7a of the National Industrial Recovery Act had been a disappointment, and the National Labor Relations Board was slow to react to union-busting campaigns. Civil rights organizations noted a lack of progress toward redressing racial injustices. They noted that Arthur W. Mitchell of Illinois, a Negro House member, had been moved against his will from his Pullman seat into a Negro coach car when the train he was riding in crossed into Arkansas.

During its 1937–1938 sittings, the Seventy-fifth Congress did pass significant legislation in the fields of housing and the minimum wage. The Farm Security Administration and a Civil Aeronautics Administration were established. The legislative achievements of the previous Congress were not matched, however. One misfortune was the Administration's proposal that the United States participate in the Permanent International Court of Justice (the World Court) at The Hague. Again, Congressional leaders complained there had been insufficient advance preparation. The proposal did not secure Senate approval.

The granddaddy of the uproars was Roosevelt's Supreme Court proposal, the so-called Court-packing bill. Two weeks after his second inaugural, Roosevelt sent to the Congress a bill to reform the Federal judiciary. Other Presidents had been faced with a hostile Court, but the Court had perhaps never before laid such a crushing judicial hand upon so many legislative programs. Roosevelt was determined to find constitutional support for programs he felt the nation needed. The core of the bill provided that one additional justice would be named to the Supreme Court for each incumbent justice who was seventy or older and had had ten-years' service on the Court. No more than six additional justices could be added however. Conservatives inside and outside Congress used the Court-packing bill as a rallying point. They now had a constitutional issue with which to belabor Roosevelt. Others, liberals such as Burton Wheeler, made common cause with them out of animosity toward Roosevelt.

Shortly after the Court fight began, the Supreme Court upheld a minimum-wage case in the State of Washington. It appeared to be a reversal of an earlier 5 to 4 decision, in which it had struck down a minimum-wage statute in New York State. Justice Roberts was the swing man in the decision. Felix Frankfurter wrote Roosevelt in March, 1937: "And now, with the shift by Roberts, even a blind man ought to see that the Court is in politics, and understand how the Constitution is 'judicially' construed. It is a deep object lesson—a lurid demonstration—of the relation of men to the 'meaning' of the Constitution. . . ."

Roosevelt lost some battles, but won the war. H. S. Commager and Samuel Eliot Morison explained it in *The Growth of the American Republic:* "For even as the bill was under consideration and before there had been any change in its membership, the Court found ways of making the constitutional sun shine on legislation which had heretofore been under a judicial cloud." The

Social Security program, a revised farm-mortgage act, a railroad labor act, and various provisions of the National Labor Relations Act, all were upheld. Morison and Commager suggest that the Senate Judiciary Committee defeated the Court-packing bill by a 10 to 8 vote, not so much on grounds of opposition to the legislation, but out of recognition that the Supreme Court had changed its tune. Soon, too, one after another of the conservative justices retired.

The 1937–1938 packet of Rooseveltian troubles had their roots in an astonishing resurgence of conservatism at a time when the nation had barely begun to mend. The core of opposition in the House lay in the Rules Committee. Eventually, as one Congressional student wrote, Rules "asserted a power independent of any party and almost without responsibility to any political institution." An element of this development was the departure of Chairman Bankhead, in mid-1934, to become majority leader. This left the committee subject to the prescription of O'Connor as chairman for the next four years. His willing aides were two future chairmen, the volatile Cox and Howard Worth Smith of Virginia, whose courtliness masked a keen mind and reactionary opinions. The three men reached across to the Republican side of the committee's meeting table. There they shook hands with Joseph W. Martin, Jr., of Massachusetts, also a seventeenth-century man.

O'Connor combined a quarrelsome nature, frustration over successive leadership defeats, and opposition to substantive economic alterations proposed by Roosevelt. Roosevelt did attempt to win over O'Connor, whose brother Basil had been a law partner of his; he failed. In explosive exasperation, Roosevelt placed O'Connor's name on a list of House and Senate members to be "purged" at the 1938 fall elections. Only O'Connor lost. He was denied the Democratic renomination, won the Republican nomination against Allen W. Dulles, and then was defeated in the general election.

Until then, he had helped hobble the New Deal. Under his aegis, the Rules Committee became transformed from a cockpit of the majority leadership into a slaughterhouse for legislative programs. The inside story of these years has not yet been told. Perhaps Howard Smith, Rules Chairman between 1955 and 1967, will tell us some day. O'Connor changed his spots fairly rapidly. The O'Connor who refused Rayburn's request for help on the utility bill in early 1935 had said a few months earlier:

> To some of you new members I might state in advance that the Rules Committee is an arm of the leadership of this House. It is sometimes called an "arm" of the administration in power in the Nation. Some people have also referred to it as the "political committee," or the committee which shapes or brings before the House the policies of the leadership of the House and the administration.

Shortly before he walked the political gangplank in 1938, however, O'Connor defiantly described the situation involving Roosevelt's executive reorganization bill: ". . . the Rules Committee has a pigeonhole and the bill is in it and the cobwebs are so thick over that pigeonhole you can hardly see it is a pigeonhole."

John L. Lewis, who had licked the mine owners, tried to lick the Rules Committee. In June, 1938, Lewis twice visited the Speaker in an effort to get action on favored legislation. Lewis particularly wanted a Walsh-Healey Act amendment, then bottled up in O'Connor's committee, that would forbid the Federal Government to contract with employers who had violated orders of the National Labor Relations Board. He also wanted changes in pending legislation to establish minimum hourly wages in businesses engaged in interstate commerce, the fair labor standards bill.

Lewis sat in the Speaker's office and talked to two Rules members, the conservative Martin Dies of Texas and a Western liberal, Lawrence Lewis of Colorado. Neither would bend. John Lewis asked Speaker Bankhead to call up the amendment under suspension of rules of the House. Bankhead, a cooperative Rules Committee Chairman only four years earlier, seemed now to envision the committee as something quite different: "The Rules Committee, I understand, by a very large majority has made a decision against it." The leonine Lewis said Rules was working under a "corporate lash."

As John L. Lewis spoke, a coalition of five Southern Democrats and three Republicans in the Rules Committee were keeping the wage bill captive. In early May, 1938, out of desperation, a discharge petition was filed. Newspapers reported members pushed and shoved so eager were they to sign. Within three hours, the necessary 218 signatures were obtained. Only two dozen were Southern Democrats. One of these was Lyndon Johnson. Rayburn was another. So were at least eight present or future chairmen, including Emanuel Celler of New York. Cox, angered that the bill had escaped captivity in Rules, led a fierce attack on it. There were efforts to riddle it with amendments, but it passed and became law in June, providing a 25-cent hourly minimum wage, with an increase to 30 cents the second year and 40 cents by the seventh year.

Let there be no doubt, there was a Republican-Southern Democratic alliance, not unlike the one spawned by the Tilden-Hayes election deadlock in 1876. Martin, Speaker in two Republican Houses, described it in his autobiography, *My First Fifty Years*. Martin called Cox the "real leader of southerners in the House. . . . He and I were the principal points of contact between the Northern Republicans and the Southern Democratic conservatives." There were enough of each on Rules to stymie progress.

If the Supreme Court was never packed by F.D.R., someone saw to it that Rules was packed with Southern Democrats. An analysis of Democratic membership on the committee shows that Southerners have equaled or outnumbered Democrats from all the other regions of the country between 1931 and 1967. New England was not represented until the 1950s; California not until 1963. In 1933, three of six Democrats were Southerners, and there were two vacancies to fill. Even so, two highly conservative Southerners were added, William J. Driver of Arkansas and Howard Smith of Virginia. Smith was given the most uncommon distinction of being placed on Rules after only one term in the House. At the beginning of the 1940 session, four of the six Democrats were Southerners, and there were four vacancies.

Robert L. Doughton of North Carolina was chairman of the nominating Committee on Committees. Two of the four vacancies were filled by one Mississippian, William Colmer, a future chairman, and one border-state member, William Nelson of Missouri. Southern Democrats, snug in their safe one-party districts, vaulted to top ranking. In combination with the four or five Republicans on the committee, they were always able to dominate it.

After O'Connor was defeated for reelection in 1938, a Northerner, Adolph Sabath of Illinois, did become chairman. Sabath was Chairman of Rules for six terms. It was a disaster. The White House suggested to Speaker Bankhead that a steadier successor than Sabath was needed, someone more aggressive and commanding. Sabath gave the impression of a man "trying to hold back a steam-roller," as one observer described him. He couldn't control his committee, whose Republicans included gut fighters such as Leo Allen of Illinois, Hamilton Fish of New York, and Charles Halleck of Indiana.

On one occasion, during discussion of a housing bill, the short-fused Cox and Sabath had a "fight" on the House floor. Sabath would become so frustrated in the face of his wilier committee colleagues that he would pretend to faint during meetings. Once, thinking his colleagues had gone, he opened one eye. Republican Clarence Brown of Ohio was watching. "Have they all gone, Clarence?" Sabath asked.

Sabath was badgered and taunted when Allen was ranking Republican. It spoke ill of Allen and the Democratic leadership that they permitted a key committee to exist in this condition. Incumbent House Democrats may be excused in believing that the current state of affairs in Rules has always been so. This is, of course, not correct. The disarray of programs and the supposedly sacrosanct seniority system had their wretched roots in such alliances that evolved on Rules in the mid-1930s, aided by listless or acquiescent Democratic leaders.

The newborn conservative coalition gained strength in the Seventy-sixth Congress that convened in January, 1939. Democrats strayed off the reservation from the beginning of the first session. Roosevelt was discontented. Twice in 1939, the Democratic leadership called a party caucus in an effort to create some discipline. On St. Valentine's day, a "harmony" caucus was held in an effort to heal discontent between Roosevelt and House Democrats, made restive by the President's political purge. The 1938 fall elections had gone badly, the Democrats having lost seventy-one House seats and seven Senate seats.

Rayburn and other leaders asked their party colleagues to "quit following the Republicans down the aisle when teller votes are taken" on amendments to New Deal bills. Cox fired back that the House was being asked to do all the "cooperating." Rayburn also asked for better attendance on the floor. That afternoon, nevertheless, only forty-five Democrats were present during a discussion of a military-preparedness bill. One Democrat from New York City suggested that the President had spanked the House leadership and the leadership in turn "was crying on the shoulder of House membership." In July, a second caucus was asked to go on record as supporting the Administration. It did, after pulling from the resolution a pledge to support specific measures.

The 1937–1938 recession, the candidate purge, memories of the court-packing bill, and continued labor unrest made members unfriendly toward new programs. George Gallup reported that 62 per cent of Americans were opposed to increased government "pump priming." Regrettably, the New Deal was partially spent and partially frustrated, although unemployment still totaled 9.5 million, or 18 per cent of the civilian labor force.

In a 1939 Presidential message to the Congress, Roosevelt acknowledged his compounding difficulties. There was no longer talk about additional "reform," but rather of preserving the established programs. In fact, the domestic patient was prematurely declared as having recuperated. Roosevelt was about to step into a new role, "Dr. Win-the-War." Roosevelt tried to put a good face on the situation. "We have now passed the period of internal conflict in the launching of our program of social reform," he told the Seventy-sixth Congress. "Our full energies may now be released to invigorate the processes of recovery in order to preserve our reforms." As it turned out, "our full energies" became focused on foreign-policy problems involving Europe and Asia.

2

Roosevelt and the War

The whole decade of the 1930s is pockmarked with aggression of nation against nation: the Japanese in Manchuria and China; Italy in Ethiopia; foreign intervention in the Spanish civil war; Hitler's occupation of the Rhine territory, Austria, and Czechoslovakia. The country and its Congress were disquieted. Roosevelt's early record in respect to international affairs was spotty. In 1932, he had become the first Democratic Presidential candidate unequivocally to repudiate our participation in the League of Nations: "I do not favor America's participation." Some accounts assign him the responsibility for rendering the London Economic Conference of 1933 useless. Yet he proposed, as had three conservative Republican Presidents before him, our affiliation with the Permanent International Court of Justice (the World Court).

Then, in 1937, he upset the Congress with his "quarantine-the-aggressors" speech in Chicago. The well-financed America First organization fought him—the Lindberghs, Wheelers, Nyes, Borahs, and the La Follettes. In February, 1937, Louis Ludlow of Indiana introduced a constitutional amendment providing that, except in case of armed attack upon us, a declaration of war by the Congress would not become effective unless ratified by a national referendum among Americans. The Ludlow resolution was sent to the Judiciary Committee, where the leadership and the President succeeded in having it pigeonholed. Then Ludlow filed a discharge petition. The resolution, disastrous in its objective, nevertheless evoked strong support in the House. In December, 1937, the necessary 218 signatures were obtained within a few days after a Japanese attack upon our naval gunboat *Panay*. The House leadership and Roosevelt were plainly worried, although a constitutional amendment resolution needs to be approved by a two-thirds vote of House and Senate. Roosevelt sent a letter urging its defeat to Speaker Bankhead. In mid-January, 1938, the House took up the matter. Bankhead took to the floor to declare ". . . this is the gravest question that has been submitted to the Congress of the United States since I became a member of it 20 years ago." Subsequently, 188 Democrats and 21 Republicans provided the 209 votes by which it was decided not to take up the Ludlow resolution. A total of 188 votes, including 111 Democrats and 64 Republicans, voted for consideration.

The drumbeat of isolationist criticism mounted. Conspicuous isolationists in the House were usually anti-British, Eastern Democrats and pro-German, Midwestern Republicans. Supporting or opposing Roosevelt were national committees of concerned citizens composed of clergy, academics, and mass intellectuals. Some House members warned Americans that they would lose their birthright if their country did not stay clear of foreign politics, while other members warned Americans they would lose it if they did not become more involved.

In January, 1939, Roosevelt told the Congress: "We know what might happen to us of the United States if the new philosophies of force were to encompass the other continents and invade our own."

That September, World War II broke out in Western Europe. Germany invaded Poland. The House and then the Senate voted 2 billion dollars for expansion of the armed services. In October, 1939, the House and Senate approved a neutrality act, repealing the arms embargo and permitting "cash-and-carry" arms transactions. That same month a German raider seized the *City of Flint*, an American ship. The Soviet Union prepared to invade Finland. In May, 1940, France fell. Britain stood alone. That was the year we gave her fifty overaged destroyers in return for ninety-nine-year leases on bases in the West Indies and Newfoundland. Roosevelt told Americans "there is a vast difference between keeping out of war and pretending that this war is none of our business."

Roosevelt sought an unprecedented third term in 1940. His intention cost him several prominent supporters, among others, Garner and Jim Farley. He had already lost Al Smith. His foreign policy outlook cost him others in the Congress.

In 1939, the Hatch Act was passed. It prohibited Federal employees from engaging in direct political activity at a national level. It also forbade political use of work-relief funds. Sponsors portrayed the measure as a protection for Federal employees from overzealous political agents of either party, but Samuel Lubell said that, as far as Garner was concerned, its purpose was to establish a barrier to a third-term election. Nevertheless, Roosevelt defeated Wendell Willkie by 55 per cent of the vote, the lowest of his three winning percentages. Now Roosevelt told Americans that their country was the "great arsenal of Democracy." American opinion edged closer to his view, yet Americans seemed to want both to stop Hitler and to stay away from any fighting. When Selective Service extension squeaked through the House by one vote in mid-1941—one foreign observer commented that the United States seemed to want to save the world in one breath, yet in the next, its Congress almost refused to have an army.

The same year, American troops occupied Iceland and Greenland, the lend-lease program of aid to Great Britain was authorized, as was a shipbuilding program. Roosevelt ordered our military to attack "at sight" German and Italian vessels discovered moving through our "defensive waters." In the House the Firsters grew louder; Roosevelt grew more adamant. The Japanese resolved the matter on December 7, 1941, at Pearl Harbor.

The Seventy-seventh was the first War Congress. In the House, Rayburn was Speaker. The legislative program consisted of price and wage controls and higher taxes to fund the war that was then going badly for us. Roosevelt informed him that national defense in fiscal 1943 would cost approximately 50 billion dollars, half of our national income. When the Congress ended, *The New York Times* editorially gave it mixed marks:

> . . . full of inconsistencies and contradictions. It acted in some cases with astonishing speed, and in others with incredible tardiness. It passed huge appropriations bills one after another without stopping to study them and often without troubling to read them. On the other hand, it took six months to pass a price-control act and an equally inexcusable time to pass revenue acts. It often rose to the demands upon it and acted vigorously and without partisanship, and just as often it slid back into inexcusable short-sightedness . . . at a time of extreme national peril, Congress, for partisan political reasons, extended the draft period from twelve months by the narrow margin of a single vote. When its members were calling upon the country to make great sacrifices they quietly passed an act granting themselves pensions—an act which they were forced to repeal by the immediate national resentment that it aroused. And when the 77th Congress came to an end there were groups still working to prevent or delay gasoline rationing, to force up the national cost of living in the interests of their farm constituents, or to prevent the use of an important metal—silver—for the war effort because a few local constituents might be adversely affected financially by such an action. . . . The new Congress must have a much clearer and more constant recognition of its responsibilities if it hopes to restore the prestige of Congress and if it expects to make a real contribution to a successful and early conclusion of the war. To do this, it needs both a new spirit and a better organization.

The Seventy-eighth Congress sat during the rationing at home and bloodshed abroad, the collapse of Fascist Italy and Mussolini, the Allied invasion of Western Europe, the liberation of France, the Moscow and Teheran Conferences, the recapture of Guam, and the Dumbarton Oaks Conference. This is the Congress that passed the Servicemen's Readjustment Act, the memorable "GI Bill of Rights."

The first session, lasting 350 days, said *The Times* correspondent, "was marked by eager cooperation with the Executive Branch in prosecuting the war and preparing for post-war collaboration to make the peace secure and by its disagreements and repeated revolts on domestic issues." The 1944 session, only five days shorter, ended on December 19 as the Germans struck back in final fury in the Belgian Ardennes. In less than five months, the European war would be ended; within less than four, Roosevelt would be dead.

Rainey, Byrns, Bankhead, Garner, Rayburn, and McCormack were Franklin Roosevelt's House helpers during those New Deal years. Each served as Speaker. The white-haired, outspokenly liberal Henry Rainey of Illinois, with his flowing Windsor tie, represented the same section of Illinois that Abraham Lincoln and Stephen Douglas once had. He was politically at odds with John Garner. Rainey, seventy-two when he was elected Speaker over Garner's opposition in March, 1933, died fifteen months later.

His successor was the more conservative John W. Byrns of Tennessee. Byrns was a kindly, considerate Speaker. A party colleague said Byrns wanted to be a good Speaker but didn't know how. He bemoaned his failing and became known as a "wailer" on the subject. This did not enhance his standing among his fellows during his eighteen-month Speakership. He, too, died in office.

William Bankhead of Alabama performed his greatest service as pathfinder for New Deal legislation through the Rules Committee he chaired. He became majority leader, then, in 1936, Speaker after Byrns died. He was less successful presiding over a fractious House no longer fully responsive to Franklin Roosevelt's legislative desires. Bankhead served slightly more than four years before he also died in office. Two Texans and a lanky Massachusetts man from South Boston, however, achieved the greatest prominence among House leaders of the New Deal era. The crusty Texan John N. Garner of Uvalde had learned his legislative trade during Cannon's Speakerships. The stubby Texan Sam Rayburn of rural Bonham began his Congressional service with the first Wilson Presidency. John W. McCormack of Massachusetts was affable, quick to do a favor and kindly regarded because, when presiding, he would permit members to speak beyond their allotted time.

Garner played poker with Cannon and drank bourbon after

hours with Nick Longworth in the latter's Capitol hideaway. After World War I, Garner became one of a dozen influential Democratic legislators in the House. Garner was considered even more taciturn than Coolidge, one biographer wrote. In 1930, "Cactus Jack" Garner had expected to serve his forthcoming two-year term as minority leader. Overall, the Republicans had won 218 seats, the Democrats 216, and the Farm-Labor party 1. An astonishing number of deaths occurred, however, between Election Day and the convening of the Seventy-second Congress in December, 1931. Fourteen members-elect, including Longworth, died—seven were Democrats and seven were Republicans. In the ensuing special elections, Democrats not only retained their seven seats, vacated by death, but also won three of the seven Republican ones by the time Congress opened. Thus, the Democrats narrowly controlled the House 219 to 214.

Consequently, Garner became, not minority leader, but Speaker, the first Democrat since Champ Clark twelve years before. Three of his votes came from invalid members brought to the floor. In all, he received 218 votes for Speaker, a majority of five. Interestingly, twenty-one of Garner's votes came from a hard-bargaining Tammany delegation from New York City.

John F. Curry, the Tammany chieftain, had breakfast with Garner shortly before the Seventy-second Congress convened. The breakfast had been preceded by reports that the Tammany group would withhold its votes and let the Republicans organize the House, unless certain demands were met. Tammany "went Texas" for Garner, after being assured of additional representation for delegation members on important committees, including Ways and Means. Other agreements were reached. Tammanyman Curry said the delegation would support Garner in opposition to the creation of a steering committee that liberal Democrats, including Byrns, wanted. Garner also secured a commitment for better attendance on the part of the delegation. *The New York Times* notes that the Tammanyites had "shown little interest in their legislative obligations. It is said that the largest number of them present in the House in the last Congress, except when some extremely important measure was being acted on,

seldom exceeded nine of the 21." Even today the New York City
delegation is regarded as part of the East Coast "Tuesday-to-
Thursday Club," a reference to the only days of the week these
members are customarily found at their Congressional work in
Washington. After the negotiation, Curry told newspapermen
that he "had a very pleasant visit here." In return, Southern
Democrats were reported as saying they had a more positive
attitude toward the Tammany delegation.

The Tammany-Texas handshake helped lift Garner into the
Speaker's chair, and because a Republican was President, Garner
now became the highest elected office holder of his party and its
titular head.

Historians have not written glowingly about Garner, primarily
because of his later disaffiliation from Franklin Roosevelt. John L.
Lewis thought him a "poker playing, whiskey-drinking, labor
baiting, evil old man." Garner could handle himself. He said
Lewis's trouble was that his neck had "just grown and haired
over." His strengths should not be obscured by his failure to
remain a political supporter of Roosevelt.

Garner knew when long-range considerations were important.
Marquis James, a Garner biographer, refers to a leadership ri-
valry in 1923. Kitchin had died and the minority leadership was
therefore vacant. Finis Garrett of Tennessee claimed the right to
the position "by right of his standing on the Rules Committee
which was senior to Garner's rank on Ways and Means." James
writes:

> Though disappointed, Garner refused to enter an open contest
> against his Tennessee colleague. Garner's behavior won over
> Garrett's friends, making the Texan stronger in the party
> councils than he would have been had he won the leadership
> by a divided vote. Actually he was leader without title, but so
> tactfully did he exercise his influence that Garrett took not the
> least offense.

Garrett ran for a Senate seat five years later. Garner then
formally became Democratic floor leader.

Garner had not served with Cannon and Longworth without

learning. He knew the correct moves and had a good intelligence network. His party colleagues complained, however, that he had a streak of the bully in him. One newspaperman described his brand of leadership as "more brutal" than Longworth's. Another thought Garner a "bruising Speaker."

Garner was aware of the great insufficiency at the White House. He stood up for some constructive legislation to help the economically distressed country, but he refused to bedevil President Hoover unnecessarily. His biographers report that Garner believed that four-fifths of legislative business could be conducted on a bipartisan basis. A disputatious tax bill is illustrative. This occasion also shows what courageous and determined Speakers can accomplish.

In February, 1932, the final measure in Hoover's emergency program had cleared the House. Emphasis was mostly on measures to expand credit and improve the circulation of money. Garner turned his attention to the unbalanced budget. Treasury had told the Congress that a 1.3-billion-dollar deficit was in sight, much more than originally forecast. Garner set out to find ways of cutting costs and, if need be, increasing taxes. Apparently, for a time, Garner and the majority leadership lost control of Ways and Means, the tax-writing committee, which brought to the floor a hodgepodge bill that included a manufacturers' sales tax. The House roared its disapproval for more than a week. On March 29, Garner set out to buck the members' mood, instead of "hunkerin' down" like cows in a storm in his native Texas. He left the Speaker's chair and went to the floor and addressed the House. He told the attentive House that he had always opposed the sales tax, but

> I think more of my country than I do of any theory of taxation that I may have, and the country at this time is in a condition where the worst taxes you could possibly levy would be better than no taxes at all. . . . I believe that if this Congress today should decline to levy a tax bill there would not be a bank in existence in the United States in sixty days that could meet its depositors.

Garner then did an astounding thing. It may even have been an unparalleled legislative gamble in public:

> At the risk of being criticized, I want to give to the world and to the country today, if I can, an expression of this House, so that the world and the country may realize we are going to balance the budget.
>
> Mr. Chairman, may I do an unusual thing? I may be criticized for it, but I want every man and every woman in this House who hopes to balance the budget and who is willing to go along with that effort to try to balance the budget, to rise in his seat. [Most did.]
>
> Now, if they do not mind, those who do not want to balance the budget can rise in their seats. ["No one rises," the *Congressional Record* states parenthetically at this point.]
>
> I think this ought to restore the American people confidence in our country.

Bascom Timmons, a Garner biographer, comments "Backwoods evangelism had triumphed."

A new tax bill was soon developed more in accord with Garner's views. Congress passed it. Arthur Krock of *The New York Times* wrote in his dispatch that "rarely in the annals of Parliaments has the intervention of one member in a crisis dispelled it so promptly and so effectively as did Speaker John N. Garner's address to the House of Representatives today." Krock further suggested that by his speech Garner had "restored the leadership of the Speaker and the Ways and Means Committee. . . ." Furthermore, *The New York Times* account said, Garner had "shamed" members who were opposing the tax bill without presenting alternatives. It all was done, the account continued, without "table thumping" or "oratory . . . His manner was that of a friend. . . ."

Garner provided leadership in other ways. Although not a "friend of Labor," he helped guide to passage the Norris-LaGuardia Act of 1932 that outlawed the "yellow-dog" union-busting contract and use of Federal injunctions to break strikes.

Overall, however, Garner was regarded by many House Democrats as too conservative in a time of disastrous economic depression. He refused to establish a party steering committee that liberal Democrats, such as Rainey, wanted. It caused Garner trouble at the end of his term.

Garner made a strong run at securing his party's Presidential nomination in 1932. He failed. Instead he became Vice President. He made only one speech during his first campaign as Democratic Vice-Presidential candidate in 1932. "Hoover is making the speeches for us," he told Franklin Roosevelt. In this position, he served with increasing surliness toward the New Deal until 1941 when Henry Wallace succeeded him.

Sam Rayburn had two characteristics in common with Garner. He kept his word and kept his mouth shut; "steam that blows a whistle will never turn a wheel," Rayburn said. Like Garner, too, he was conservatively inclined. Attributed to him is an observation that there is "room in the country for free men and free enterprise—rural skepticism and rural conservatism." Rayburn became Chairman of Interstate and Foreign Commerce in 1931, where he guarded Texas oil and gas interests. Discussing regulatory agencies, over which the committee has charge, Rayburn said "legislation should never be designed to punish anyone. It must be fair and ordinarily it's a question of regulating the minority—the pistol-toting minority."

As chairman, he worked to regulate these minorities. He played a major role in securing passage of the Securities Act of 1933, designed to prevent fraud in sale of securities, and the 1934 Securities Exchange Act, designed to prevent unfair practices by stock exchanges. Unlike Garner, however, he never crossed over into political insubordination against Roosevelt. Rayburn had greater stretch to his mind. He stayed the route through the New Deal and Fair Deal and into the New Frontier.

Rayburn, the "Texas Squire," was no novice when he entered the House in 1913. He had entered politics, an admirer once wrote, with a "pony, a smile, and determination." At twenty-nine, he had become Speaker of the Texas House of Representatives. "I like responsibility because I enjoy the power responsibility brings," Rayburn said frankly. He also had a winner's instinct—"I hate like hell to be licked. It almost kills me," he confided to a friend.

Rayburn served as Garner's aide when Garner became Speaker. They worked together politically, not always successfully. Their losing effort on behalf of McDuffie was followed two years later by an effort of Garner to elect Rayburn after Speaker Rainey had died. Garner, however, was thwarted by Senator Guffey, boss of the Pennsylvania Democratic machine. Guffey reached into the House to place the twenty-three-member Pennsylvania delegation behind Majority Leader Byrns of Tennessee for Speaker. Guffey, the Senator, had outreached Vice President Garner, the Senate's presiding officer.

Rayburn, however, did climb the leadership ladder after Speaker Byrns died. Majority Leader Bankhead became Speaker. John J. O'Connor of New York, Rules Committee Chairman, was named acting majority leader. By this time, O'Connor had become rabidly anti-New Deal. Rayburn contested O'Connor for election in January, 1937. Rayburn won by fifty-seven votes. When Bankhead died four years later, Rayburn was elected Speaker. In that capacity, Rayburn served twice as long as Clay. He served as Speaker for nearly one-third of his forty-nine years in the House. His rural constituency in Texas was not always appreciative. Several times it provided him with a strong opponent. There were fierce campaigns and a near defeat or two. However, he survived to be elected twenty-five times, a length of service exceeded only by Carl Vinson of Georgia, who served one day longer than Rayburn. Rayburn wielded great personal influence as Speaker, far more than most.

He usually led a large but volatile Democratic majority, and he could always depend upon Republicans to be combative. Strategically, Rayburn sought both as majority leader and as Speaker to persuade President Roosevelt to curtail his more extreme tendencies to order people about. On the other hand, he also tried to keep alive the party-loyalty instincts of the anti-New Deal Democrats. An observer, watching Rayburn work, wrote that perhaps the most "impossible political pairing" in history consisted of Roosevelt and Gene Cox of Georgia, prime mover in the anti-New Deal conservative coalition on the Rules Committee.

Rayburn compiled a good record of advancing his party's programs. He did it largely through his immense personal influence. He avoided promising opportunities to enhance the powers of the institution of the Speakership itself, however. Rayburn's persuasiveness as an individual is best illustrated by a hair-raising episode in connection with selective service extension on one day in August, 1941. It also illustrates his oft-repeated opinion privately expressed that "one can run the House from the Chair or the floor." It once again demonstrates the benefits of a strong individual in the Speaker's chair.

At this point in time, the country was of two minds about Roosevelt's tendencies in foreign policy. A draft law had been enacted, which was scheduled to expire in October, 1941. Newspapers reported that the acronym, OHIO, was appearing on walls on and off Army camp sites—Over the Hill in October. Roosevelt viewed the situation uneasily. Robert Sherwood, in his biography, *Roosevelt and Hopkins*, wrote that Roosevelt was even inclined not to do battle over extension, to "let the matter go." Secretary of State Stimson and General Marshall are portrayed as pushing hard for extension. American troops were occupying Greenland and Iceland; the lend-lease program had been authorized; there were rising tensions between the United States on the one hand and Japan and Germany on the other; Nazi troops had advanced to the Black Sea; Marshall Pétain had turned over France to the pro-Nazi Admiral Darlan. At home, Burton Wheeler, Charles Lindbergh, and the Hearst press led the isolationist phalanxes.

Rayburn supported extension of the draft to the degree that he violated his own working principles. He risked a vote on this major measure without the assurance that it would pass, although he persuaded several members to promise to support the bill. The bill to extend the draft for eighteen months came to a final vote on August 12. The occasion was not unnoticed by others. Sherwood called the occasion "disagreeably synchronized," because the decisive vote occurred on the concluding day of the then secret conference between Roosevelt and British Prime Minister Winston Churchill on a naval ship on the North Atlantic. "It proved to be one of the narrowest escapes of Roosevelt's wartime career," Sherwood wrote. Members sat in the full glare of publicity. Newspapers had announced the day the vote was scheduled. Members saw mothers, holding small American flags, sitting in the public galleries above. Also in the galleries were young men in Army uniforms with a more than casual interest in the voting.

The floor discussion was tense. The Military Affairs Committee had made major changes in the Administration bill in an effort to pick up votes. Even opponents, such as Everett Dirksen of Illinois, a *Chicago Tribune* isolationist, thought the measure was sure to pass. Supporters thought so, too, when a motion to recommit was defeated by twenty-five votes: 190 to 215, with 27 recorded as Not Voting. Then came the roll call on final passage. A dozen members switched sides. The clerk's tally recorded the result as 203 yeas, 202 nays, and 27 not voting. A total of 182 Democrats and 21 Republicans had voted for extension; 133 Republicans and 65 Democrats, 1 American Labor party, and 3 Progressive party, against—a one-vote margin, the razor's edge.

There were confusion, conferences, and cries of protest. An outspoken isolationist, Dewey Short, demanded a recount. When it was finished, Rayburn quickly rattled off the parliamentary language: "No correction in the vote, the vote stands and the bill is passed and without objection a motion to reconsider is laid on the table." The gavel he held banged conclusively. Opponents were outraged when they realized the consequences of the fast gavel. Several members protested, H. Carl Andersen of Minnesota prominently among them. Rayburn countered, "The Chair does not intend to have his word questioned."

Four months later, the Japanese attacked us at Pearl Harbor and elsewhere in the Pacific. We had an Army four times as large as we would have had, if the draft-extension legislation had not been passed. We were better prepared because of Rayburn.

Unlike Garner and Rayburn, there seem to be no recognizable high points, or high point, in the Congressional career of John

McCormack. He is loyal, helpful, uncomplaining, and outraged when told that, as a devout Roman Catholic, he is sometimes referred to by members as "The Archbishop." His sonorous oratory ("sound and affirmative Americanism") is of the sort congenial to a state legislature; his had been Massachusetts, where in the 1920s he served as a representative from South Boston, first in the state House and then as floor leader in the state Senate. He was elected to the United States House of Representatives in 1928. By means of generous impulses and the common coinage of political favors, McCormack has developed a base of influence that is heavily Southern. It's called the Boston-Austin axis.

To use a military comparison, McCormack's failures are at the strategic and tactical levels. He understands and works very hard and effectively at the job of corralling individual votes for Administration programs. His appeal is usually to loyalty, to the Democratic party, to the Democratic President, or to John McCormack. In fact he fits the self-description of an Army general of World War II who, coming under enemy small-arms fire, picked up a rifle and supposedly said, "I may not be much of a general but I'd make a hell of a corporal."

There are, however, no evidences of the leadership, determination, and courage that distinguished the Congressional careers of Speakers Reed, Cannon, Longworth, Garner, and Rayburn. First as Democratic whip and later majority leader, McCormack's weakness for partisan overstatement during floor debates often drove wavering Republicans back into the arms of their own party whips. His militant anti-Communism is fully faithful to the views of his Roman Catholic Constituency. In 1939, McCormack demanded we recall our ambassador to the Soviet Union because Premier-Foreign Commissar V. M. Molotov had criticized Roosevelt. At a later press conference, the President let it be known that bad manners shouldn't beget bad manners. The next year, McCormack offered a motion to delete an appropriation to pay the salary of our ambassador to the Soviet Union on the grounds that the Russian diplomatic mission engaged in subversion in this country. The motion was adopted by a standing vote but subsequently lost on a teller vote.

McCormack has seldom strayed into the suburbs of party orthodoxy. He doubtlessly was a bit out of line with his Irish constituency in supporting Roosevelt's foreign policy in the 1930s. Father Coughlin and isolationism with an anti-British bias were not unpopular in "Southie." He did support Hamilton Fish, a rabid isolationist and Roosevelt hater, in efforts to delay compulsory selective service, pending an effort to rely upon volunteers, but this and a tax vote or two in the 1930s were exceptions. He's a regular, and regulars are by definition regular whether a President wants one, two, three, or four terms. McCormack supported foreign-assistance programs and civil rights legislation. His constituent-servicing operation is excellent. It probably helps to provide him with a cushion against parochial, working-class constituents who prefer their cultural ghetto and whose political enthusiasms embrace candidates such as Louise Hicks. He served conventionally and as best he could the Democratic National Administration. Party regularity bears fruit.

Speaker Bankhead died in mid-September, 1940. Rayburn moved up from majority leader to Speaker. Lindsay Warren of North Carolina, designated by Roosevelt to become comptroller general, became temporary majority leader. Members seeking to succeed Rayburn began campaigning. McCormack, who reportedly made a motion to name Rayburn as Speaker, was Chairman of the House Democratic caucus at the time. He became a candidate. So did Clifton Woodrum of Virginia, a senior on Appropriations and recruiter for anti-New Deal majorities. Others included Majority Whip Boland, Rankin of Mississippi, and Jere Cooper of Tennessee, a colleague of McCormack on Ways and Means.

An effort developed to postpone election of a permanent majority leader until the following January, 1941, only a few months away, when a new Congress would convene. Senior Democrats, such as Vinson of Georgia, took this position on the grounds that a party row before the fall elections would hurt. McCormack supporters wanted an election immediately. A petition to gain the requisite fifty signatures was circulated in order to force holding a caucus.

A caucus was held September 25. There, Vinson is said to have argued that, if the Democrats kept control as a result of the coming elections, one type of majority leader would be needed. If not, then a different type of man would be needed as minority leader. Vinson moved to delay a permanent election. His motion was defeated, reportedly by seventeen votes. According to reports, all prospective candidates except McCormack voted in favor of the delaying action. There was never anything official or public, but the caucus was encouraged to believe that President Roosevelt favored McCormack. This seems to have helped McCormack. With the delaying motion defeated, only McCormack and the conservative Woodrum were on the board as candidates. Voting was by tellers, that is, in the open, rather than by secret ballot. McCormack had support in the South. Identified supporters included Gene Cox. McCormack was elected by a vote of 141 to 67. Woodrum successfully moved to make the election unanimous.

Key Southerners had boosted McCormack into leadership in 1940. Twenty years later, his election to the Speakership was similarly approved. He was seventy. With one exception, Rainey, no member had been older upon becoming Speaker. And no one had served as many years in the House, thirty-four, before being elected Speaker as had McCormack. His years as Speaker would not be looked on favorably.

IV

CONGRESS IN THE POST-WORLD WAR II PERIOD

I

The Cold War Successes

Politics, Albert Einstein once remarked to Franklin Roosevelt, is much more difficult than physics. Yet of course it was Einstein's revolutionary physics which made politics even more difficult. His famous energy equations injected a highly combustible component into already volatile relationships among nations. No President could ever again conduct his Administration without keeping these consequences continually in mind.

When Roosevelt died in mid-April, 1945, in Warm Springs, Georgia, Harry Truman became the first "A-Bomb" President. Ironically, while Truman knew nothing about the secret project until he became President, for years selected members of the House and Senate appropriation committees were being kept informed, because requests for developmental funds for the A-bomb had to be disguised in various overall departmental budget submissions. Truman, the honest judge (county commissioner) in the Jackson County Courthouse in Kansas City, Missouri, seat of the corrupt Prendergast political empire; Truman chugging along as effective Chairman of the Defense Investigating Committee during World War II; Truman drinking bourbon with Speaker Rayburn in a Capitol hideaway when unexpectedly called to the White House. "Boys, if you ever pray, pray for me now," he later asked reporters at the White House the day after being sworn in as Franklin Roosevelt's successor.

Truman, unlike Harding, believed America could not go home again after a world war. Truman, and the Eightieth Congress he presumed to despise, did not let America come home. Her troops remained overseas. America assumed many of the imperial obligations of Great Britain. Furthermore, America sent tens of billions to repair shattered societies in Western Europe. Other billions were forwarded, with less success, to build or restructure less developed societies on other continents. America and her adversary, the Soviet Union and its client states, confronted each other in mounting open and undercover combat, until, in the eighteenth year of the Cold War, a cool and determined young President stared down the Cuban missile crisis. This hair-raising confrontation sobered the two superpowers.

The episode in Cuba had its roots in the Cold War. At the end of World War II military victory was within reach in Europe (the end would come May 7, 1945) and in sight in the Pacific. Yet Roosevelt's advisers, if not Roosevelt himself, had returned from the Yalta Conference in the Crimea in February, 1945, with forebodings about a postwar world in which the Soviet Union appeared to be America's only rival.

Truman had become Franklin Roosevelt's Vice-Presidential candidate when the convention sent down Henry Wallace on waivers, Truman being one of those border-state politicians useful in mediating disputes among national Democratic factions. Roosevelt had encountered more and more difficulty with the Congress during the war. He felt obliged to reach into the Supreme Court and tap Justice James Byrnes for fence mending on Capitol Hill. Byrnes left the Court to become "Assistant President," just as Arthur Goldberg would do when President Johnson wanted him for duty at the United Nations.

As Vice President, Harry Truman was just another occupant of an office which John Garner had disdained as "not worth a pitcher of warm spit." In the subsequent nuclear age, Presidents, though still on their own constitutionally, have attempted to make the Vice Presidency an office of *de facto* responsibility, but this was not so in the spring of 1945. An uninformed Vice President, Truman as President was now asked both to administer an end to a devastating war and to undertake to secure a certain peace. Truman inherited the Seventy-ninth Congress. It was a product of the same 1944 campaign that led to the election of Roosevelt to a fourth term. It was a victory-and-reconversion Congress, with a Democratic majority.

Truman, of course, had little to do with its composition. As a result, it was during the life of the Seventy-ninth that his weaknesses dominated his relationship with the Congress. Truman was growing into a role he would ultimately manage well, but at this point he was growing. He did not fully realize what being President entailed. Furthermore, he had not yet decided on the strong advocacy of the bold foreign and domestic policies which make his Presidency memorable. Events helped him to assume these policies. His foreign policies would become enormously successful, the European Recovery Program, for example. His domestic policies, equally farsighted, were correspondingly unsuccessful. Their failure, in large measure a responsibility of the Congress, has had dreadful consequences in the worsened problems of poverty and racial conflict in the 1960s.

In midsummer the Potsdam Conference, held in a Berlin suburb, apparently convinced Truman that the holdover Roosevelt advisers were correct in their surmise of Russian tactics and strategies. Four days after conclusion of Potsdam, an atomic bomb was dropped on Hiroshima, Japan; three days later on Nagasaki. A minimum of 119,000 persons died as a result. On August 14, five days after the Nagasaki bombing, the Japanese formally surrendered.

The untidy business of dismantling wartime controls dominated the remaining months of 1945 and 1946. Truman received conflicting advice both as to which controls should be first disassembled and, more important, at what pace and to what degree. The Seventy-ninth Congress wanted them down, although the House agreed to a one-year extension for the Office of Price Administration. The War Manpower Commission lifted its controls however. The War Production Board jettisoned more than 200 regulations restricting consumer production. Truman closed the War Labor Board. The Wage Stabilization Board assumed its duties. The United Auto Workers struck General Motors. In 1946, approximately 4.6 million workers were involved in strikes. John L. Lewis's United Mine Workers sought and gained admission to the A.F.L. Price controls were ended except on sugar, rice, and rents.

In foreign affairs, the House and Senate approved an extension of Presidential authority to negotiate reciprocal trade agreements; implemented the Bretton Woods International Monetary Agreement; broadened the lending authority of the Export-Import Bank; approved a 3.7-billion-dollar loan to Britain over protests that the funds would underwrite nationalization; and extended the lend-lease program. By a vote of 89 to 2, the Senate ratified the United Nations Charter in late July, 1945, within one month after it was drafted at the San Francisco Conference. In this connection, the House asserted, as it occasionally has, a claim to share in treaty-making power. Overwhelmingly but futilely, the House approved a resolution to amend the Constitution to require that the House, as well as the Senate, should give its "advice and consent" before a treaty became operative. The Senate took no action.

In midsummer, 1946, the Senate discussed the degree to which the United States should submit to the jurisdiction of the International Court of Justice (the World Court). The Senate adopted, 51 to 12, a compromise amendment authorized by the Chairman of its Foreign Relations Committee, Tom Connally of Texas, that, in matters where the United States is involved, it is within our discretion to determine whether a dispute is domestic or international in character.

The Congress enacted several major pieces of domestic legislation designed to meet unmet needs that had accumulated during the war years. Among these was the Hill-Burton program to provide Federal funds for additional hospitals and a Federally assisted program of airport construction, as commercial aviation entered its postwar boom period. After a fierce fight, the Atomic Energy Commission was established, in which civilian control of atomic energy development was stated as a first principle. With the memory of the great Depression still keen, a President's

Council of Economic Advisers was established as part of a truncated Employment Act of 1946, whose objective was "to promote maximum employment, production, and purchasing power." Significantly, in the course of the bruising legislative fight, the word "maximum" had been substituted for the word "full." For itself, the Congress established a Joint Economic Committee. These two examples illustrated the general acceptance of the idea that the national Government had a role to play in building a strong and prosperous economy. The Congress also approved the La Follette-Monroney Legislative Reorganization Act of 1946, designed to modernize Congressional operations and procedures. In the process, members' pay was increased to 12,500 dollars a year, a 2,500-dollar increase.

The ending of the war meant that the split between the Democratic leadership in the House and the conservative coalition that ran the Rules Committee could no longer be camouflaged. The Democratic leadership could no longer rely upon Rules to abide by, much less assist, its legislative program. More than ever, Rules was looking at the substance of measures passing before them and making decisions whether to report them to the floor, and the committee majority was cleverly using the kind of rule they reported to assist in achieving the legislative result they desired.

Very often the way in which a bill is considered can determine whether it passes intact, is mangled, or even defeated. Rules recommends to the House the way to consider the bill. Nearly always, a majority of the House accepts that recommendation. For example, when the majority of Rules favors a tariff bill, but knows that, if subjected to the amendment process, special interest logrolling will endanger the bill's final passage, it recommends a rule providing for lengthy debate, but no amendments, a so-called *closed rule;* or the bill may be subject to a motion to recommit the bill to its legislative committee. This is the prerogative of opponents, usually a member of the minority party.

In 1945, a conservative majority on the Rules Committee successfully demanded alterations in a housing bill which the Banking and Currency Committee had already approved and reported, as a price for letting the bill go to the House floor. Furthermore, it successfully demanded advance commitment that the Banking and Currency Committee would not seek to restore the original provisions during the floor debate. Earlier, during World War II, the Rules Committee sought to block an Administration bill dealing with the Office of Price Administration, which conservatives both mocked and hated. A majority in the Rules Committee approved a rule for the bill under which a substitute, partially nongermane bill, hostile to O.P.A. but favored by the conservatives, could be easily offered on the floor of the House.

This was too much for Speaker Rayburn. He took to the floor when the rule on the O.P.A. bill came to the floor: "I take this time," Rayburn said, "to warn the members of this House . . . the Committee on Rules was never set up to be a legislative committee. It is a committee on procedure to make it possible that the majority of the House of Representatives may have the opportunity to work its will. . . ." Rayburn won his point. By a vote of 177 to 44, the House turned down the rule.

Meanwhile, downtown, Truman was getting used to being President. The adjustment takes longer for a man not elected to the Presidency in his own right. There were counselors, official and unofficial, to be tried and found acceptable or not. There were Cabinet feuds based on policy differences. The major one involved Secretary of State Byrnes and Secretary of Commerce Henry Wallace. The issue was foreign policy. Republicans asserted that unpublicized commitments and understandings, contrary to our national interests, were conceived at Quebec, Moscow, Teheran, and other wartime conferences attended by Roosevelt. Furthermore, Western Europe was politically and socially shaky, Italy particularly. There had been trouble in Iran where the Russians had sought to establish a puppet regime in the northeast region. French colonialists in Indochina were reestablishing their administration, while the home government in Paris was promising a different future for the Vietnamese. Truman, reflecting on the Cabinet and advisers he had inherited from Roosevelt, once remarked, "I don't know how I ever got out of that mud-hole." Now he had troubles within a Cabinet largely of his own choosing. The feud involved an interpretation of Soviet maneuvers in Europe.

Today, Byrnes would have been called a hawk; Henry Wallace, a dove. From London, Byrnes cabled Truman to the effect that the Cabinet was simply not large enough to accommodate both men. In September, 1946, Wallace left, the first of Truman's two famous firings. Wallace thought Truman was falling in line with anti-Soviet warmongering. He noted that President Truman had been on the platform at Westminster College in Fulton, Missouri, the previous March, when Winston Churchill had said that "an iron curtain has descended across the [European] continent. . . . I am convinced that there is nothing they [the Soviet Union and its allies] admire so much as strength, and there is nothing for which they have less respect than for weakness, especially military weakness. . . ." A further chill was in the air.

Truman also had to bone up on the Roosevelt Administration—its agreements, understanding, and direction, and he faced a Congress exhibiting both wariness and weariness toward domestic innovation in social policy. For the most part, Truman did not really campaign to secure a friendly Eightieth Congress. In a broad sense, therefore, the Eightieth Congress was a product of his uneven Presidency, then nineteen months in existence, and an adverse national response to it.

A Boston advertising agency had caught the mood in a four-word campaign slogan "Had Enough? Vote Republican." A majority of American voters did. In November, 1946, they elected a Republican Congress. For the first time in fourteen years, the Democratic party no longer had a majority in either the House or the Senate. The Republican party controlled the House by fifty-seven seats and the Senate by six, approximately the same margins that Democrats had held in the previous Congress. In terms of domestic issues, however, there were about 300 conservatives to 125 to 135 moderates and liberals in the Eightieth.

Too little thoughtful attention has been given to this Eightieth Congress. In large measure this is because Truman achieved his election to the Presidency in 1948 by attacking "that notorious Republican 80th Congress . . . that no-good, do-nothing 80th Congress." The maligned Eightieth deserves study, however, because Congresses since then have generally supported the policy positions its bipartisan majority assumed in both domestic and foreign affairs. The Eightieth set the pattern advantageously in foreign affairs and disadvantageously in domestic. In foreign affairs, Presidents since Truman have, deliberately or not, used their persuasive powers to urge their Congresses to emulate the Eightieth. With the exception of Dwight Eisenhower and the 1959–1961 Congress (Eighty-sixth), every President has unsuccessfully asked every Congress to enact important domestic legislation too liberal for the conservative coalition. If, in the late 1940s, the Congress had gone along with Truman in domestic affairs as it had in foreign affairs, our terrible problems today would be closer to resolution.

The first session of the Eightieth lasted almost the entire calendar year, 1947. When completed, the United States was more deeply involved in the world than ever before. In February, the British notified the Truman Administration it could no longer afford to maintain troops in Greece, where it had been involved for more than a century, although Greece was now torn by civil war. The British had been similarly involved with Turkey. The next month, Truman went to the Congress. He took the advice of Senator Vandenberg that, to put over such a program as Truman and his advisers felt necessary, the President would have to "scare hell out of the country." In this context, Truman asked for 400 million dollars for economic and military assistance for both Greece and Turkey to offset the pressure from the Soviet Union and its bloc states. The request was approved. With the Truman Doctrine, the United States was committed to "support free peoples who are resisting attempted subjugation by armed minorities or by outside pressures." In May in Mississippi, Dean Acheson, then Under Secretary of State, outlined the European aid program, and in June Secretary of State Marshall formally proposed it in a speech at Harvard University. Secretary of State Marshall asked that European states establish a long-range economic recovery program, which the United States would financially support. This evolved into the European Recovery Program (E.R.P.) or Marshall Plan.

In December, Truman proposed to Congress that there be authorized a four-year, 17-billion-dollar loan-and-grant program, with 6.8 billion dollars requested for the first fifteen months. In April, 1948, final Congressional action, overwhelmingly adopted in both House and Senate, produced a 4.3-billion-dollar authorization for the first twelve months, plus a 1-billion-dollar increase in the lending authority of the Export-Import Bank. Two concessions helped the bill to pass. First, Paul Hoffman, a Republican, was named the first E.R.P. administrator. Secondly, a ransom of more than 460 million dollars was authorized for military and economic assistance to the fatally wounded Chiang Kai-shek Government.

Certain bizarre additions to the Marshall Plan luckily did not get the backing of the majority. One was an attempt to reduce assistance to Britain unless the partition of Ireland was ended by 1951; another, a proposal to incorporate Franco's Spain into the European Recovery Program.

In July, 1947, the military forces were placed under the administration of a Secretary of Defense. In September, James Forrestal became the first Secretary. Expenditures for the military, which had tumbled from 90 billion dollars in 1945 to 9 billion dollars two years later, now began a steady ascent upward to reach 80 billion dollars in the fiscal year of 1969. The House and Senate also approved establishment of the Central Intelligence Agency. While authorizing the financial and programmatic sinews for an expansionist foreign policy in an unstable postwar world, the conservative Congress also did some domestic business during its first year. In March, it passed and sent to the states for ultimate successful ratification the Twenty-second Amendment to the Constitution limiting future Presidents to two terms. "There! That'll fix Roosevelt," said conservatives who couldn't beat him at the polls when he was alive. The Speaker and then the President *pro tem* of the Senate were placed, respectively, in line of succession for the Presidency, behind the Vice President. This order was changed after the Kennedy assassination by the Twenty-fifth Constitutional Amendment ratified in 1967, whereby more precise procedures are established for a Vice President to assume executive leadership in case of death, resignation, or incapacity of the President.

The major at-home legislative achievement was passage of the so-called Taft-Hartley Act over Truman's veto. The bill was aimed at organized labor whose members then represented one out of three nonfarm workers. The act outlawed secondary boycotts, the closed shop, and jurisdictional strikes. If it has not proved to be a "slave labor act," as the labor leaders had asserted, it has, at a minimum, indisputably slowed organizing efforts. Later its chief sponsor, Senator Taft, tried to correct the unintended results of the secondary boycott provision in respect to picketing by unions at construction sites.

In 1948, international issues dominated the Congress. Czechoslovakia, "a window on the East," acquired a Communist government by coup in February. On the second day of April, the Marshall Plan received full Congressional approval. A strong Communist effort was beaten back at the Italian elections, and, the day before, the Soviets imposed a blockade upon divided Berlin that lasted until September, 1949. In such an atmosphere, the Congress in June passed a peacetime selective service act. It proved less cooperative in respect to extension of reciprocal trade. Truman asked for a three-year extension of his negotiation authority. The strain on the bipartisan coalition was appreciable. One year was authorized.

As in the previous year, the Congress was backward in its attitude toward domestic needs, the House, particularly. Truman twice vetoed a tax-reduction bill. The Congress persisted; the bill became law. Upper-income taxpayers received as much as a 48 per cent reduction and lower-bracket ratepayers 3 per cent. The Congress's contribution to the Social Security program was to exempt newspaper boys from coverage. This, too, survived a Presidential veto. In April, 1947, the Senate passed a 300-million-dollar elementary-secondary-school bill, sponsored by Taft. Even Taft had an uphill pull in the House, however, where conservatives were occasionally too conservative for Mr. Republican himself. Thus, the House Education and Labor Committee, whose chairman was Fred Hartley, Jr., of New Jersey, killed the bill by parliamentary maneuvering. As he had in late 1945, Truman again requested passage of the Wagner-Murray bill providing for a comprehensive, prepaid medical-insurance plan for Americans of all ages, financed through Social Security taxation. Taft again said it was "socialistic." Taft in rebuttal introduced a 230-million-dollar-a-year grant program by which states could offer comprehensive care for the medically indigent. Hearings were held on both bills, but there was no further action.

In late August, during a hearing of the House Committee on Un-American Activities, Whittaker Chambers, a self-styled former courier for the Communist party, identified Alger Hiss in a direct confrontation as one he knew to have been a Communist. Hiss, then with the Carnegie Endowment for International Peace, had worked for both State and Agriculture departments. Hiss denied the accusation. Unfortunately, Hiss's innocence became a touchstone of liberal faith, as much so as the innocence of Nicola Sacco and Bartolomeo Vanzetti had been in the late twenties. Hiss was convicted after two trials. Richard M. Nixon, then a member of the House Committee on Un-American Activities, got his start as a national politician as an investigator in the case. His Presidential ambitions were inflated and those of others deflated as a result of the Chambers-Hiss episode. Such was the record of the Eightieth Congress, written largely by Robert Taft and Arthur Vandenberg. They were the guides in the House, as well as in the Senate.

Vandenberg was only recently a convert to "internationalism." In his private papers, he wrote that the Sunday the Japanese bombed Hawaii "ended isolationism for any realist." Another factor in his conversion was the influence of a nephew, Hoyt Vandenberg, who became Air Force Chief of Staff. The export-minded automobile industry in his home state of Michigan was a third. He played a shaping role in the Republican Mackinac Island conference in 1943. It met to draft broad policy positions for the postwar period. Vandenberg assigned himself the role of "hunting for the middle ground between those extremists at one end of the line who would cheerfully give America away and those extremists at the other end of the line who would attempt a total isolation which has come to be an impossibility." Taft didn't think isolation an impossibility at all, however; he remarked that Vandenberg just couldn't resist the blandishments of "those internationalists." This Marshall Plan business, he said, was "a global New Deal." Vandenberg disagreed. During the war, he had served on a special Senate Committee on postwar plans, known as the Committee of Eight. Vandenberg wielded his decisive influence in foreign policy matters as second most senior Republican in the Senate and Chairman of the Foreign Relations Committee.

Although the House Foreign Affairs Committee lacks the constitutional endowment of the counterpart committee in the Senate, the House is not without influence in foreign policy matters. For example, the Agriculture Committee, under the Chairmanship of Harold Cooley of North Carolina, assigned heavily lobbied sugar-import quotas in such a mystifying fashion that they not only caused trouble to our foreign policy administrators but also to the less favored foreign governments. In recent years, the Armed Services Committee has overridden recommendations of the executive-branch policy makers by earmarking authorizations for the development of anti-antimissiles and for a specific number of Air Force air groups. Government Operations itself investigates our far-flung foreign aid operations. Ways and Means legislates tariff authority. Merchant Marine and Fisheries legislated a requirement that half the cargoes procured under American foreign aid programs must be shipped to their destination in American flag ships. In 1951, the Rules Committee blocked for two weeks a famine relief bill for India until the measure was altered to require that India borrow funds to buy our domestic grain.

The House's main power to shape foreign policy, however, lies within the Appropriations Committee. For example, the Congress authorized 4 billion dollars in the first year, fiscal 1949, of the Marshall Plan. Congressional procedure consists of two steps, first, authorization of a program, and then appropriation. The Appropriations Committee is not obliged to fund the full authorization of any program. It may refuse to provide any funding, or it may provide funds between one cent and the authorization. In the case of the Marshall Plan's first-year authorization, it provided about 3.75 billion instead of the authorized 4.3 billion dollars. Moreover, it applied the funds to a fifteen-month period rather than the customary twelve-month fiscal year. It made other changes which Administration officials translated into an actual reduction of nearly 1 billion dollars. An explanatory report accompanying the foreign-aid appropriation bill indicated that these changes were based on a conflict of attitude between a majority of the committee and the Marshall Plan administrators. The former saw the aid program as a dole or relief undertaking. The latter, of course, envisioned a broad, comprehensive, long-range recovery undertaking.

The original premise of the Marshall Plan was restored during the appropriation process in the Senate. In recent years, the Chairman of the Foreign Operations Subcommittee of the House Appropriating Committee has been Otto Passman of Louisiana. Passman is on record as saying there is no such thing as a good foreign aid bill. During committee deliberations on the fiscal 1968 foreign aid bill, Passman was chided by the chairman of the full committee, George Mahon of Texas, on the grounds that he was not acting responsibly. This is another instance of a program favored by the majority being turned over to unfriendly hands by a leadership careless of the effects of seniority.

Appropriately, Taft was chairman of the Senate's Labor and Public Welfare Committee. From his captain's chair there, he led, even dominated, this Congress on domestic affairs. In this century, surely, there has been no other Congress in which the responsibility on major policy sectors can be so clearly attributed to two men. The House had no Republican leaders of the stature of Vandenberg and Taft, and so the two men were House members without portfolio. Certainly, seniority, their fortuitous committee assignments, experience, and the personal legislative interests of the two men must have played a role in the division of responsibilities between them: Taft to lead in domestic matters; Vandenberg in foreign. It constituted a tacit "leadership truce." I had no experience with Vandenberg. Taft and I, however, served together on the Joint Congressional Economic Committee. He was a man of such intellectual power, self-assurance, and force that it seems inconceivable he would have lent himself to such a division. Perhaps his single-minded purpose to dismantle the New Deal left him no time for other than cursory attention to foreign affairs. Perhaps Taft realized that his essential allies in the Congress, the Southern Democrats, were then internationalists in large measure because of the export orientation of those states. They might be less cooperative if he imposed his isolationist foreign policy views on them.

Vandenberg realized the consequences if Western Europe collapsed. His support immeasurably helped Truman's wise counselors, George Marshall, George Kennan, and that remarkable politician-diplomat, Dean Acheson. American foreign policy, thanks to Vandenberg, became not nonpartisan but bipartisan. With his backing, Truman was able to muster large support in the country for restoring Europe to health. It must be remembered, however, that though the cloak of bipartisanship covered military assistance, economic assistance, and the United Nations, it could not be spread widely enough to cover substantively other foreign policy sectors, such as agricultural exports, tariffs and trade barriers, and specialized United Nations organs.

The situation was different in domestic affairs. Taft and his allies in both parties in both House and Senate intended to undo the New Deal. These Republicans and Democrats demonstrated an incredible isolationism in respect to domestic affairs. Their sincerity and honesty of purpose only served to make their undertaking more dangerous. The tragedy of the late 1940s and the 1950s was the failure of understanding and vision on the part of such influential men as Taft, who did not know their country or their countrymen.

Most Americans did not want the New Deal programs eliminated. They wanted to retain Social Security, minimum wage, and housing programs, for example. They had accepted trade unionism. The intervention of "big government" was no longer automatically bad in their eyes. Taft must have missed the point of the Employment Act of 1946, whereby the national Government assumed some responsibility for the maintenance of prosperity. True, the majority wanted greater efficiency and economy in government. The overwhelming support received by the first Hoover Commission on reorganization of the Federal executive is interesting proof of this. The point that the majority wanted increased economy and efficiency but not massive changes in policy direction was made clear by the relative lack of success of the second Hoover Commission, which went beyond efficiency and economy into basic policy in the recommendations it made in the first Eisenhower term.

Taft's domestic program by and large won out over President Truman's in the Eightieth Congress. His masterwork was the Taft-Hartley Law. The Eightieth also inadvertently enraged the farmers by not supplying sufficient storage for their crops. It worried present and prospective recipients of Social Security by cutting several hundred thousand off the rolls. It did little or nothing constructive about health, education, welfare, natural resources, housing, and so forth.

Although Presidential appropriation requests were reduced, it passed the usual highway, public works, Federal salary-increase bills that had voter appeal, but it was largely negative in domestic matters. It managed to out-Taft even Taft when, in 1946, the Rules Committee killed off a Senate-passed four-point Wagner-Ellender-Taft housing bill that would provide more favorable F.H.A. mortgage terms, research, and development efforts, including 500,000 public housing units and urban redevelopment grants. In 1948, a diluted and renamed Taft-Ellender-Wagner bill, containing only the first two items, was approved by both the House and Senate. Then in 1949, in the Eighty-first Congress, a promising 1949 Housing Act, containing the other two points, was passed, after being wrestled from Rules only when Rayburn threatened to invoke the new twenty-one-day rule.

The Republican Eightieth Congress was organized and run efficiently by the Taft-oriented Republican leaders, ably aided and abetted by their conservative Democratic cohorts. The latter, in fact, had become even more anti-Truman, because he dared seek action from the Eightieth in the then forbidden area of civil rights. Every single committee of the House was firmly controlled by Republican conservatives. That power center, ancient and modern, the House Committee on Rules, consisting of eight Republicans to four nominal Democrats, actually had only one dependable Truman supporter, its former ineffectual Chairman, Adolph Sabath. When the Republican leadership of the House wanted a bill scheduled at a certain time with a specific rule providing for debate on terms most advantageous to the leadership's objectives, with the one exception of the housing bill, Rules promptly produced what they wanted. In the Eightieth Congress, the committees were organized in such a way that Republican domestic policy could most effectively be brought forward and acted upon in the House.

There were those then, and there are many now, who believe that Southern cooperation on domestic matters was part of an arrangement, a deal that is. The assumption is that Southern support on Taft's domestic program would be the payment for inaction by the Eightieth on civil rights legislation. My guess is that Taft would be too shrewd to make such an explicit arrangement. There was no need to do so. The Southern conservatives knew where to find birds of the same feather.

In his acceptance speech at the Democratic convention in Philadelphia in 1948, President Harry S. Truman described American foreign policy as successfully bipartisan, dismissed it as a campaign issue, and proceeded to take the Eightieth Congress apart on the domestic issues that bore Taft's brand. He called a special session, with brazen partisan gall, giving the Republicans in Congress an unwanted opportunity to demonstrate how unlike Republican Congressional deed was to the words of the platform of the just adjourned Republican party convention.

Truman ran against Thomas Dewey on the issue of Taft's platform. Dewey could not evade the domestic record of the Eightieth; Truman would not let him. Dewey could not accept or reject it; one or another wing of the Republican party would not let him. I wonder, when I study the relatively light vote cast (51.5 per cent in the Presidential year of 1948), whether, if Taft had really fought for election on the issues, he might not have won the Presidency in that year as he did his reelection to the Senate in Ohio in 1950. Honest conviction and vigorous advocacy go a long way in American politics, as Truman's victory proved.

On every occasion when he discussed foreign affairs, Truman repeated the ancient cliché honored by all partisan politicians, "politics must end at the water's edge." He thus avoided having to admit that the Eightieth Congress had responded to his foreign affairs leadership in a wholly responsible and realistic fashion. There really was no campaign issue on foreign policy between Truman and Dewey, not because either was *non*partisan but because both partisans knew that parties equally involved in *bi*partisan policies could not attack each other with much effect. As events since 1950 have shown, it was to Truman's advantage not to highlight the constructive nature of the Vandenberg role in leading the Eightieth Congress on foreign affairs, and since Dewey needed the support of many isolationist Republicans, Dewey played along.

Thus Truman was left free to attack the Taft-led Eightieth Congress on domestic affairs. For example, a crucial component in his election was his success in garnering "the farm vote." He played on fears of economic depression. Truman told farm audiences that the Eightieth Congress had appropriated insufficient funds for storage of crops. Farm prices worked against Dewey. Corn, selling for approximately 2 dollars 15 cents a bushel when Tom Dewey was nominated in late June, had fallen by nearly half, to 1 dollar 20 cents a bushel, on the eve of election day over four months later.

An episode at the Democratic nominating convention also played an influential role in the Democratic party within the House. The episode was the bolt of Southern delegates, Dixiecrats, from the convention. It was precipitated by the adoption of a mild-sounding, but politically potent substitute for the innocuous civil rights section of the platform draft, authored by Representative Andrew J. Biemiller of Wisconsin. Hubert H.

Humphrey, then Mayor of Minneapolis, gave an eloquent and fiery speech in support of the stronger draft. Truman's own Missouri delegation voted against it. The bolters formed their own party, the so-called States' Rights party, and nominated for President Strom Thurmond, then Governor of South Carolina. Nevertheless, the bolters, including Mississippi delegates, many of whom were members of the House, were concerned about the consequences of their action when the Eighty-first Congress convened in January, 1949, following Truman's surprise victory over Thomas Dewey. Wallace had no strength in the House. The Mississippi electoral votes had gone not to Truman but to Thurmond.

Democrats had regained control of the House by ninety-one votes and of the Senate by twelve. The election brought to the Senate those Democrats who would be its first-rank leaders for many, many years: Paul Douglas of Illinois, Humphrey of Minnesota, Estes Kefauver of Tennessee, and Lyndon Johnson of Texas. That year, too, Illinois voters elected Adlai Stevenson as their governor. Elation about the election results was ill-founded, however, as I, a freshman member of the House, discovered when I analyzed the composition of the new House by issues. The line-up was about 213 votes for Truman's domestic programs to about 221 against. Compounding this situation was the control of the organizational structure of the House by conservative Southern Democrats and conservative Republicans, including three major committees, Ways and Means, Appropriations, and Rules, all of which were dominated by conservatives. It was a situation for a Speaker to remedy. In their day, Clay, Reed, Cannon, and Longworth maneuvered their party legislative program so that Congress would act on it. Rayburn might have, but didn't.

Of course, Sam Rayburn knew the strength of the Southern Democrats on important committees and recognized, at least in part, their significance for the legislative process in the new Eighty-first Congress; but the combination of nearly fifty years of service in the House with the fact that Rayburn belonged to the majority party for all but four of the last thirty years, made it possible for him to hold great power longer than anyone in the history of the House and to rely on that power to achieve his Party's ends.

Short, stocky, erect, and shiny bald, Rayburn exuded strength. He knew more about the ins and outs of the legislative process in the House than any member. He sucked up information about the House, its committees, employees, members, and activities like a giant vacuum cleaner. The result was that he knew nearly everything that was going on. He had done ten thousand favors for hundreds of members. When the House was in session, it was his whole life. A childless, unmarried,* single-minded man he devoted twelve to fourteen hours each day to the House, those connected with it and its affairs and then retired early to his lonely, quiet apartment. He was kind and helpful to all new members and to all old members, too, unlike most House seniors. He took a personal interest in their families, their private and public problems, and their careers in the House. He could be remarkably persuasive. He seemed simple but was complex; he seemed open and frank but kept his own counsel to a degree not often comprehended by even his closest associates.

In 1949, he had vast personal power. Even before he became Chairman of the Committee on Interstate and Foreign Commerce in 1931, his skills, abilities, and knowledge of the House and its history must have been well above average. Since 1931, he had played a key leadership role in virtually every significant legislative action of the House. Nevertheless, apparently he did not recognize the long-range significance of the Dixiecrat bolt. Still he must have understood the short-range consequences in the House of Representatives of allowing those members who had supported the Thurmond Presidential candidacy against that of the regular Democratic nominee to retain their seniority and thus to influence the forthcoming Truman legislative program.

President Truman probably thought of Rayburn when he thought of the House. No doubt he knew he did not know very

* Rayburn had married early in his political career, but the marriage lasted only a few months. As the years went by, the marriage was so thoroughly forgotten that experienced House members and Washington correspondents referred to Rayburn as a bachelor.

much about the House, its members, or how it worked. Ten years as a Senator may make one an expert in the legislative process and the underlying power structure in the Senate, but few Senators know the House.

Thus Rayburn had the power of decision in the matter of the Dixiecrat bolters. He made that decision in some fashion; perhaps, even by taking no action, he made the destructive decision to allow the bolters to retain their seniority status in the House, in the Democratic caucus, and on the committees. After all, like most members with their two-year terms, he, too, was given to living from hand to mouth legislatively. Very knowledgeable about America's past history, he was not much given to long-range planning about our future. His methods of leadership were so personal and time consuming that he really did not have time.

The day before the new Eighty-first Congress convened, the Democratic party caucus was held in the Hall of the House of Representatives. Our candidate for Speaker was chosen. Sam Rayburn, of course. John McCormack for majority leader, unanimously, too, of course. I remember no rows about those who might not be entitled to be a member of the caucus. At any event, no concrete action was taken to exclude from the caucus anyone who might have supported Dewey or Henry Wallace or Strom Thurmond. The members of the Mississippi delegation took their places there just as did those who had supported Truman, although the very same Mississippi members, including William Colmer, as members of the Mississippi delegation to the Democratic convention, had walked out and refused to participate. Here at the caucus, they walked in and were allowed to stay without protest.

The significance of this failure to act was not foreseen by anyone at the time. In fact, nearly everyone would have been truly shocked and startled if in January, 1949, an attack had been made in the caucus on the sanctity of the iron rule of seniority. No doubt Speaker Rayburn did not want to rock the boat. He took the position that only the performance of a member in Washington mattered. Rayburn had decided that it was not his business what a member did about politics back home. No doubt President Truman took the lead from Rayburn. After all, he really had to trust his old friend Sam, the senior Democrat in the House.

The liberal Democratic leaders, Andrew J. Biemiller of Wisconsin, John Blatnik of Minnesota, John Carroll of Colorado, Herman Eberharter of Pennsylvania, and Chet Holifield of California, settled for a gimmick to bypass Rules. This was the so-called *twenty-one-day rule*, adopted first by a vote of 176 to 48 in the Democratic caucus and then by 275 to 142 in the full House. Under its provisions, if a piece of legislation were reported by a legislative committee and after twenty-one days a resolution to bring it to the floor for action had not been acted on favorably by the Rules Committee, then the chairman of the legislative committee could call it up for consideration on either the second or fourth Monday of each month. This new rule was apparently Rayburn's response to liberal pressure for a way to bypass the Rules Committee. Adolph Sabath of Illinois, Rules Chairman, welcomed the device, because he could not control his committee. It is my understanding that the language of the twenty-one-day rule was drafted by Lewis Deschler, the parliamentarian, at Speaker Rayburn's direction. The use of this rule or the threat to use it made it possible to bring to the floor for action legislation blocked in Rules; during its brief life bills covering flood control, statehood for Alaska and Hawaii, the establishment of a National Science Foundation, an antipollution program, and a resolution relating to participation in international organizations won via the twenty-one-day rule. Threat of its use freed other bills, including a major housing measure.

Nevertheless there were inherent imperfections in the twenty-one-day-rule. It was not really enough just to bypass Rules. A demagogic and irresponsible legislative committee could use it and thus add to the burdens of the House, without check from the Speaker, the leadership, or even a bipartisan majority. Also the rule further weakened the already frail institutional power of the Speakership. The Speaker *must* recognize the chairman of the committee under the rule. This was a further strengthening of the already too strong dukes, the committee chairmen. Considering the circumstances, however, the twenty-one-day rule was useful. The conservative coalition disliked even this slight trimming of its power in the nominally Democratic House. In the second session, a strong effort, led by Cox, was launched to repeal the twenty-one-day rule. It failed by a vote of 183 to 236. However the next year, when the Eighty-second Congress met, the coalition did succeed in repealing it.

How much more useful it would have been to deprive the Mississippi members of the House of their seniority. We have seen that each of them was a member of the convention delegation which had bolted the convention. There was no justifiable reason for rewarding these men with the fruits of Democratic victory which they had opposed. Accepted as members of the majority party in good standing, they were automatically endowed with their committee seniority. This meant that John Rankin was in line for the Chairmanship, not only of the Committee on Veterans Affairs but also of the House Un-American Activities Committee. He was maneuvered out of the latter chairmanship by a series of expediencies which carefully avoided any overt breaching of the seniority system. William Whittington by virtue of seniority became Chairman of the House Committee on Public Works. Jamie Whitten became Chairman of the key Agricultural Appropriation Subcommittee of the Committee on Agriculture. Thomas Abernethy, Arthur Winstead, and John Bell Williams took their places on Agriculture, Armed Services, and Interstate and Foreign Commerce, respectively. Abernethy became the Chairman of Agriculture's important cotton subcommittee; Winstead played his negative role in military legislation; Williams held an aviation subcommittee chairmanship in Interstate and Foreign Commerce.

Southern Democrats, themselves, ignored seniority when it suited their purposes, as in the 1950s when Graham Barden of North Carolina, Education and Labor Committee Chairman, passed over the second-ranking Democrat, Adam Clayton Powell of New York, a Negro, when subcommittee chairmanships were allocated.

The case of William Colmer of Mississippi is particularly fascinating. It was not only the inaction by the caucus in 1949, but also a typical "mistake" by Majority Leader John McCormack, which restored him to Rules, which he now chairs.

Colmer for several Congresses had been a junior member of the Rules Committee. When the Republicans became the majority in the Eightieth Congress, Colmer lost his place on the committee, since its Democratic membership was cut to four. It had not been a rigid rule that once a member lost his position on a committee because of change in the party control of the House, he would get it back when his party next became the majority party. The story both Rayburn and McCormack told is that, after the 1948 election, Colmer asked McCormack for assistance in regaining a seat on Rules. McCormack, without thinking, agreed. Rayburn felt that he had to abide by the commitment.

The consequence of the failure of the Democratic leadership to punish bolters (unlike Longworth in similar circumstances) is particularly noticeable in the case of Colmer. That failure delayed beyond toleration needed domestic legislation, such as school aid and civil rights. The obstructionist nature of Rules would have been thwarted years earlier if, instead of Colmer, an able, loyalist Southerner had been named, such as James Trimble of Arkansas. Instead, the restoration of Colmer meant there were seven die-hard conservatives on the twelve-member Rules Committee. Within a few years, there would be nine out of twelve. The masquerading Mississippians had slapped their party leadership, and the leadership simply turned the other cheek. All the other conservative Southern Democrats, who kept quiet during the election, quickly understood the real meaning of the Democratic leadership's failure to act. So did the trapped liberal Southern Democrats, whose ultimate fate, defeat, was sealed by the tolerance of Rayburn and the majority of House Democrats toward the Dixiecrat defectors.

What incentive was there for a Southern Democrat in Congress to be loyal to his party and his party's Presidential nominee—much less to his party's program—if the Mississippians could walk out of the Democratic convention planning to defeat the party's nominee? Then when the nominee, despite their efforts against him, was reelected to the Presidency and the party they had deserted was once more in control of the Congress, they were permitted to return with impunity to share in the power they had tried to prevent their party from regaining. These Democrats delayed, emasculated, and destroyed the program of their own party, but they could say truly to their Southern colleagues, who supported the Democratic program: "What good does that do you? What does your support of the party program and the party's nominees get you? Nothing! But my seniority makes me Chairman of Public Works, of Veterans Affairs, and puts me back on the Rules Committee." They also told their constituents about their unassailable positions, and they told the constituents of the Southern liberals about it. The result also was to delay the growth of a two-party system in the South. "Why elect a Republican who won't have any power as a member of the minority party? Our conservative Democratic congressman thinks like a Republican and votes like a Republican but his seniority as a Democrat and an accepted member of the majority party gets him power which he uses to destroy Democratic programs."

The Southern conservative Democrats (helped by their like-minded Republican colleagues) also took care of their own with vital public works projects and other Federal expenditures for their districts. The amount of Federal money spent in the past twenty years in the lower Mississippi Valley area, largely represented by Southern conservatives, greatly exceeds the amount of Federal funds expended in the Tennessee Valley, until recently largely represented by Southern Democrats who supported most Democratic programs. This is no coincidence. Nor is it a coincidence that most of the hard-core Dixiecrats have survived (with some losses to Republicans), while nearly all of the Southern party loyalist Democrats have been defeated, conceded, or have been just plain run out of politics by reactionaries and racists who use the Democratic party label but subscribe to Republican social and economic principles.

There were also less dramatic results of the failure of the House Democrats under Rayburn's leadership to organize its committee appointees so that it could control Truman's domestic legislative program. For example, the Appropriations Committee was divided nominally into twenty-seven Democrats to eighteen Republicans. Its programmatic division was seventeen moderates to twenty-eight conservatives. Program control was important because the amount of money appropriated usually determines the effectiveness and scope of an authorized program. Program control also was lacking on Ways and Means, which deals with taxes, Social Security, unemployment compensation, and trade. Of its twenty-five members, twelve were down-the-line conservatives, eight down-the-line Rayburn supporters, and five were doubtful. When the conservatives picked up the support of one of the five, they had a majority.

Judiciary, whose jurisdiction included the critically important area of civil rights legislation, was divided by label, seventeen Democrats to ten Republicans, but the division on issues was eight moderates and nineteen conservatives. The chance for meaningful civil rights and immigration legislation was much impaired.

Rayburn, McCormack, and the majority of House Democrats tolerated committee assignments to be made that gave advantage to the opposition. By pretending that all those who wore the Democratic party label shared a common outlook, Rayburn, in effect, transferred the power of the majority party to the political opposition, the coalition of most Republicans with sixty to eighty Dixiecrats.

Truman continued to score better in foreign affairs than in domestic in his second term. His inaugural address in January, 1949, contained a proposal for a program making available to underdeveloped nations our scientific and industrial skills and techniques, the so-called Point Four program. Congress authorized it in May of the following year. The North Atlantic Treaty Organization (NATO) came into being in the spring, and the Russians lifted the Berlin blockade in September, but these advantages were overshadowed by the knowledge that the Soviet Union had developed an atomic bomb and by the Communists' military successes in China.

The labor-liberal wing of the Democratic Party looked forward to the enactment of a broad and effective domestic legislative program by the Eighty-first Congress. After all, the conservative coalition had lost its *total* control of the organizational structure of the House. The twenty-one-day rule had diluted the power of the Rules Committee, but, the coalition's effective control of the Appropriations Committee still provided a strong base from which to hack at adequate funding of liberal programs. A stranglehold over the flow of legislation had been loosened but not eliminated. Strong rear-guard actions, pitched battles from ambush, and constant harassment were well within the capability of those old allies, the conservative Republicans and conservative Democrats.

Stalemate was the order of the day. The conservatives in the Eighty-first Congress did not have the strength to undo the New Deal, but they could block Harry Truman's Fair Deal. Sometimes they mustered a bare majority to strike down some familiar established program. President Truman, however, had that most powerful of all legislative weapons, the veto. In the Eighty-first Congress, unlike the Eightieth, the conservative coalition simply could not muster the two-thirds vote necessary to override the veto. Knowing this, they seldom tried.

After hard fighting overcame determined delaying actions and bitter debates, a major housing bill was enacted in 1949. Taft was the sponsor of its Title I, which embraced the concept of urban redevelopment. It was the only major step forward in the social welfare field that year. Bedrock conservative that he was, Taft still accepted a Federal role in education, housing, and health. The new program, in effect, rested upon a Congressionally mandated national housing policy, "the realization as soon as feasible of the goal of a decent home and a suitable living environment for every American family."

Two other achievements of the Eighty-first were equally hard fought. Social Security benefits were increased. The hourly minimum wage was increased from 40 to 75 cents. Yet when other changes were made, the coverage of the act was shrunk so that 500,000 *fewer* workers were protected. There were other failures. An attempt to repeal the Taft-Hartley Law, a major issue in Presidential and Congressional elections of 1948, ended in disaster in the House. Only a parliamentary maneuver and Rayburn's ability to get a few votes switched overnight prevented the House from passing a bill more antilabor even than Taft-Hartley. The Brannon plan for agriculture—direct production payments—was defeated. The Truman health insurance program and Federal aid to education could not even get out of the committees to which they were referred. This again demonstrates how inadequate was the control of the legislative structure of the House by the pro-Truman leadership. Twice rejected was Truman's proposal to establish a cabinet-level Department of Health, Education, and Welfare. The House passed a Fair Employment Practices Bill. Despite the fact that no one really believed the Senate would act favorably on the matter, the conservative coalition in the House could not resist removing all effective enforcement provisions from the bill just prior to its passage.

The year 1950 was an inauspicious one. It marked the beginning of a period some called "the dreadful decade." "Intellectual" became a dirty word. UNICEF and fluoridation were regarded as Communist plots. Taft criticized Acheson for assuming the innocence of Joe McCarthy's ill-starred victims. Americans suspected other Americans. They were particularly upset by the USSR's development of the atomic bomb. In September of 1950 Americans reasoned, Eric Goldman wrote in *The Crucial Decade*, that we had cleared and developed a continent and shown our superiority in all ways thereby, so surely then an inferior economic system (Communism) could only make progress by conspiracy, spying, and subversion. Hiss, that New Dealer, was convicted in January. In early February, Klaus Fuchs, the physicist spy, was exposed. The same month, Julius and Ethel Rosenberg were arrested and later tried, convicted, and in 1953 executed on charges of carrying on espionage on behalf of the Soviet Union. Great Britain extended diplomatic recognition to Communist China.

Nineteen days after the Hiss conviction, Senator Joseph McCarthy made a speech at Wheeling, West Virginia, in which he said there were 205 Communist card carriers in the State Department—or was it 75? The number was elusive and never proved. McCarthy found willing allies in the House, especially in the Committee on Un-American Activities. Judith Coplon was found guilty of espionage. McCarthy, until he was censured in late 1954 by his Senate colleagues, paralyzed the State Department and impaired foreign policy by totally irresponsible and false defamations against domestics, dentists, and Army generals.

The Korean War broke out in June, 1950. Next year, Senator Estes Kefauver exposed on television the extent of organized crime. Democrats in city halls were not amused; neither was Truman. Republicans orchestrated a crime, Communism, and corruption theme that reduced Democratic majorities in the Congress in the 1950 elections. (Two years later, the same theme was to put Republicans in charge of the House, Senate, and White House for the first time in nearly twenty-five years.) The conservative coalition reassumed total control of the House. Domestically, the Congress was a cipher. The war in Korea was the dominant issue.

In April, Truman carried out his second major firing. General Douglas MacArthur, dismissed but intractable as ever, flew home a few days later to address an adoring joint Congressional session. ". . . and like the old soldier of that ballad, I now close my military career and just fade away. . . ." He did, too, rather sooner than the misleading adulation of the moment portended. In one of its last acts, the Eighty-second Congress overrode a Presidential veto of the restrictive McCarran-Walter Immigration Act. Congress adjourned and headed for the Presidential nomination conventions. Harry Truman a few months before had told a Jackson-Jefferson Day Dinner he would not seek re-election. Bitter conventions and a bitter Presidential election lay ahead.

2

The Eisenhower Years

Dwight David Eisenhower, the grandfatherly, Republican Presidential candidate, said he'd go to inflamed Korea if he was elected. "Ike" made the promise during the campaign, after a supporter commented publicly that he was "running like a dry creek." Actually, Korean truce negotiations had begun in June, 1951, but Communist intransigence kept the war going for another two years before an armistice was signed. During the twenty-four months that the truce talks dragged on before an effective cease-fire was achieved, enemy forces inflicted the following casualties on United States troops: 12,700 dead; 49,501 wounded.

The pleasant, sincere, nonpolitical Eisenhower found a warm response among Americans. The Republican rallying cry of Communism, crime, and corruption, plus the Korean War, drowned the "talk sense" campaign of the witty, erudite Adlai Stevenson. A majority of Americans had come to distrust the Democratic party. Others felt, perhaps rightly, that the Democrats had been in power for too long. Walter Lippmann felt a tour of duty in the White House would housebreak the frustrated Republican party to the realities of mid-twentieth century domestic and foreign affairs. Ironically, it was not Taft, Mr. Republican, who gained the White House. It was Eisenhower, whose supporters outgunned the Taft forces in a bitter battle at the nominating convention. Eisenhower, whom the liberal Democrats wanted to run in 1948, won the election for the Republicans by more than 6.5 million votes over Stevenson. At the same time, John Kennedy and Barry Goldwater were elected to the Senate.

Quite probably, if Taft had been nominated, he could have won, also. However, his monumental ignorance of foreign policy would have been even more damaging to the United States than Eisenhower's monumental ignorance of domestic affairs. A succession of conservative, able advisors, including Arthur Burns and Gabriel Hauge of the Council of Economic Advisors, checked Eisenhower's unerring instinct for childlike views and bad judgments in respect to matters domestic. Brave campaign talk of repudiating and dismantling the New Deal was forgotten. The fault would consist of insufficient financing of New Deal programs and unwillingness to meet or anticipate new major domestic needs.

Eisenhower was deferential to his Eighty-third Republican Congress. Admittedly, this Congress was a peculiar animal. For example, a breakdown showed that among forty-eight Republican Senators, nineteen were inclined toward Eisenhower, an equal number were Taft-oriented, another ten were uncommitted. In the House, 42 per cent of the Republicans were Taft men in policy. The convention wounds still were unhealed. A difficult situation obviously confronted the politically inexperienced President. A clue to Eisenhower's attitude toward the Congress is provided by his chief administrative lieutenant, Sherman Adams: "The influential Representatives in Congress were, for the most part, conservatives who did nothing to help Eisenhower get the nomination nor did they accept the fact that he virtually saved their party from a deepening oblivion," Adams wrote in his book, *Firsthand Report*. "They gave him only intermittent support and considerable opposition and personal aggravation. . . . The weekly meetings with the legislative leaders became a chore that a President, without Eisenhower's unfailing patience and determined optimism, might have soon crossed off his calendar as not worth the effort."

Overall, the Eighty-third Congress, and the three others that sat during the Eisenhower Administration, provided him with solid bipartisan support on matters of European collective security and, to a lesser degree, foreign aid. In the domestic field, a largely Democratic bipartisan coalition, with a somewhat different membership than the foreign affairs coalition, attempted to make improvements in health, education, and welfare programs. This grouping was not sufficiently strong or large to force through domestic legislation that Eisenhower would predictably veto, however. In fact, behind his "Modern Republican" rhetoric, Eisenhower was probably more conservative than Robert Taft in respect to health, housing, and education needs.

His appointments had an odd ring. T. Colman Andrews, who was against the income tax, became Commissioner of Internal Revenue. John Baker Hollister directed the foreign aid program, and it developed that he, too, was unenthusiastic about the premise on which it rested. Oveta Culp Hobby was named the first Secretary of the new Department of Health, Education, and Welfare. It became clear she believed in "not too much" of any of the three. The new antipolio Salk vaccine was mishandled, and Mrs. Hobby subsequently returned to Houston. His Secretary of Labor, Martin Durkin, a plumber in a cabinet of millionaires, held office barely long enough to find his way to work. Also a few of Eisenhower's other appointees made misjudgments similar to those which Truman appointees had been flayed for. For such a misstep, Eisenhower's strong right arm, Adams, resigned in September, 1958.

During the first session of the only Republican Congress in his eight Presidential years, Eisenhower and his Congressional advisers seemed content simply to get the departmental appropriation bills passed and the excess-profits tax extended. Wage and price controls, left over from the Korean War, were jettisoned. Shredded rent controls hung on a while longer. Defense Department budget requests for fiscal 1954 were curtailed by about 5 billion dollars, but a stubborn overall Federal deficit postponed a prime objective—tax cuts.

Eisenhower seemed unwilling to destroy the rump "State Department" run by Joe McCarthy, William Jenner of Indiana, and those tragically ludicrous aides, David Schine and Roy Cohn. This critically wounded the real State Department.

John Bricker of Ohio sought a constitutional amendment to restrict the treaty-making power of the Presidency. The role Bricker envisioned for the Congress would have created a state of affairs analogous to that under the Articles of Confederation. As the legislative battle over the Bricker proposal developed, Eisenhower's viewpoint seemed typically murky. Both sides claimed his support. In February, 1954, the Senate defeated a modified Bricker amendment, which failed by only one vote to secure the necessary two-thirds approval needed for a constitutional-amendment resolution.

In March, 1953, Stalin died. In July, unrest developed into an uprising in East Germany. The high-pitched Dullesian rhetoric of "interventionism" was not translated into action in this case nor three years later during the uprisings in Hungary and Poland. Taft died, to be succeeded as majority leader by William Knowland of California, "the Senator from Formosa." There seemed to be more emphasis on Asia. A geopolitician, Admiral Radford, was chairman of the Joint Chiefs of Staff. He sought American involvement in the fading French fortunes in Indochina. Eisenhower vetoed the suggestion. In May, 1954, the French forces were defeated at Dien Bien Phu. In July, the French and Vietminh signed a cease-fire accord and Vietnam was provisionally divided into two territories at the seventeenth parallel. The Soviet Union detonated a hydrogen bomb in August, and the next month Dulles generated a Southeast Asia Treaty Organization (SEATO). Dulles said the United States would place "more reliance on deterrent power and less dependency on local defensive power." Sloganeers translated Dulles's "massive retaliation" into "more bang for a buck." Outstanding military leaders, among them Matthew Ridgway, James Gavin, and Maxwell Taylor, dissented.

In the Congress, about two-thirds of Administration requests were approved. Rayburn supplied more votes from among his 213 Democrats than Speaker Martin could recruit from among his 221 Republicans for such foreign policy staples as reciprocal trade. Crusty Dan Reed, Way and Means Chairman, repeatedly opposed Eisenhower on tax and tariff matters. The Congress approved a tax-reduction bill strongly in favor of the wealthy, authorized the St. Lawrence Seaway, outlawed the Communist party, and improved Social Security and unemployment compensation. The House adjourned without taking any action to improve its own security arrangements after four Puerto Rican nationalists from the public gallery shot five of its members during a floor session. The Republican-controlled committees showed a weakness for character assassination and a compulsion to exhume the New Deal. (Democratic committees tend to be no less partisan but are more inclined to assassinate impersonal economic interests—private power in the Dixon-Yates case for example—and to develop hearing records of support for remedial legislation or for new programs.)

Rayburn watched the Eisenhower performance with growing discontent. When a Presidential message implied that Democrats were less than loyal, Rayburn took to the floor and in ungentle terms pointed out the indispensable Democratic votes that put across Eisenhower's foreign policy requests. Eisenhower summoned Rayburn:

"Mr. Sam, we've been friends too long to have a falling out now," the President said. "What made you so mad?"

Without comment, Rayburn handed Eisenhower the message with the offending passages underlined.

The President replied, according to Rayburn afterward, "Did I sign that?"

Discontent became disillusionment, but Rayburn did not tell all in public. The country had just one President, Rayburn said, and the office should be respected. The President, perhaps in part because of a heart attack he suffered in September, 1955, remained beyond criticism for an extraordinary length of time. The immunity began to break down only after the Soviet Union announced it had orbited a satellite, *Sputnik*, in 1957.

The 1954 elections had put an end to Republican party control of the Congress. It has never since held a majority of seats

in either the House or the Senate. Republicans held only the
White House. Macauley, the British historian, said that, in such
a time of divided government, our Constitution is "all sail and no
anchor."

Rayburn resumed his position as Speaker and McCormack his
as majority leader. In the Senate, Lyndon Johnson became
majority leader. An Associated Press interview printed in *The
New York Times* quoted Johnson as scoffing at reports that he
had Presidential ambitions. Johnson is also further quoted: "I
think it's fair to say nobody but my mama ever thought I'd get
as far as I am." The same interview also quoted Senator Russell
of Georgia: "Lyndon Johnson hasn't got the best mind in the
Senate. He isn't the best orator. He isn't the best parliamentarian. But he's the best combination of all those qualities." Both
Rayburn and Johnson played a brand of cooperative, consensus
politics with the Eisenhower Presidency that would cause considerable discontent and sporadic mutinies among Senate and
House Democrats.

Eisenhower continued to have his way in foreign policy.
Trouble in Vietnam, the Formosan Straits, the Suez Canal crisis,
uprising in Eastern Europe, the U-2 incident, and the isolationist
Bricker amendment in the Senate proved that Eisenhower, much
less the Republican party, had no magic wand that would make
the world orderly and leave white middle-class Americans to
their material affluence. The Democratic party apparatus in both
House and Senate acquiesced in the foreign policies advanced by
Dulles, Eisenhower's Cardinal Richelieu. These policies were not
imaginative, innovative, subtle, or perceptive—but neither were
they, at that time, disastrous. Time bombs ticked but had not
yet exploded in Vietnam, Cuba, the Middle East, Africa, Latin
America.

In domestic affairs, cooperation also ruled for the most part.
In May, 1954, the Supreme Court ruled that enforced racial seg-
regation in public schools was unconstitutional. Two years later,
seventy-seven House members, including such seniors as Wilbur
Mills of Arkansas, and nineteen Senators, including J. William
Fulbright of Arkansas, signed a "Southern Manifesto" pledging

themselves to fight by "all lawful means" the "unwarranted decision." In 1962, the Court would rule against inequitable districting for state-legislature representation and, two years later, for Congressional districts. The latter was an area in which the Congress should have acted under authority derived from its constitutionally assigned obligation to conduct a census every ten years. It didn't. Sometimes, Eisenhower spoke as if he disapproved of the school decision. At other times, he seemed to view it as an unfathomable decision by a foreign court on a distant planet. When red-necked whites harassed Negro school children at Little Rock in September, 1957, the President could no longer ignore the inflamed situation. In the 1950s, the most substantial impact in domestic affairs was the work of the Supreme Court, not the Congress. It alone behaved in superior fashion during the period of panic and legislative cowardice provoked by McCarthyism and the internal strains brought on by the Cold War.

In 1956, a 41,000-mile, interstate, "defense" highway system was authorized, with 90 per cent of the cost paid for by the Federal Government. A good case can be made for the view that this was the major domestic legislative accomplishment of the eight Eisenhower years. The Congress turned away from the need for comprehensive medical care, school aid, and adequate low-income housing. There were two catch-up legislative achievements forced upon the Congress by events. The National Defense Education Act was made possible by the reaction to the successful launching of space satellites *Sputnik* I and II in 1957 by the Soviet Union. In the midst of the school violence at Little Rock, Arkansas, the Civil Rights Act of 1957, the first in eighty years, became law. Speaker Rayburn played a unique role in the enactment of this bill. During our many long conversations about many subjects, I discovered that, despite his deeply ingrained Southern attitudes, he firmly believed that everyone, including Negroes, should have the right to vote. As a result of this knowledge and many hours of work and maneuvering by members of both parties in the Congress, the Executive and outside groups, a right-to-vote bill was devised. Rayburn gave it his all-out support and helped push it through the House, first in

1956 when the Senate could not act, and again in 1957. Much of his work was behind the scenes, but very soon the knowledgeable insiders in the House and the more sophisticated outsiders were aware that my work in behalf of civil rights legislation had the backing of the Speaker.

Perhaps even more important to the bill's final enactment, and, in part at least, because of the Speaker's persuasive powers, the majority leader of the Senate, Lyndon Johnson, decided that he too must gain enactment of a right to vote law. When the bill got to the Senate, he cajoled and drove it through in one of the most amazing examples of legislative broken field running in the modern era.*

Some Democrats and Republicans were aware of mounting unmet needs directly traceable to the conservative's coalition politics. When they discussed these with Rayburn, he gave the impression that, though he could not force, he could persuade Smith, for example, to let a particular piece of legislation go to the floor; Rayburn relied on personal influence rather than the structural power of the Speakership. Sometimes, Rayburn could persuade; many more times he couldn't.

Rayburn, with a Republican as President, stood as the number one leader of the Democratic party. He dominated the Democrats in the House. Any member born after March 4, 1913, was younger in years than Rayburn's entire career in the House. Very few had served in the House for as long as he had wielded great power there. He would ultimately serve as Speaker twice as long as anyone else. In his various capacities, including presiding at his party's nominating conventions, he had done so many favors, small and large, that there were few in either party in the House who were not in his debt in some way.

As the Democratically controlled Eighty-fourth Congress convened, *The New York Times* accurately described Rayburn's position as Speaker by saying that he held a "kind of balance of power" among the Democrats in both houses. Rayburn's protégé, Johnson, was then about to assume the role of Senate

---

* The full story of my involvement in this civil rights act appears in my book *House Out of Order*, published in 1965 by E. P. Dutton.

majority leader for the first time. Essentially, Rayburn resisted any formal change in the ways of the House. He resisted changes in the Rules Committee; he resisted changes in other committees; he resisted any change in the way the Democratic party was operated in the House. This judgment is based upon my service as his aide. With all his wisdom, he liked to operate on a hand-to-mouth basis legislatively. Knowing that the next election might drastically change the complexion of the House, he failed to plan beyond the current session's short-range problems.

Rayburn believed that the seniority system, rigidly applied, was a sound guide to committee assignments. He was not sure that there was a better one. Occasionally, he would depart from seniority but in no way that basically modified the concept. He knew how change could have unexpected results, so he refused to risk the unknown. He believed so much in the "system" that he refused to support those very changes that would have strengthened him as Speaker and would have put down the committee chairmen. As a result, he tolerated many a defeat, both public and private, in the pursuit of causes to which he was committed.

During the earliest New Deal years, the Northerners and Southerners were thrown together by the Depression. A flat-broke, Southern dirt farmer is, after all, in the same difficulty as a flat-broke Northern workman. As the severest difficulties eased, however, the basic differences reemerged in respect to labor-management relations, welfare, social injustice, and the role of the national Government. "States rights" was the Southern password. The civil rights issue dissolved the paste holding together the traditional coalition of the Democratic party. The walkout at the 1948 Democratic convention was an early example. It was business as usual with Rayburn, however. There was the matter of organizing the House in the Eighty-fourth Congress in 1955. There were five vacancies on the Democratic side in Ways and Means. Southerners were awarded three of the seats. This gave Southerners seven of the fifteen Democratic seats, including the Chairmanship. These fifteen, in turn, as the

Committee on Committees, selected other Democrats for seats on other committees. Thus, the Committee on Committees functions in the nature of a supervisor over Democratic legislative policy by virtue of its appointive power.

The Committee on Committees was heavily weighted with Southerners unsympathetic to the larger purposes of the Democratic party. Its Chairman, Jere Cooper, was a Southerner, as was the Chairman of Rules. The Appropriations Committee Chairman, Clarence Cannon of Missouri, preferred a balanced budget, whatever the country's needs. Two-thirds of committee chairmen were Southerners. In the late stages of the Eighty-fifth Congress in 1958, Southern Democrats refused to support their party's platform on more than eighty crucial roll calls in the House.

One result of this disinclination on the part of Rayburn was aggravated misery for the city of Washington, D.C. Deprived of local self-government, the nation's capital was hostage to the intense segregationist outlook of the House District Committee, nominally led by its Chairman, John McMillan of South Carolina. This state of affairs prevailed during the years when Washington was becoming the first major city to have a predominantly Negro population and an overwhelmingly Negro school population. Also, beginning in 1959, Southerners increasingly lost their historical internationalist outlook. As the South became more industrialized, it veered toward protectionism.

The decline of party responsibility and neglectful leadership infected the Rules Committee. It became a policy committee manned by political primitives. Until its back was broken during the Kennedy Administration, it functioned as if it were a "third branch" of the Congress. It would have been easier to move a cemetery than to change the Rules Committee. John Kennedy would have had to possess a geologist's appreciation of time had he been content to sit and wait for the Congress to pass his program. James Robinson, in his book *The Role of the Rules Committee in Arranging the Program of the United States House of Representatives*, states that between 1947 and 1959 eighty-three requests by the leadership for rules for bills were denied by the

Committee after hearings. Yet he also reports that, between 1939 and 1956, Rules reported out forty-two bills not acted on by legislative committees. On major tax and housing legislation, it had successfully demanded alterations in the committee-approved bills in return for providing rules.

In 1953, for example, Rules Chairman Allen, responding to his Republican President, buried an unwanted tax-reduction bill reported out by Ways and Means under Dan Reed of New York. In retaliation, Reed sat on an Administration revenue bill. Allen simply had his Rules Committee report out a revenue bill favored by the Eisenhower Administration that never passed through Ways and Means, the committee of jurisdiction. In the summer of 1957, Howard Smith, then Rules Chairman, dropped out of sight in order to prevent action within his committee on a civil rights bill. Occasionally, Rules played the role of David Harum, releasing a minimum-wage bill to the floor in return for being permitted to bury a construction-site picketing bill desired by the building trades. When the hapless Democrat Adolph Sabath of Illinois was Rules Chairman, the ranking Republican, Allen, once said mockingly, "Adolph has a right to be heard. Let him speak for two or three minutes." In 1960, the House and Senate each had passed differing versions of an elementary-secondary-school assistance bill. The next step was to send the measure to conference, where a mutually acceptable version could be devised by a board of House and Senate members. The Rules Committee refused to let the House version go to conference. The bill died in September, when the Congress adjourned for the fall campaigning. "The will of both the House and Senate had to yield to a little group of willful men on the Rules Committee," said Frank Thompson of New Jersey, a leader of education legislation then pending in the House.

In 1960, Colmer, who would become Rules Chairman during 1967–1968, campaigned for independent Presidential electors in his home state of Mississippi, not for his party's Kennedy-Johnson electors. Surely, this was sufficient reason not to reappoint Colmer to Rules when the new Congress convened in January, 1961. Colmer went untouched. So, with the Republican-Southern Democratic coalition in firm control of much of the House machinery in the Eisenhower-Rayburn years, it is not surprising that the domestic problems of American society, now so tragically obvious, were almost entirely neglected. The fate of a remedial depressed-areas bill is one illustration of how this condition in a Democratic Congress caused unfortunate delay in meeting domestic problems.

Perceptive members of Congress, among them Senator Douglas of Illinois, a professional economist, sensed that behind our gaudy, chrome-laden, consumer-oriented "affluent society" lay deep social and economic rot. Chronic unemployment existed in New England and Appalachian states. Douglas sponsored S. 2663, which authorized 100 million dollars in industrial-development loans and another 100 million dollars in public-works grants, both for economically depressed areas. Eisenhower was persuaded to recommend a 50-million-dollar revolving fund for capital-improvement grants and technical assistance, to be administered by the Commerce Department. An independent agency would be the administrating authority in the Douglas bill. The Senate passed an amended Douglas bill in July, 1956. Goldwater thought it an "unwarranted invasion of private rights." The House Banking and Currency Committee favorably reported an altered version. It died in that *abattoir*, the Rules Committee.

In the next Congress, the Senate again passed a bill at a time when three-fifths of the major labor markets in the country were categorized as containing "substantial labor surplus." This meant unemployment exceeding 6 per cent of the civilian labor force. The measure cleared House Banking and Currency; it then went to Rules. Chairman Smith and his allies released it after insisting that the financing mechanism be direct appropriations, not borrowing authority. The House passed it. In September, Eisenhower vetoed it, a pocket veto, on grounds there was insufficient local discretion involved.

The bill then went around the legislative track for the third time, after the Eighty-sixth Congress convened in 1959. In March, the Senate passed a Douglas bill similar to the vetoed one. In May, House Banking and Currency Committee again reported favorably a somewhat modified version. Again, it went to legislative death in Rules. Smith and his bipartisan conservative coalition sat on the bill throughout 1959. Under extreme pressure, Rules was obliged to vote in April, 1960, on whether to release it for floor action. The vote in Rules was a tie, 6 to 6; thereby the bill was lost. Rayburn was then forced to attempt to bypass Rules by getting the bill to the floor under the Calendar Wednesday procedure. It was a rare success, passing the House 202 to 184. In mid-May Eisenhower vetoed it. He said the bill was larger in scope than the situation warranted. The bill's proponents sought to override the veto but failed by eleven votes of securing the necessary two-thirds. Such a bill was eventually passed five years after it was first proposed. John Kennedy then sat in the White House and a crimp had been placed on the freedom of movement of the Tory coalition in Rules.

The anti-Democrats, who nevertheless wore the Democratic party label—Smith of Virginia and Colmer of Mississippi—cast the deciding votes on Douglas's bill. If Rules had been staffed only by program Democrats, the Republicans on Rules would have been outnumbered. Rayburn had good reason to bar both Smith and Colmer from reassignment to Rules. But neither he nor the Democratic majority were yet ready for drastic steps.

How much better might the situation be today in our blazing urban ghettos, swollen with unskilled unemployment, if Douglas's depressed-areas bill and a wide array of civil rights and social welfare legislation had been passed in the 1940s and 1950s instead of a decade or two later. Our domestic history might be brighter if Southern domination of the Democratic party in the Congress, reinforced by Republican collusion, had been uprooted.

This bipartisan collusion also set back education legislation. The history of Federal aid to education had perfectly respectable antecedents, the Northwest Ordinances and the Land Grant College Act of 1861 among them. The Congress had passed legislation to help those school districts whose pupils included an appreciable number of children of Federal employees. There was a National Science Foundation and the 1958 National Defense Education Act providing 1 billion dollars to improve teaching of science, mathematics, and foreign languages at all school levels, by means of student loans, equipment, graduate fellowships, counseling and guidance services, and teacher training for public schools.

The obscurantists in both parties managed to conceal the true question, which was not should there be Federal assistance, but how should Federal assistance be applied. Elementary-secondary-school legislation was blocked by members elected as "Democrats," occupying key positions. Howard Smith on Rules was one. A second was Graham Barden of North Carolina, whose powers as Education and Labor Committee Chairman would eventually be curtailed when committee liberals forced a re-writing of the committee rules of procedure. President Eisenhower proposed a general school-aid bill in 1955. It languished in Rules. A revised version arrived on the House floor in 1956. A nondiscrimination amendment, bearing the name of Adam Clayton Powell, was adopted 225 to 192. It resulted in defeat of the school bill—against the legislation, 224 (105 Democrats and 119 Republicans); in favor, 194 votes (119 Democrats and 75 Republicans). Interestingly, 96 of the Republicans who voted for the Powell civil rights amendment then turned around and voted against final passage of the bill. This is a political trick little understood by the public. It enables a member to seem to favor something which he votes for only in order to kill it later along with the legislation to which it is attached. The conservative coalition, therefore, drove off enough anti-civil rights Southern and border-state Democratic supporters of Federal aid to public elementary and secondary schools by first having the Powell amendment adopted.

These were dismal years, the Eisenhower-Rayburn years. Some may question the coupling of Rayburn with the President. Many would suggest Lyndon Johnson as the Democratic legislative counterpart of the Republican President. The facts are to the contrary. In every way, Rayburn was the senior partner of the Texas leadership team in the Congress. In fact, it was not until 1960 that Johnson, though dominant in the Senate, became a full partner in the Democratic leadership. Rayburn shunned publicity, but behind the scenes, his voice was more often than not the decisive one. Newspapers, radio, and television, however, made Johnson the star of the legislative arena. His fleetness of foot and his flashy legislative coups kept him in the public eye. Soon Johnson was portrayed as a master of legislative *legerdemain.*

Johnson, despite earlier denials, thirsted for the Presidency. Rayburn fought for his fellow Texan's nomination. They had been close political associates for a dozen years and more than acquaintances for decades. Rayburn believed in Johnson's proved and matured abilities. He believed Johnson would make a good President, but part of this attitude stemmed from negative considerations in respect to Senator Kennedy. "That kid" was often Rayburn's phrase for John Kennedy. Rayburn believed that Kennedy's ambition outreached his ability. He had not been impressed, nor had I, for that matter, with Kennedy's House service. Moreover, Rayburn believed Kennedy would not be nominated, or, if so, Rayburn was sure he could not be elected. Rayburn was not anti-Catholic but just convinced that American voters were not yet ready to elect a Roman Catholic as President. He was almost right.

In truth, Rayburn was typical of the group which dominated the Johnson campaign for the Presidential nomination. The Texans were highly skilled legislative operators, whose political skills were conditioned to the faction-ridden politics of Texas. They could not begin to grasp the high quality and creative imagination of the Kennedy generalship. Most of all, perhaps, the Johnsonites misjudged both the rank-and-file Democrats and the American people. A Presidential campaign was not similar to making arrangements at a Democratic state convention in Texas.

The preliminaries took place in the Congress. Both parties and their Presidential aspirants were each jockeying to make a record. The Democratic majorities became larger in both House and Senate beginning in 1956; it was nearly 2 to 1 in both houses in the 1959–1960 Congress. The restiveness increased correspondingly. Liberals of both parties were aghast at the continued failure of substantive health, housing, welfare, and education legislation. They pressed for large programs in these areas even if such legislation should be cut down by Presidential vetoes. Johnson in the Senate and Rayburn in the House usually would not go much beyond support for programs reduced in scope, to prevent an increasingly conservative Eisenhower from using the veto. The Senate was particularly restive.

In 1959, Majority Leader Johnson was in trouble with his Northern Democratic colleagues. For example, the Senate voted 57 to 35 to extend Korean-war excise taxes. All 35 negative votes were cast by Northern Democrats. Johnson's winning majority was composed of Republicans and Southern Democrats. Senator Clark of Pennsylvania suggested that the Democratic victory in the 1958 Congressional election meant voters wanted the Senate to progress beyond mere ratification of Eisenhower proposals. On the other hand, Johnson and Rayburn did not often emphasize party differences; they worked to subdue or prevent attacks upon Eisenhower and to emphasize low-key legislation.

Would the Senate be the playing field on which the Presidential nomination would be won? Perhaps. Senators Humphrey, Kennedy, and Symington were among the players. They had an outside ally in Paul Butler of Indiana. A Democratic Advisory Council, ignored whenever possible by both Johnson and Rayburn, was established as an arm of the party's national committee. The council had a Stevensonian air about it. Rayburn already had his candidate selected—Johnson.

Meanwhile, Eisenhower was losing his gloss. His buffer at the White House, Sherman Adams, had resigned in 1958. Dulles had died in May of the following year. The social Darwinism of his Secretary of Agriculture, Ezra Taft Benson, had alienated farmers. In January, 1959, Fidel Castro, a crypto-Communist, overthrew the fascistic Batista regime in Cuba, ninety miles away, right in our own backyard.

Leaders of organized labor, with its approximately 16 million members, were persuaded that the 1959 Labor-Management and

Disclosure Act was as much an Administration effort as it was that of the Congress. This was the Landrum-Griffin Act, a response to the testimony about racketeering, collusion, abuse of union members' rights and handling of their funds that the McClellan Committee had heard. The intraparty wounds caused by that bitter battle have not yet healed. An Eisenhower veto was overridden by the Congress on the issue of a pay raise for Federal employees. The fiscal 1959 budget deficit would be approximately 12.4 billion dollars, four times that of the previous fiscal year. The Joint Congressional Economic Committee issued a report deploring the growth rate of the United States economy. It pointed out that the rate amounted to approximately 2.3 per cent a year between 1953 and 1959. Unemployment had risen from 2.9 per cent in 1953 to 5.5 per cent of the civilian labor force in 1960. The Negro rate was double. It was time to get the country moving again. There were new frontiers to be secured.

3

The Kennedy Years

In 1960, John F. Kennedy's Roman Catholicism, his youth (forty-three), and his purported inexperience caused other Democratic contestants to believe he could not get the nomination. Even after his victories in Presidential-preference primaries, rivals consistently underrated him, his political skill, and the scope and skill of his organization, all of which were strongly demonstrated when, on the road to nomination, Kennedy demolished the candidacy of Senate Whip Hubert Humphrey in fundamentalist, Protestant West Virginia.

Not long before the Democratic Convention was to meet in Los Angeles in July, Speaker Rayburn called me to his office late one afternoon and, with few preliminaries, told me that he wanted me to go to the convention to help him work for Lyndon Johnson's nomination there. I promptly replied that I could not do so because the senior Senator from my state of Missouri, Stuart Symington, was also a candidate. His answer was that he did not have a chance. I agreed but insisted that nevertheless I must honor my commitment. I then volunteered that I was positive Kennedy was going to be nominated on an early ballot, possibly the first one. I added my hope that he would not put himself in such a position that Kennedy's nomination would be a personal humiliation for him.

In July, the convention met at Los Angeles. There, the Kennedy forces overwhelmed the candidacies of Symington, Adlai Stevenson, already more legend than man, and, most significantly, Johnson, the Senate majority leader. Actually, there was little significance in the defeats of Symington and Stevenson. Symington's campaign was never really airborne; Stevenson's two previous defeats to Eisenhower weighed heavily against him, as did his diffidence in presenting himself as a candidate.

The defeat administered Johnson was more profound. It was worse than a defeat. It constituted a humiliation in the eyes of Johnson and his political coach, Sam Rayburn. The Speaker viewed Kennedy as if he were still a backbencher. Kennedy's service in the House had not shown great promise. Neither had Lincoln's. Kennedy and McCormack were not congenial; at least, from McCormack's point of view they weren't. He was offended, for example, when Kennedy declined to sign a petition asking Truman to pardon "the Purple Shamrock," James Michael Curley of Massachusetts, whom McCormack greatly admires and who was serving a prison term for using the mails to defraud. The young pro Kennedy taught the old pros Johnson and Rayburn a lesson in national and conventional politics. The fact is that neither Rayburn nor Johnson were truly national politicians, never having really gone beyond their regional, or less tactfully, parochial political bases. Massachusetts politics was no less parochial, but Kennedy had the capacity to grow.

In retrospect, Kennedy's offer of the Vice-Presidential nomination to Johnson eased the pain of humiliation for Rayburn, Johnson supporters, and even Johnson himself. It also, of course, made possible Kennedy's election by preventing much of the Southern Democratic vote from defecting to Nixon.

The weeks following the Democratic convention were inauspicious for the Democratic nominees. There was a treacherous postconvention session of the Congress, apparently previously desired by Johnson on the grounds that he would become the Presidential nominee and a productive session could be developed to help him in the White House. Johnson had not been nominated, and the session was not productive. It met in August for three weeks. House Rules killed the school bill; the

House conferees killed a Senate-passed minimum-wage bill bearing Kennedy's name; the Senate turned down a health-care bill,
not exactly a session "to point with pride at." The Presidential
and Vice-Presidential nominees of the Democratic party, both
Senators, and the politically wise Speaker failed to pass out a
single piece of pending legislation related to the platform on
which they were standing. The session taught Kennedy one so-
bering lesson, however—he had to break the back of the obstructionist Rules Committee.

Rayburn had opposed this rump session but was forced to
accept it, since much essential legislation was incomplete. He had
already been finally convinced by his experiences in the regular
sessions of this Congress in 1959 and 1960 that he must take
some steps to curb the power of the Rules Committee. The
rump session strengthened his resolve. In addition, events in this
Congress had revealed to many that, though Speaker Rayburn
was himself a strong man, the Speakership he had held so long
was not vested with the power necessary to achieve prompt consideration of even essential legislative programs. Rayburn's un-
equaled legislative skills, his almost unfailing ability to anticipate
legislative difficulties, and his great personal power obscured his
losses. The myth of his invincibility had a strong hold on the
minds of nearly everyone. Few realized until this Eighty-sixth
Congress how often he had been defeated.

Richard Nixon campaigned in each of the fifty states; Kennedy in forty-eight. The campaign was exhausting, rough, bitter,
and, in respect to the religious issue, which Kennedy had courageously faced in Houston at a specially arranged ministers' meeting, an unlovely kind of dirty. Eisenhower made his first public
campaign appearance for Nixon only eleven days before election
day, November 8. I had not participated in the convention at all,
nor had I been in the Kennedy camp prior to that time. Therefore, I had expected to spend the campaign in my own district.
To my surprise, the Kennedys enlisted me at once in several
jobs. The one that took me into twenty states and occupied
nearly all of every long day from early September to November
8 was as Chairman of the Democratic National Committee's

Congressional Liaison Committee. In that position, I was charged with coordinating the Presidential campaign with each of the 400-plus House campaigns. Among other things, the job gave me a fine opportunity to further the cause I had been promoting for six years—the need to break the hold of the conservative coalition in the Rules Committee. Rayburn fully approved my activity. During the campaign it was obvious that he had changed his mind about Kennedy and had come to admire him greatly.

By the morning of November 9th, by the thinnest margin of votes in seventy-six years, 112,881, Kennedy's victory was achieved. There hadn't been such a squeaker since the Cleveland-Blaine election in 1884. In retrospect, the Kennedy victory was a godsend. During the 1950 decade, it was not compellingly apparent how sluggish America had been, how neglectful of her cities and rivers; how careless of her people's well-being; how heedless of her 19 million black citizens; and, as a result, how frozen the energies of her young men and women had become. In the late 1950s, the Gaither Report, designed to study the state of civil-defense readiness, had in fact illuminated a neglected society.

The President-elect faced a House divided in the same ratio as in 1948 after Truman's surprise election. This time, however, no one mistook an 89-seat Democratic margin as a meaningful one on issues. There were 263 members labeled Democrats, 60 of whom, mostly Southern, were strong conservatives. Ten Republican liberals therefore only brought the total of Democratic program-oriented votes to 213. Against them, there were 174 Republican members. These, minus the 10 liberal Republicans, joined with the 60 defecting Democrats to give 224 conservative-oriented votes, a majority of 11 on the conservative side. The legislative tasks ahead seemed ever harder when we realized that, in the preceding Eighty-sixth Congress, there had been a majority of 18 on the liberal side, and still virtually no forward-looking legislation was passed because of the Rules coalition. The coalition had to be busted. There were several ways. After some delay during which many alternatives were seriously considered, Rayburn made the decision as to how to do the job.

Without his all-out effort, no change could succeed. His decision—the least "painful" as Rayburn characterized it—was to expand the Rules Committee from twelve to fifteen members, rather than to remove Colmer and other obstructionists. Two of the three additional seats would be for Democrats, bringing their total to ten; and one would be for a Republican, for a total of five. Even this change, incorporating the existing members, would only provide a shaky eight to seven leadership-oriented margin on most bills.

Expansion of the Rules Committee was necessary before the Kennedy program could move through the House. The President, tactfully and humorously as "an interested citizen," participated publicly in the struggle for mastery by the majority party for the majority of Rules. Behind the scene, however, the Kennedy political apparatus was also committed to the struggle. I surmise that in the process there evolved the new Kennedy concept of the way to organize a liaison operation between the White House and the Congress, an operation that would ultimately be so enormously effective under the able supervision of Lawrence O'Brien. The activities of this apparatus were completely coordinated with those of allies outside the House—the civil rights movement and the labor movement, principally. Within the House, the impetus came from Rayburn's personal efforts and those of his senior allies and from the operation headed by Frank Thompson of New Jersey and myself. We collaborated on this, as on many other liberal causes. Information was pooled and assignments given. Our counts were so accurate that we came within one of the actual figure several days before the votes were cast.

It was a bruising, all-out battle, but eleven days after Kennedy's inauguration the deed was done. Rules was enlarged by a vote of 217 to 212, a five-vote margin. The winning coalition consisted of 195 Democrats and 22 Republicans. Three out of five Southern Democrats voted against expansion. The other Southern Democrats voted for expansion, as a result of masterful efforts by Rayburn and Carl Vinson of Georgia, the loyalist Democratic leaders. The larger component of votes was supplied by the Democratic Study Group, a loose-knit association of House liberals.

The O'Brien Congressional liaison operation was another indispensable element for the success of the Kennedy legislative programs. "Delicate" is the only description for the handling of the involvement of the President and his executive-branch departments in the legislative process. The myth that a President should not interfere in the law-making processes of the Congress is as pervasive as it is ridiculous. A President holds the most powerful, single legislative weapon that exists, the veto. Americans would not think much of an elected President who sent his legislative program to the Congress one day by messenger and then forgot about it for the four years of his term.

Fortunately, President Kennedy neither believed the myth, nor was he intimidated by it. Neither was his politically intuitive brother, Robert, the Attorney General. Larry O'Brien, a counselor during the campaign, was a sound choice to head up the President's Congressional relations. He was affable and practical. His aides came from all sections of the nation. Their political techniques were pragmatic, whatever their political outlook; their quality was quite high. The concept of a Congressional liaison staff was not at all a new one, although its scope had never been as large as the Kennedy apparatus became. The distinctive characteristic consisted of tight centralized control. In the past, an executive-branch department had furnished members of Congress directly with no more than routine information about departmental programs and constituent service, usually without going through the White House. The White House, if the President were Truman, would send Charlie Murphy, for example, to the Hill to garner support for a bill or a policy. With Eisenhower, it was General Persons, Bryce Harlow, or Gerald Morgan who worked the Hill.

During the Kennedy Administration, however, the director of a department's Congressional liaison was made directly responsible to the White House, that is, to Kennedy. Such a director had probably already worked in some phase of the Kennedy election campaign. The directors were selected by O'Brien and then assigned for payroll purposes to a particular department. This is not to say that a Congressional liaison director was not loyal to the legislative program of his assigned department, bureau, or agency. A department secretary and his assistants, however, often have an understandable self-interest in the primary importance of their own particular legislative program. A disgruntled department head may go to the Hill, "behind his President's back" so to speak, to gain advantage for a program in defiance of his President's priorities. The Kennedy approach helped substantially to mitigate this knife cutting, because, if a conflict should develop, the Congressional liaison director knew, or had better know, where the priority belonged.

The new operation also made it possible to coordinate the vast resources of the President in lobbying for a bill of unusual importance. The pressures, the promises and trade-offs, as well as the threats, which are staples of executive-legislative lobbying relationships, could be better coordinated and, one could hope, used with maximum skill and effect. In 1962, an Administration farm bill was forcefully lobbied, almost excessively so, by Congressional liaison chiefs assigned to Labor and to Health, Education, and Welfare Departments, as well as to the Agriculture Department.

The liaison work was difficult. The Congress, particularly the House, was not particularly cooperative. Again, it was a period when an assertive President presided—"the Chief Executive led—Congress altered or vetoed." There was a downward conservative pull, particularly in the House. This was offset somewhat by the inaugural address. Changes of tone in politics are intangibles of great importance. The note of high purpose caused Americans not normally interested in government to participate. Idealism, President Kennedy said, is the pragmatism of the day. His inaugural speech rightly told America that freedom abroad and opportunity at home should not die out of commitment to a balanced budget. His summons to choose between "public interest and private comfort" not only stimulated the more intellectually minded but inspired the professional politicians in the wards and the senior "old bulls" on the front benches. Several, notably Vinson, became quite enthusiastic supporters. Rayburn was a great admirer of the President; he no longer called him "that kid." It was a fascinating fermentation to watch and experience.

Style became a fashionable and overused word in connection with the Administration. Nevertheless, there was real imagination, innovation, and flexibility in the new Administration, as opposed to the churchly solemnity, black-tie pomposity, and country-club conformism of the outgoing one. The idealism survived even a big blunder: the CIA-sponsored invasion by 1,200 refugees from Castro's Cuba during three days in April, 1961. The President manfully shouldered the blame and typically recalled a gifted phrase, "success has many fathers; failure is an orphan." There were also successes, among them an Arms Control and Disarmament Agency, the Peace Corps, the Trade Expansion Act, a 4.9-billion-dollar comprehensive housing bill (the most comprehensive in twelve years), and several antirecession proposals. In March, Kennedy announced a ten-year program to make the 1960s an "historic decade of democratic progress" in Latin America, the so-called Alliance for Progress.

The economy was suffering from severe problems, Kennedy told the Congress in his economic message in late January: slow economic growth; a decade of falling farm prices; and an unacceptable level of unemployment. An Area Redevelopment Administration bill cleared the Congress in March. It provided a 300-million-dollar revolving fund to underwrite public facility projects, rural and industrial development, and job retraining for those in chronically depressed communities. The minimum wage was raised to 1 dollar 25 cents an hour. The Social Security system was improved. There were other major antipoverty measures, which comprised the building blocks of an over-publicized, under-financed "war against poverty" that would be authorized in 1964 during the Johnson Presidency. Besides ARA, the Trade Expansion Act provided training for workers going jobless because of competition with foreign firms and imports.

The 1962 revision of public welfare also provided a program for job training for those on public assistance, in order to enable them to become self-supporting. Most importantly, the Manpower, Training, and Development Administration authorized a training program to offer new skills to workers whose existing skills found no market. A 900-million-dollar, accelerated public-works program was launched.

There were defeats: mass transit; a proposed Department of Housing and Urban Development; and, in 1961, the farm bill, which sought to keep commodity surpluses off the market, never got out of committee.

Again, education assistance was a legislative casualty. The Administration asked for an extension of the National Defense Education Act, which provided scholarship money; a 2.3-billion-dollar, three-year program for classroom construction and teacher salaries in public schools; and a five-year, 2.8-billion-dollar program for construction of academic facilities at institutions of higher learning. Catholic bishops protested the omission of private schools in the elementary-secondary-school program, which was covered in a separate bill. Kennedy replied it would be unconstitutional. Compromisers went to work. It was agreed to insert a provision in the NDEA bill authorizing low-interest construction loans to private schools to promote the teaching of "defense" subjects, such as foreign languages and mathematics. The elementary-secondary-school aid bill reached Rules. Wary Catholics wanted no action on it until the amended NDEA bill also arrived in Rules. When it did, they were skeptical of a tandem effort by which both bills would be taken up simultaneously on the floor. They feared the public-school bill would be passed and the NDEA bill left in the lurch. Maneuvering and suspicions grew. Finally, James Delaney of New York City, out of deep conviction and very much in accord with the views of those he represented in his district, combined with conservatives in Rules to kill off all bills.

Job training for youth was a great need, manpower surveys showed. The situation was particularly desperate among Negro youths, where the unemployment rate was approximately twice

the white rate. In 1961, nevertheless, Rules killed three remedial programs, each of three-years' duration. On each of these
occasions, I led the unsuccessful fights for favorable action by
Rules on these bills, with Rayburn's specific approval. One was
training for service with local and state governments; a second
authorized on-job vocational training; and the third, a youth
conservation corps. The first emerged later as the Job Corps section of the Office of Economic Opportunity (antipoverty) program authorized in 1964. The second became the VISTA component of O.E.O. The last was included in the MDTA program.

In late summer, Sam Rayburn, who had become ill in July,
went home to Bonham to die of cancer. In January, 1962, the
House had a new Speaker, John McCormack. Some weeks prior
to his election in the Democratic caucus, I had announced my
candidacy for majority leader. When it became apparent that I
could not win, I withdrew. When the caucus was held, I made
the motion which made possible the unanimous election of Carl
Albert as majority leader the same day.

The year had its silly note. The previous year, in the absence
of the ailing Rayburn, the House had adjourned precipitously
and ineptly. As a result, the Senate, its leaders in a rage, was
forced to accept an unpalatable supplemental appropriations bill.
Consequently in 1962, the Senate struck back. Its Appropriations
Committee Chairman, Carl Hayden of Arizona, asserted a co-
equal role in the appropriations process, an assertion the House
has vigorously rejected since the First Congress. Hayden and
Clarence Cannon of Missouri, House Appropriations Committee
Chairman, both in their eighties, wrangled over conference arrangements—where to meet, who should preside, and other mar-
ginalia. At one point, Cannon denounced the new Speaker, John
McCormack, on the grounds that McCormack had let him down
during the dispute. "I have sat under ten Speakers," Cannon
thundered, "but I have never seen such biased and inept leadership."

For three days in April, the President butted heads with the
giant steel industry and forced it to cancel price increases which

he felt most inappropriate in view of the noninflationary contract settlement between the industry and the steelworkers'
union ten days earlier.

There were flare-ups abroad, too. The newly independent
Congo was an African trouble spot. Kennedy returned disheartened
in June, 1961, from a meeting, with Chairman Khrushchev. The
following month he asked Congress for additional billions of dollars for the military. In August, the Communists erected a wall
separating the East and West sectors of Berlin. Congress did endorse a supportive 100-million-dollar bond issue to help ease the
financial difficulties of the United Nations.

The midterm elections in 1962 were a standoff in the House.
Considering the pattern for off-year elections, it was a Kennedy
victory. Kennedy had campaigned actively. He asked for a gain
of five to ten seats in the House as a boost to accelerate his legislative program. Instead, there was only a small net loss of five
Democratic seats. In terms of issues, there were, in the 1963–1964
Congress, approximately 208 votes for the Administration on
domestic matters and 227 against. Quite probably, the harrowing
preelection crisis, created by placement of Soviet missiles in
Cuba, created a solidarity among voters for the Democratic
party. This may have helped reduce customary losses.

Somewhere in this period, the President made a realistic and
remarkable forecast. Kennedy decided, I surmise, that in all
probability Senator Goldwater would be his Republican opponent in 1964. He further sensed that such a candidacy would
result in a devastating Republican defeat across-the-board and,
therefore, a grand Democratic margin in the Congress. Usually,
of course, a President's greatest legislative triumphs occur during
the first two or three years of his first term. But virtually everything of consequence that Kennedy did in politics was proof
that neither did precedent dominate him nor historical anal-
ogy deter him.

Based on our conversations, I believe Kennedy decided in 1963
to concentrate his domestic efforts on one major issue which
would have had wide voter appeal, a reduction in individual and

corporate income taxes. It was much more than a vote-getting proposal. It would be a major departure from the classical, backward American approach to economics. In their failure to use fiscal policy as a flexible instrument of economic management, successive Administrations, both Democratic and Republican, had proved themselves to be decades behind the economic management of any other government of any other industrially developed nation.

Kennedy proposed to cut taxes when the economy was functioning at a relatively high level (though growing more slowly than other industrialized nations) and the Federal Government was running a substantial deficit. He proposed to do so on the grounds that a reduction would give the economy a kick that would lift it out of economic stagnation. He set out to convince the Congress and the business community that the choice was really between "chronic deficits arising out of a slow rate of economic growth and temporary deficits stemming from a tax (reduction) program designed to promote fuller use of our resources and more rapid economic growth. . . ." In January, 1963, he proposed a tax cut of 10.5 billion dollars.

His decision was a result of much greater knowledge and sophistication in the field of general economics than he was then, or for that matter is now, being given credit for. Once, in late 1960, we discussed at length a need for updating the Federal Government's economic thinking. That night, we discussed both the possibility of a tax reduction, such as the one he proposed in early 1963, and also the urgent need for tax reform. We agreed that tax reform, that is, restoring equity to the tax structure, was infinitely more difficult to achieve, although in the long run it was probably as important as that the country accept what has come to be somewhat misleadingly known as "the new economics." President Kennedy pressed on a balky Congress the new-economics view that budget deficits were rooted in the restraints of the existing tax structure on the economy. He proposed a substantial reduction in income taxes that would lead to more rapid economic growth at the risk of a temporary deficit.

The other side of the coin, that would provoke corresponding opposition in 1967–1968, is that if the economy becomes overly active a tax increase should be applied. Tax reform has yet to be achieved. The tax cut, Kennedy's proposal, was not achieved in his lifetime, but its enactment in 1964 was a consequence of his courageous advocacy.

Tax policy aside, Kennedy found himself confronted with a deeply rooted, festering social problem that now broke into open warfare, the wretched state of the American Negro. There had been brave campaign talk on both sides, but little was being done in the form of legislation to secure "open housing," for example. Kennedy's proposal to the Congress in late February, 1963, was insubstantial. Events changed that. The Negro burst from his rural and urban ghettos and spilled over into the white man's streets. In sections of the South, whether urban Birmingham or rural Neshoba County in Mississippi, white communities raised the flag of insurrection. Negroes were beaten, bombed, and bullied. In June, the President sent the most ambitious civil rights bill in modern times to the Congress. In August, approximately 250,000 white and black Americans marched to the Lincoln Memorial in a "jobs-and-freedom" march. This keenly sought objective of Kennedy would not be achieved during his lifetime; however, the bill was enacted in July, 1964, a testimony to his concern and to the pressure exerted by his successor.

Other progressive measures included a program to combat mental illness and a construction and scholarship bill to assist medical and dental schools was established. In September, the Senate approved a limited, nuclear-test-ban treaty, a first step "on a journey of a thousand years" toward a peaceful world in an atomic age.

Then on November 22, 1963, Kennedy was assassinated, and the nation, faced with a consequence of its violent nature, fell into collective shock, numbed and horrified by the incredible, senseless deed in Dallas. Somehow a fundamental strength, deep within the bereaved nation, brought it through its constitutional crisis. It was immeasurably assisted by two differing personalities—the firmness of the new President, and the magnificent outward composure of the widow Jacqueline Kennedy. The behavior of the Eighty-eighth Congress was fundamentally changed by the assassination.

4

The New President

It was painful for Lyndon Baines Johnson to enter upon the Presidency that bleak November afternoon in Dallas. No man wants to take the office in such circumstances. Another Vice President named Johnson had also become President as a result of a murder, and assassination has enabled four men to become Presidents of our violence-stained land.

Lyndon Johnson, as thirty-sixth President, had placed upon him the lonely burden of administering the leading industrial-military country in its age of great power and responsibility. It was an unenviable position. First, Johnson had to reassure his countrymen and to quiet the world beyond. In countries where political murder had often struck down kings and eldest sons, ministers and commissars, no one could believe that "Dallas" could be the act of one deranged. Many, probably General De Gaulle among them, still do not. At home, the Warren Report is not dogma in every home, either. The United States had to renew confidence in itself and remake its image in the eyes of both its allies and its enemies. This was Johnson's first order of business.

Presidents, emperors, and first ministers, arriving for the state funeral, were given crucial words of reassurance to carry back. Five days after the funeral, President Johnson addressed a joint session of the Congress. Invoking the name of John Kennedy

several times, Johnson conveyed a spirit of continuity, reconciliation, and rehabilitation, and Congress and the country approved.

Congress had been Johnson's "home" for thirty-two years,
with the exception of service as a lieutenant commander in the
Navy and a stint as boss of the National Youth Administration's
operation in Texas. Beginning in 1931, he had worked in the
House as an assistant to Representative Richard Kleberg, of the
monster King Ranch. Seniors in the House remember him as
"Speaker" of a "little Congress," a mock assembly composed of
staff employees of members. In the spring of 1937, he had been
elected on a strong New Deal platform to fill a vacancy caused
by the death of James Buchanan of Texas. At the time, as the
story goes, Franklin Roosevelt was fishing in the Gulf of Mexico
off Corpus Christi. Always glad to have a friendly face in the
rebellious House, Roosevelt asked the Representative-elect, then
twenty-eight, to come to see him. Roosevelt was impressed; the
feeling was mutual. Johnson rode on the Presidential train on its
return to Washington, D.C. There and over the years, he
formed an alliance with an elder colleague, Sam Rayburn. Rayburn had known Johnson's father, also Sam, when both had
served in the Texas state legislature.

Lyndon Baines Johnson was not a particularly outstanding
member of the House. He voted New Deal on bread-and-butter
and education issues but "Southern" on such measures as regulation of labor unions, poll tax, and Federal regulation of oil and
gas producers. He served on the Armed Services Committee and
stayed longer in the House than he had hoped. In 1941, he ran
for the Senate against W. Lee (Pass-the-Biscuits, Pappy) O'Daniel and lost by about 1,300 votes. In 1948, he won a Senate seat
over "Calculating" Coke Stevenson by an even closer margin,
eighty-seven votes. Three years later, he became an assistant
floor leader. Only two years after that, in 1953, he became
minority leader in a Senate where the Republicans had one more
seat than the Democrats. This leadership position became available when Ernest McFarland of Arizona was defeated by Barry
Goldwater in the 1952 fall elections. An outspoken admirer of

Johnson's, William White, then of *The New York Times*, wrote that Johnson's role was to serve as a bridge between right-wing conservatives, such as Harry Byrd of Virginia, and the Northern Democrats. At forty-six, he may have been the youngest man ever to be minority leader.

In 1955, the Democrats took control of the Senate by just as narrow a margin as Republicans had had during the previous two years. With Southern backing, Johnson was elected majority leader. He would hold two other party positions in the Senate, chairmanships of both the Democratic Conference and of the Policy Committee. At the time, one observer saw him as a "political centralist," to the left of most Southern Democrats and to the right of Northern Democrats. A second wrote that Johnson's position was "about half way between right-wing Southerners and the 'regular' Northern Democrats." A newspaper interview quoted Johnson as scoffing at reports that he was a young man in a hurry—toward the White House. "Talk about my being a potential candidate is a lot of foolishness," Johnson is quoted as saying. "I have no interest, no ambitions in that direction. I'm conscious of my limitations."

There is no doubt that Johnson was a most effective leader in the Senate. Newspapermen fashioned a myth out of his able performance however. They endowed him with almost supernatural skills. Johnson was at his best in those years as a politician dealing with politicians. Neither Johnson in the Senate, Rayburn in the House, nor Eisenhower in the Presidency initiated much legislation. Both Johnson and Rayburn cooperated with skill and patience. Occasionally, Johnson would venture forth to do battle with Eisenhower on such bills as depressed-areas legislation. Toward the end of Johnson's Senate stewardship, Senator Proxmire and other Democrats accused him of being excessively inclined to compromise. This inclination seemed explicable in the first two of the Johnson-led Senates, when the Democrats had only a one- or two-seat margin. But in the 1959–1960 sessions, the Eighty-sixth, there was nearly a 2 to 1 Democratic margin in the Senate.

Johnson, a consummate compromiser, evidenced no desire to

innovate; he practiced consensus politics. The latter was often a good tactic; but, as a strategy in a time of accumulating unmet national needs, it boded disaster. Its politically insidious consequences were aggravated for national Democrats when an increasingly conservative and unassertive Republican occupied the White House.

Johnson's skills and successes as majority leader, plus the secretive nature of his personal political style, so common among Texans, proved almost meaningless when he sought the Presidency. Mastery of the Congressional cloakroom is not much use in national politics. The Kennedy forces squashed his ambitions without strain in the 1960 convention. That he took the Vice-Presidential nomination startled as many people as did the fact he was offered it. His enormous energies were frustrated as Vice President, but he simmered quietly and was loyal to his President. John Kennedy was aware of the box Johnson felt himself to be in. He was asked to sit in at meetings of the National Security Council, at infrequently held Cabinet meetings, and at the regularly scheduled meetings with the Congressional leadership. Johnson found himself chairman of both the civil rights-oriented Committee on Government Contracts and the National Aeronautics and Space Council. President Kennedy sent Johnson on official visits to Southeast Asia, Scandinavia, and Berlin. He was the President's representative at the funeral of Pope John.

Johnson's assumption of the Presidency under ghastly pressures constituted a near-perfect taking over of the responsibilities and powers which burden that office. It was a remarkable performance in the acceptance and use of power. Early in the Johnson Presidency, Senator Fulbright of Arkansas, later among his most biting critics on Vietnam, ventured a prophecy: "I think there is a much better than average chance," Fulbright said, "he will be a great President." In his first joint session address, Johnson aimed, he told the Congress, "to continue" John Kennedy's work, "to honor" the young President's memory, and to honor the same commitments "from South Vietnam to West Berlin."

Johnson, the first true Southerner in the Presidency in one hundred years, made a symbolic and significant shift in the Kennedy program. He put civil rights legislation ahead of tax reduction. Both bills were enacted into law. The myth of his legislative skills fed on this fresh publicity. Still, there is no question that Johnson worked for these bills with skill and energy. The fact is, however, that even before John Kennedy's death, both bills were set to pass; so were others. As the fiction of Johnson's mastery of the Congress grew, so there has grown an equally ill-founded fiction that John Kennedy was a butter-fingered, fumble-footed President in his relations with the Congress. In its extreme form, the myth makes the Kennedy legislative program a bust. The record does not bear this out.

To the contrary, when John Kennedy boarded the Presidential airplane for Dallas, his mental-health bill had passed; his tax-reduction bill had passed the House; hearings had been held on his civil rights bill in both House and Senate, and the bill was in the Rules Committee, certain to come to the floor; his youth-employment bill had cleared the Senate; his higher education bill, passed by both House and Senate, was in conference, as was his foreign aid bill, the latter badly mauled; and his limited test-ban treaty had been ratified. Elementary-secondary-school aid and Medicare bills were badly bogged down in committees. Johnson, however, couldn't move either one of them while he served out the remainder of John Kennedy's term. It wasn't until the electorate provided an indispensable ingredient, the most liberal Congress, the Eighty-ninth, in thirty years, that these two measures became law in 1965.

The strong civil rights bill of 1964 was assured of passage because of the Negro revolution, supported by organized labor and the belatedly awakened religious communities, and, not least, by the ability of John Kennedy to reach agreement with the legislative leaders of both parties in the House. This latter I know from personal experience. Johnson's personal contacts and skills hastened the House-passed tax bill through the Senate. Insiders believed, however, that its enactment was inevitable, regardless of his efforts.

Early in 1964, three great Presidential messages had to be sent to the Congress: a State-of-the-Union message, giving broad policy outlines; the budget message, providing revenue and expenditure details; and a message dealing with the state of the economy and its problems and remedies. Taken together the three would tell the nation Johnson's intentions. Inevitably, President Johnson had to adopt the bulk of the program already in preparation. Preparation of one fiscal year's budget begins almost as soon as the last is "put to bed," but, understandably as political leader, Johnson wanted to place his own brand on the new Administration. In less than a year, he would seek election to the Presidency in his own right. He wanted to run, not on memories of John Kennedy, but on a current assessment of himself, Lyndon Johnson.

Thus, the New Frontier was superseded by the Great Society as the tag line for the Johnson Administration. This was symbolic of the new President. It was expansive, implied a state of affairs already achieved, and was hyperbolic, like the tall tales of Mark Twain.

President Johnson cleverly consolidated the separate Kennedy-proposed bills into omnibus legislation, exaggeratedly titled a War on Poverty. An Office of Economic Opportunity served as the command post. The antipoverty program would prove to be underfinanced and oversold by the O.E.O. administrator, Sargent Shriver. Disappointingly, it was more skirmish than war. The ghetto walls were papered with promissory notes. Most city halls were unprepared, indeed frightened, by the rising expectations generated by the public relations aspects of the antipoverty effort. City halls around the nation fought back. In 1967, the Congress, after a bruising legislative battle, agreed to make the Federally assisted community action programs of O.E.O. subject to the authority of these city halls, some of them ill-equipped to handle the job and some simply unsympathetic to the larger aims of O.E.O.

The antipoverty effort, of course, was overdue. Americans had not sensed the ironic flavor in economist John Galbraith's phrase, "the affluent society." There was a whole other America, a domestic new frontier to be identified, crossed, and the land beyond explored, evaluated, and developed if American society was to survive. Unseen by most Americans, there had grown vast communities of the poor within the great and lesser cities. Their residents were more than just poor in income. They were cut off from society. They were born of the poor, who, in turn, were sons and daughters of other poor. Often, there was no family in the accepted sense—no home, no adequate diet, no medical care, no meaningful education or training, no skills, no opportunity, no equality, no hope. There was no relevant Horatio Alger urging them on. The Constitution, the Bill of Rights, and the other writs of privileges and freedom known to most Americans did not, in actual practice, extend to these communities. The residents were black, yellow, and also white. If black, their difficulty was critically aggravated by the fact they were brought here as property before the Civil War. Since then, brutal repression had withheld from them all but a tattered humanity.

Thirty-five years after the Civil War, lynchings were weekly occurrences in the South. In the 1920s, they were not uncommon. Among Negroes in both South and North, there was timid leadership and little self-respect. Soon their hopelessness, their distrust of those who ruled the society of which they were not a part would lead to eruptions, first at the lunch counters and on the buses and then on the streets as riots. These riots were almost surely spontaneous, but, once started, they might be exploited by Klan members, Russian-oriented, Chinese-oriented, or Cuban-oriented Communists, and black racist revolutionaries.

This "other America" Lyndon Johnson inherited was as much in need as Vietnam and as much in the throes of a revolution. It was the revolution brewing in this other America at which the War on Poverty was aimed—too little for the young, too late for the old, but at last. The Johnson omnibus proposal was realistic in the light of a generally uncaring Congress and a country filled with pleasure-oriented families with middle-class incomes but lacking a traditional middle-class sense of responsibility.

The anti-poverty program, called the Economic Opportunity Act of 1964, was authorized in August. Its principal provisions included:

1. A Job Corps for deprived young men and women. It was based on the Youth Conservation Corps first suggested by Senator Humphrey five years before and submitted to the Congress by John Kennedy.

2. A work-training program similar to the hometown corps legislation sent to the Congress in 1963 by John Kennedy.

3. VISTA, Volunteers in Service to America, analogous to the Kennedy proposal for a National Service Corps or domestic peace corps.

4. A number of work training, vocational adult, and supplemental education programs designed for the educationally disadvantaged of all ages.

The intense problems encountered in execution of the 1962 Manpower Development Training Act had been one factor which revealed the scope of poverty in America. The studious also found much information by reading the voluminous 1960 census reports. The awareness grew first in the academic community, then filtered into the Federal bureaucracy. Michael Harrington wrote tellingly about poverty in his book, *The Other America*, which received wide attention through a long article by Dwight Macdonald in *The New Yorker* magazine. The MacDonald article was placed in the *Congressional Record*, which brought it to the attention of members and their staffs. The problem of poverty, it seemed clear, required a total program in which the physical, mental, and social ills of the poor were attacked in coordinated fashion. Young black man, John Jones, a name his slave ancestors may have taken from their master, could not be trained to hold a job, even if he were physically in good health, highly motivated, and, equally improbable, even if he had escaped psychological damage as a result of being raised in a nonfamily in a segregated, exploited ghetto. It turned out that John Jones could not really read, and he could barely write. He had been passed along through the legally required number of grades at a crowded, unsanitary firetrap of a segregated school, where overworked, often professionally and temperamentally unqualified teachers taught from irrelevant instructional manuals and outdated textbooks in overcrowded classrooms. His learning situation was further impaired because he had a rather common sight difficulty which had never been discovered and could have been easily corrected. It was truly "death at an early age." The Rotarian-type pep talks, a Dale Carnegie smile, and Sunday sermons wouldn't set right John Jones's askew world.

The House passed the War on Poverty bill by a vote of 226 to 185, not an inspiring margin considering the dimensions and depth of the long-festering problem. A total of 144 Northern Democrats, 60 of the 100 Southern Democrats, and 22 Republicans voted for passage. A total of 145 Republicans and the remaining 40 Southern Democrats voted against. Phil Landrum of Georgia, whose name was on the House bill, provided able assistance in weaning the vital number of Southern Democrats away from their usual antiwelfare position. In this connection, a most important concession was made to the Southerners in the form of a floor amendment that provided a limited veto to the governors over the most promising section of the bill, the community action programs.

This C.A.P. section authorized Federal grants to local, state, and private nonprofit agencies for improvement programs in a variety of sectors, health, welfare, legal assistance, and remedial education among them. It required that these improvement programs be undertaken with the "maximum feasible participation of residents of the areas," that is, the poor themselves. This phrase may have been the most profound statement of policy in domestic affairs issued from the Congress since the National Labor Relations Act about thirty years earlier. It was given casual attention during floor discussions. In a newspaper article, three years later, Adam Yarmolinsky and Richard Boone, principal assistants in drafting the Administration's bill, discussed the intent of the phrase. They said the poor were to be encouraged to participate in the operation and administration of specific programs. It was not intended, they said, that the poor should occupy policy-making positions.

Anyway, the phrase was a remarkable invitation to the dispossessed to participate in a remaking of American society. Since then, both those who voted for and against the bill have attempted to withdraw it. The phrase remains, but, in 1967, concerned Northern liberals combined with conservatives of both parties to circumscribe the invitation.

Slightly less than 1 billion dollars, less than 1 per cent of the Federal budget for that year, was appropriated to finance the undertaking. Certainly, of the major bills, it was the one for which the new President deserved the most credit, no matter what its origins, more so than for passage of the civil rights and tax-cut bills.

A promising 375-million-dollar Federal program of assistance to public and private transit companies, food-stamp and long sought conservation programs, and expansion of NDEA were other legislative achievements. Despite Congress's temporary willingness to go along with a new President, important legislation was passed over. Medicare was again laid to rest. Its House sponsor, Cecil King of California, announced in June, 1964, that he could corral only twelve favorable votes within the twenty-five-member Ways and Means Committee. It would take the forthcoming Democratic election sweep to compel the chairman, Wilbur Mills, to stop sitting on it. School legislation was dead. Unsuccessful, too, were consumer-protection legislation and a measure to uproot a discriminatory national origins quota imbedded in the immigration statutes.

In foreign affairs, trouble persisted. Foreign aid had done a good job in Europe, but the memory was running out. Foreign aid appropriations would steadily decrease; in the fiscal 1963 budget, foreign aid was reduced one-third. In May, Nehru had died. In October, a Labor Government was elected in Great Britain and Khrushchev was deposed, to be succeeded by Brezhnev and Kosygin. De Gaulle's challenge stiffened; the war in Vietnam worsened, as did relations with China. Congress adjourned in early October. Members left to get themselves re-elected. Johnson, sensing a big win, campaigned to make it the biggest of all.

5

The Goldwater Congress

Johnson succeeded. He received the largest Presidential vote, 43.1 million, ever received by a candidate. This was 16 million more than the rightist Goldwater received. The political right had long yearned to offer a "choice, not an echo." The nation had chosen.

The Democratic party held a 155-seat advantage over the Republican, 295–140, the largest in thirty years. It amounted to a net gain of 38 seats. In the Senate, there was a net gain of 2 seats for the Democratic party; more important, the half-dozen or so promising Democratic Senators elected in the 1958 election were reelected. Democrats held 68 seats; Republicans 32.

As the racing-form chart would have said, Johnson "won breezing." Nevertheless, America showed an ugly side during the election, first at the Republican nominating convention, when noisy delegates, including some white-collar thugs, nominated Barry Goldwater of Arizona. He certainly deserved the nomination. Sincere, honest, and wrongheaded, Goldwater and his aides had worked hard. Other than Nelson Rockefeller of New York, Goldwater's Republican opponents acted like boys in velvet suits and Buster-Brown collars, whose blood had run, oh, so thin. They were bruised, too, by Eisenhower, who kept endorsing a different aspirant from one edition to the next. The rampaging, roguish Republican elephant seemed mortally wounded.

The election really was no contest. Johnson and Humphrey ran an active but low-pitched campaign, designed to wrap a cloak of consensus around as many million voters as possible. On the Republican side, it had to be an insane campaign, highly distasteful to orthodox Republicans. Goldwater selected his Vice-Presidential running mate on the inexplicable ground that the individual bugged Johnson. Clifton White seemed to be the only quality politician on the Goldwater team. They all seemed to be glint-eyed, snarly Poujadists, for whom the tax rates were the measure of all things. In a sense, the country suffered. There is an abundance of bunkum in any Presidential campaign, but it usually lards a more or less responsible presentation of the major issues. The Goldwater campaign, however, was neither responsible nor serious, and, therefore, it was frightening. Remarks made during and after the campaign indicate Goldwater himself knew he was defeated from the day in August the Democrats broke camp at Atlantic City. There are indications that Goldwater himself was rather lighthearted about the whole thing. Goldwater didn't campaign meaningfully; Johnson wasn't put under pressure, therefore, to explain himself and his policies. The country suffered thereby.

The Eighty-ninth Congress provided a Democratic President with a program majority for the first time since 1938. In the House, there were 295 Democrats. Subtracting the 60 conservative Southerners, and adding the 10 liberal Republicans gave 245 Democratic program votes. Conversely, the 140 members labeled Republican, minus the 10 liberals, plus the 60 conservative Southern Democrats gave 190 antiprogram votes. In sum, Johnson had a "real" 55-vote margin. It was an uncommon opportunity to "catch up and go ahead," if the legislative tillers were reasonably well handled.

Program Democrats outnumbered both the conservative Southern Democratic colleagues and their silent allies on seniority, the big-city, machine-oriented Northern Democrats. Therefore, they were emboldened to make changes.

They first stripped seniority from two Southern Democrats who had supported the Republican Goldwater. One, John Bell

Williams, a racist reactionary in his tenth term, was denied the chairmanship of Interstate and Foreign Commerce. Williams sulked for two years and then returned home to get himself elected Governor of Mississippi. Also punished was a second termer, Albert Watson of South Carolina. Recognizing that he had no future in the Democratic party in the House, Watson resigned his seat and ran successfully as a Republican for the House seat he had just vacated. As a Republican, he properly belonged to the party whose policies he had consistently subscribed to even when he had masqueraded as a Democrat. With these acts, the Democratic party in the House had substantively departed from the seniority system. Its belated action had short-range significance and, one hopes, long-range meaning. In this effort, program Democrats received no help from the President. The White House staff took no action that would betray his position. On the other hand, Speaker McCormack in private made clear that he would prefer that Williams and Watson not be displaced. In public, however, he adopted a hands-off policy.

Next, the Democrats forced three significant changes in the rules of the House:

(1.) A revised twenty-one-day rule was adopted. This one, unlike its predecessor sixteen years before, did not merely strengthen the power of a legislative committee whose legislation was bottled up in Rules. Instead, it actually expanded, although slightly, the authority of the Speakership. Specifically, it gave a Speaker discretion as to whether to recognize a committee chairman who wished to invoke the twenty-one-day rule. At first, Speaker McCormack balked at this slender grant of authority being thrust upon his office. Ultimately, he was persuaded to support it.

(2.) Another change was designed to eliminate the situation in which an objection by one member from the floor prevents a bill from being sent to a reconciliation conference with the Senate. In that event, the bill can go to conference only if it is re-routed to the Rules Committee for a rule granting a conference, and this rule, in turn, is approved by the House. In 1960, the elementary-secondary-school aid bill suffered such an objection, was sent to Rules, keeper of the legislative keys, and kept prisoner there. Under the new revised procedure, a bill could be sent to conference by a simple majority vote of the House.

(3.) Obstructionist members were denied a right to delay final action on a bill by requesting an engrossed copy of a bill, that is, the final certified version as passed by the House.

Toward these changes the President was silent, but it was understood that he favored them. Speaker McCormack supported them publicly. These three were useful changes. Even with a slender program majority of 8 to 7 on the Rules Committee, the twenty-one-day rule was resorted to successfully eight times during the Eighty-ninth Congress. In addition, several bills were helped when notice of intent to use the rule was served.

Thirdly, the Democrats changed the party ratio on committees to provide program control. From 1947 on, the ratio, with exception of Ways and Means and Rules, had been misleadingly based upon the actual number of Democrats to Republicans in the House. This practice further aggravated the problem caused by the slavish adherence to seniority. The application of the new ratio resulted in legislative progress. Program Democrats even achieved a slight majority on Appropriations—an unheard-of situation. The ratio on Rules was unchanged. If the standard apportionment had been followed on Ways and Means, the twenty-year-old battle for Medicare would have continued to be unresolved. Consequently, McCormack did support a ratio of 17 to 8 on Ways and Means, which finally gave Medicare supporters an adequate majority.

These structural and procedural changes were the vital preliminary to making this a "catch-up and go-ahead" Congress. They made possible the great accomplishments of the first session, accomplishments analogous to the 1911–1912 Clark-Underwood House, Wilson's 1913–1916 Congress, and the ninety-nine-day session under Speaker Rainey in 1933. A formula designed to resist successful constitutional challenge was established in the elementary-secondary-school bill that provided assistance to pupils in public and private schools. The measure was passed. Health and medical care for persons sixty-five and older, largely

financed by Social Security funding, was passed. A Department
of Housing and Urban Development, to be headed by the first
Negro of cabinet rank, Robert Weaver, was authorized. Existing
veterans' benefits, Social Security, and programs for higher education were improved. A series of other additions and improvements to Federally assisted education programs provided a
pleased President an opportunity to call the Eighty-ninth "the
Education Congress." Most of the final battles of the big wars
over "catch-up" programs ended in success.

There were still problems, however. Much "go-ahead" legislation barely moved. There were exceptions. One major "go-
ahead" bill provided for a comprehensive, coordinated attack on
urban decay, with Federal money. Originally, this was called a
"demonstration cities" program, but, because of urban unrest,
the name was changed to "model cities." A second surprise legislative achievement was Federal action in the neglected area of
automobile safety. In part, Ralph Nader, the one-man gang,
embarrassed the Congress into taking up the matter.

The new antipoverty program was given nearly 300 million
dollars more than the Administration requested, but it was impossible to jettison the limited gubernatorial veto. A housing
provision to enable F.H.A. to provide mortgage insurance for
developers of "new towns," analogous to Reston in Virginia and
Columbia in Maryland, never reached the floor. Then there was
the example of the proposed rent supplements. Under the program, low-income families would be paid a varying subsidy so
that they could afford decent and adequate private housing.
President Roosevelt once observed that a Congressional authorization is in the nature of a New Year's resolution, it may or it
may not be carried out. The rent supplements program was authorized in drastically narrowed form, but it was denied funding
in 1965. In the second session, funding was only approved by
narrow margins, ranging up to thirteen votes in the House.
Much the same fate awaited the Teacher Corps, designed to provide teachers skilled in ways of instructing educationally neglected children. It, too, was authorized but denied funds in
1965. Since then it has been on quarter rations. The Administra-

tion's bill to overhaul the immigration laws survived, though maimed, through skillful handling in the Senate by Edward Kennedy of Massachusetts.

One claim of those who believe that our involvement in Vietnam should be reduced is that this would free large sums of money which could then be spent to solve the problems of the poor and of the cities. It is true that military expenditures have risen sharply with the war. The fiscal year figures in millions of dollars for 1963, 1967, 1968, and 1969, obtained from the Bureau of the Budget, are as follows: 1963 actual—52,275; 1967 actual—70,095; 1968 estimated—76,491; 1969 estimated—79,792. In early 1968, the Bureau of the Budget published a "Table of Estimated Funds for Programs Assisting the Poor." These figures include trust-fund payments, such as health insurance for the aged and various retirement programs. The comparable figures in millions of dollars for the years are as follows: 1963 actual—12,500; 1967 actual—21,100; 1968 estimated—24,600; 1969 estimated—27,700. By category the figures, all in millions of dollars, show a jump from .100 (one hundred thousand) in 1963 to 2,500 in 1969 in education for the poor; less than .050 in 1963 to 1,600 in work and training; .900 to 4,700 in health; cash benefit programs, such as public assistance, Social Security, and other retirement programs, from 10,400 to 15,900.

The real significance of these figures demonstrates what the Eighty-ninth Congress with its overwhelming Democratic majorities did to escalate expenditures for the poor. What happened to the poverty program in 1967 was not the result of the rising military expenditures starving domestic programs but of the 1966 election, which cost the poverty program more than forty supporters in the House, and of the inept leadership in the House of Representatives.

Nevertheless, a laundry list of passed bills again led to uncritical rave notices about the legislative acumen of the President and of Speaker McCormack. It was futile for a close observer to warn that success was a result of overwhelming numbers. It was futile to suggest that, in fact, those numbers were not being used legislatively as well as they could be. Also, it was futile to warn that the political futures of many new Democratic members were being unnecessarily and pointlessly endangered.

The 1964 election returns must not only be read in gross but also in detail. Many new Democrats were elected in normally Republican districts. An unknown number would revert to Republican custody in 1966, but a substantial number could be retained if members were given a reasonable opportunity to cultivate their constituents. This meant, in part, not asking them to walk the political plank for no purpose in their first terms. Yet these new members were asked to walk it for no purpose not once, but twice.

In the first session, a major drive was made in the House to repeal the so-called right-to-work provision, section 14b of the Taft-Hartley Act. It permits states to prohibit the union shop provision in collective bargaining agreements. Now such a political issue is hazardous or worse in marginal Congressional districts, because repeal would alter the balance of power between organized labor and management. No member should be asked to vote on such an issue unless (a) there is reasonable assurance that the repeal would pass both House and Senate; or (b) he is well established politically; or (c) organized labor exercises a decidedly strong influence in the district. This three-point checklist the leadership ignored. New members fall in the a category; a war-horse such as myself would be classified in b; and c applies to a down-the-line member from a steel or coal town with strong union membership.

Committed supporters of repeal, such as myself, were horrified to discover that the Democratic leadership was leading its yearlings to slaughter without having the slightest assurance that the Senate would act favorably. The House passed the repeal bill by a vote of 221 to 203. The Senate, however, balked both in 1965 and again the following year. The vote in the House served no purpose except to help defeat a number of promising members.

The second walk-the-plank issue came up in 1966 in the form of the open-housing section of the Civil Rights Act of 1966, brought to the floor in July under the twenty-one-day rule.

That year, with cities social tinderboxes, nothing could have been politically more dangerous than having to vote on an issue of open housing. It had been successfully portrayed to whites as legislation that would result in a flow of Negroes into their cloistered neighborhoods, which, in turn, would bring about a deterioration of "property values." Of course, such contentions were false, but they were believed to be correct. White suburbanites were to vote on the basis of their apprehensions, not upon a set of facts they were not acquainted with.

The bill was being pulled in several directions. Civil rights groups were skeptical about success through legislative action. They had asked President Johnson to ban segregated housing by issuing an Executive order. When this was denied, they moved to support the bill, but some liberals wanted to widen and strengthen the open-housing provisions adopted by the House Judiciary Committee, while other liberals, both Democrat and Republican, estimated correctly that the committee version should be modified in order to gain acceptance in the Senate.

Again, the same three-point checklist should have been applied. This time, I personally sought and was given assurance by the House leadership that Senate action was a certainty. I was further informed that chances were quite good that the Senate would act favorably, if the full House were first to modify the open-housing section of the bill reported by the Judiciary Committee. Therefore, the political risks involved seemed to me necessary and justified. It was my vote that broke a 179-to-179 tie, permitting the open-housing section to be modified in respect to action of real estate brokers acting as agents for homeowners. It soon became obvious the leadership man who gave me those assurances didn't know what he was talking about. A filibuster in the Senate, acquiesced in by the Republican leader Everett Dirksen, killed the bill. The primary responsibility for the scheduling of these bills rested with Speaker McCormack. It is poor generalship to waste your troops in assaults which achieve no objective.

Another primary defect of the Speaker's leadership is in the area of legislative scheduling. It was a factor in sending freshmen

Democrats to their political deaths. The first session was an unnecessarily long one, ending on October 23. The second session
was even more unnecessarily long and inexcusably so, because it
was an election year. In my opinion this was due to poor legislative scheduling. It was another factor that sent these freshmen
to their avoidable defeat. New members never did know when
they could plan to be away from Washington to do necessary work in their Congressional districts. This condition during
the first session did not seem so consequential. After all, there
was always next year. The condition persisted through 1966.
Long periods of inaction were mixed with frantic periods of
long-delayed catching up.

  Politics is making of policy. One who votes on policy must be
afforded an opportunity to explain his vote to his constituents.
The second session ended only seventeen days before Election
Day. During the session, new members never could plan when
to be back home even to meet constituents, much less to take the
time to persuade them as to the soundness of their votes. New
members never knew whether the next week would be legislative lull or legislative frenzy. In the meantime, their Republican
opponents, some of whom they had only narrowly defeated in
1966, had been carefully chosen, well financed, and, in many
cases, were working full time to defeat the upstart Democrats. A
freshman was damned if he stayed in Washington with no
chance to campaign and damned if he left Washington and
missed a crucial vote. It reached a point when more than one
new member came to me to ask if I believed the President and
the Speaker were deliberately trying to get them defeated. I always replied that, of course, neither wanted them defeated, but
that the Speaker, in particular, was out of touch with the kind
of problem that they faced. Facing a strong election challenge in
his South Boston district was only a dim memory to John
McCormack. When faced with a long session in an election year,
seniors would advise their juniors to tell constituents that, although their opponents might spend their time speaking and
playing politics, members of Congress have to be in Washington
doing the people's business. The people were not persuaded.

Freshmen grew more and more desperate and more and more uncooperative.

Speaker McCormack is responsible for flow and scheduling of legislation for floor action. It would have taken only a slight effort on his part to plan that, even if the sessions must be long, members would know well in advance when they would be getting some time to spend in their home districts. During the first three months of 1966, virtually no important legislative business was acted on in the House, but there was never assurance that something important might not come up next week or the week after.

President Johnson was compiling a remarkable record of achievement. In the House, however, there was more concern about lost elections to come and less about legislative acumen. Speaker McCormack appeared more as a loyal ambassador from the White House to the Democrats in the House than as the leader of the Democrats in the House, whose interests and welfare must be his concern. In the November election, the Democratic party in the House lost its program majority. The well-organized, well-financed Republicans, campaigning early and earnestly, acquired a net of forty-seven House seats. Heavy casualties occurred among first-term Democrats. The party line up in 1967 was 247 Democrats to 187 Republicans, with one vacancy—the Harlem Congressional district, whose Representative-elect, Adam Clayton Powell, was not permitted to take his seat. Republicans achieved a net gain of 3 seats in the Senate, where the apportionment was now 64 Democrats and 36 Republicans.

Obviously, there were many causes for the results, such as a growing political protest against American participation in the Vietnam War, inflation, and high interest rates that severely crippled the home-building industry. Skillful Republican propaganda convinced many that the large amount of long, overdue legislation and the pitifully small amount of innovative legislation represented a "great excess" of unneeded action, perpetrated on an already overburdened taxpayer by a willful President abetted by a "rubber-stamp" Congress, but most House watchers believe the casualty list could have been shorter. The losses were partly due to two excessively long sessions and the poor weekly scheduling of bills for floor action, and partly to politically lethal civil rights and labor bills that should have been kept off the floor, since there was no real chance of Senate passage. Speaker McCormack could have controlled all three elements. His lack of planning and lack of foresight worsened the results of the 1966 elections.

McCormack was Speaker during the years 1962 through 1966. The promise of an energetic Kennedy Administration accounted for the legislative gains in 1962–1963. A sense of atonement for the assassination, coupled with the limited legislative objectives of Johnson's first year as President, accounted for the achievements in 1964. Legislative output during 1965–1966 was a direct bequest of the Goldwater candidacy. Thus, up to 1967, the weakness of McCormack's leadership had not yet been clearly demonstrated to the country.

The first session of the Ninetieth Congress opened January 9, 1967. Within a few ghastly weeks, serious defects in the McCormack leadership, long obvious to the insider, became clear to an outsider who cared to look. Admittedly, the loss of seats created a difficult problem for the best of leadership. In translation, the 247 members labeled Democrats, minus 60 conservative Southern Democrats, plus 10 liberal Republicans equaled 197 votes for moderately liberal programs; 187 members labeled Republicans, minus the 10 liberal Republicans, plus the 60 conservative Southern Democrats equaled 237 votes that would be cast against these programs. The tide was running against program Democrats, but leadership breakwaters to stem the flow should have been established. None were.

6

The Ninetieth Congress: A Study in Frustration

Even with the program Democrats in a minority as far as the whole House was concerned, the Democratic leadership was still in a position to plan how best to retain what slender advantages it had. Three possible techniques that can be used in such straitened circumstances are the program-control of the key committees, such as Appropriations, Rules, and Ways and Means; attempt to modify seniority in order to further party purposes, as was done in the Williams-Watson cases; legislative programming tailored to take advantage of every opportunity to advance specific bills. This programming means, for example, that one should not court unnecessary legislative battles. It means one should not simultaneously schedule a highly disputatious but needed bill that has no constituency, such as foreign aid, back-to-back with another major controversial bill. Such scheduling simply whets the appetite of the primitives. This particular elementary lesson was ignored in the previous Congress and again in the Ninetieth. These three techniques can be applied effectively by whoever is in charge, Democratic program liberals or Republican program conservatives.

COMMITTEE CONTROL

Control of a legislative committee plays a major role in determining the manner in which its bills are treated on the floor by its friends and opponents. In turn, that treatment helps substantially to shape the manner in which newspapers, magazines, television, and radio present these bills to their audiences.

The Appropriations Committee, for example, reports a bill supplying funds for programs administered by the Department of Health, Education, and Welfare. Program Democrats control the committee. Therefore, the bill probably contains the full amount requested by the President. Assume, however, that individual amendments to reduce funds for several of these programs are adopted on the floor while the bill is discussed in a Committee of the Whole House, wherein votes are tallied by numbers, not by a roll call of names. Under House rules, such fund cutting amendments adopted by the Committee of the Whole are then subject to a roll call. In these circumstances, each member unfriendly to the bill is now confronted with a policy choice. He is forced to make a public record which indicates whether he did or did not vote to cut the appropriation requested to finance health, education, and welfare programs. Assuming he doesn't turn tail (as does happen), he must record in public the vote he had previously cast during the anonymous Committee of the Whole process.

Assume a different situation, however, one in which the Democrats maintain nominal but not program control of Appropriations. Now, the same fund reductions can be made in the privacy of the committee room that in the first example were made on the floor of the House. The knife wielding accomplished, a reduced bill emerges from Appropriations. It comes to the floor and is discussed in the Committee of the Whole. Now the supporters of the program must undertake the tremendous job of garnering votes to restore the deleted funds on the Floor. This is far more difficult than preventing cuts in Committee. Overall, funding bills are rarely substantially increased on the floor after they have emerged from Appropriations. Now the unfriendly member of the first example and his scores of like-minded colleagues are free to pose as "supporters" of the bill on any roll call, because the work of reducing funds has already been accomplished in committee. So these false friends are able to vote for the passage of the reduced appropriations. Accordingly, their constituents are misled, especially those friendly to the purposes of the programs the bill finances. The unfriendly member, in sum, has been able to avoid making public his policy choice; thereby, his constituents are denied their simple rights to know his position. Consequently, he is further free to fashion a political reputation based not on policy choice, but on such relatively less important matters as constituent service and appeal of personality.

Likewise, Democratic program control of Ways and Means is important. Tax legislation can originate in no other place than the House, according to the Constitution. Ways and Means is the committee of jurisdiction, as it is for Social Security, international trade, Medicare, unemployment compensation, and other programs with a tax feature.

In 1967, if Ways and Means maintained the conservative majority it had had since 1947, the Democratic party would control the committee in name only. A Democratic delegation met with Speaker McCormack. They urged retention of Democratic program control of the key committees, but they were not successful, as was only too apparent when the House organized itself. Speaker McCormack permitted a reduction on Ways and Means from a seventeen-Democratic and eight-Republican seat apportionment to a fifteen-Democratic and ten-Republican one. In practice, this means conservative control by thirteen to twelve, or perhaps fourteen to eleven on some issues, as well as, of course, by a Chairman who had blocked Medicare for years. Speaker McCormack permitted an even greater deterioration on Appropriations. On that committee in the Eighty-ninth Congress, there were thirty-four Democrats and sixteen Republicans. For some years previously, there had been thirty Democrats and twenty Republicans. Speaker McCormack did not even fall back to the thirty to twenty allocation. The Republicans talked their way into an additional seat. This made the allocation thirty Democratic seats and twenty-one Republican seats, which meant conservative control of Appropriations in the magnitude of thirty-three to eighteen votes. Yet there is precedent for the

Speaker taking steps that could have provided the Democratic leadership with program control of these two key committees.

Rules, a third major committee, escaped the conservative crunch when Chairman Smith, legislative leader of the crunchers, had been unexpectedly defeated in his primary.

SENIORITY

Smith's successor was Colmer of Mississippi. Colmer, now the second senior Democrat, since Rayburn and McCormack had not removed him from the committee in 1948 when he defected to the Dixiecrats, equaled Smith in his conservatism but not in legislative leadership. Colmer was fully as skilled in maneuvering the legislative process, however. Although he talked of retiring, he now found himself in line for the Chairmanship. The disciplining of his fellow Mississippian, John Bell Williams, in 1964 constituted a departure from iron-clad seniority. Why should not Colmer, then, be denied a chairmanship? I argued this in a magazine article that was widely distributed shortly before the opening of the Ninetieth Congress. Speaker McCormack energetically opposed this proposal.

The problem was related to a much more publicized member, Adam Clayton Powell, the flamboyant Negro representative from Harlem, who had been Chairman of Education and Labor in the previous three Congresses. There was a great public outcry that Powell must be denied his seat in the House. Some of us were opposed to this move on both constitutional and practical grounds. We were convinced, however, that Powell had so abused his prerogatives as Chairman that, like Colmer, he, too, should be stripped of his seniority and denied his cherished Chairmanship. Speaker McCormack opposed both Powell's unseating and deprivation of seniority.

Democrat Powell had bolted the Stevenson Presidential candidacy in 1956 to support Eisenhower. Afterward, there was a suggestion that he should be punished, but the necessary support could not be mustered. In 1967, McCormack did not even seem to take the public outcry about Powell seriously. At first, McCormack simply let the matter drift.

The Powell affair is a classic example of Speaker McCormack's inability to anticipate trouble. When he finally could not avoid seeing trouble, his countermoves were poorly thought out and badly implemented. His tactics led not only to a serious constitutional mistake by the House but also to a significant political defeat for the Democratic leadership and the Democratic party. The Democrats could have been kept together to support Powell; they had a nominal majority, yet Powell was denied his seat.

Powell was in deep trouble. He had abused his trust as Chairman of the Education and Labor Committee. It distressed the country. It distressed many House members, including me. But McCormack felt there was no problem, although he was warned that mail demanding Powell's head was arriving by the boxcar to many House members from their constituents. A few of the old-bull chairmen, no friends of Powell, shared McCormack's view. Take away Powell's chairmanship and seniority, they reasoned, and who knows what other committee chairman might be dislodged?

Perhaps forewarned by my article, Speaker McCormack showed awareness of the problem of Colmer, who so strongly opposed the domestic programs of the Democratic party. In an unprecedented act, Speaker McCormack appeared at a caucus of the Democratic Study Group, an informal organization of liberal Democrats. The D.S.G. had met to consider both the Colmer and the Powell matters. It was clear that McCormack was using the full weight of his office to support both Powell and Colmer in their claim to chairmanships. The D.S.G. membership was split down the middle regarding Powell; so no group position was attempted on that subject. Conversely, however, a substantial majority of the D.S.G. members attending the closed meeting did vote to support action to prevent Colmer from becoming Chairman of Rules. Nevertheless, the vote made it clear that in the Democratic caucus to come fifty of the about one hundred fifty liberal Democrats would join the one hundred Southern and border-state members in supporting Colmer for Chairman of the Rules Committee. This assured the defeat of the effort to deprive Colmer of that position. There being no point in engaging in futile battles, especially in the secrecy of the Democratic caucus, it was decided not to pursue the matter further.

Subsequently, the Democratic caucus met on the eve of the opening of the Ninetieth Congress. It voted to strip seniority from Powell, a deserved rebuke, despite McCormack's ineffective opposition. On this vote the majority was made up of nearly all Southern and border-state Democrats and about fifty liberal Democrats.

There is evidence that Colmer and Speaker McCormack had collaborated to defend Colmer's seniority and his chairmanship. Prior to the Democratic caucus, McCormack let it be known that Colmer had agreed, if he should become Chairman, to a regular meeting day each week for Rules. This step had been urged unsuccessfully for years. Business in Rules had been held up by Chairman Smith, to whom, except under extraordinary circumstances, the power to call meetings was left. Sometimes Smith would leave Washington to avoid having meetings. Colmer also agreed to have a written set of rules of procedure, a requirement of the rules of the House honored in the breach by the Committee on Rules. Speaker McCormack also appointed program Democrats to the vacancies on Rules: Spark Matsunaga of Hawaii and William Anderson of Tennessee succeeded Smith and James Trimble of Arkansas. The latter had been a regrettable loss to the program Democrats in the House. His Southern constituents had finally turned against him. The margin on Rules for Democratic programs became nine to six. This helped. With even an eight to seven majority, the Democratic leadership and a Democratic President are always, in a sense, at the mercy of one of the eight. A legitimate absence by one of the eight can stymie action on an Administration measure, or one of the eight may want to trade his vote on an Administration measure in return for assistance of some sort. This game of "trade off" is common practice, but the leadership or the President does well to avoid the trap whenever possible. The nine-to-six program control was such an avoidance. Even if three of the nine are absent, the opposition six cannot work any mischief because a six to six vote would result, and a tie vote does not pass a motion.

In the shaky Democratic House, therefore, by a turn as unanticipated as the obstructionist conservative coalition ironically spawned by the 1936 Roosevelt landslide election, the Rules Committee became again the potent arm of the leadership it was designed to be. The thirty-year obstructionist role of Rules had been broken. It would belong to program Democrats, just as it always had to program Republicans when they were in power. It hadn't just happened, of course. It was a direct product of years of work inside and outside of Congress by those who were loyal to the programs of the Democratic party.

In sum, Speaker McCormack struck out on two issues (seniority and legislative programming) out of three (committee control) major organizational problems in the Ninetieth Congress. Even on the matter of committee control, Speaker McCormack failed as to Appropriations and Ways and Means, although Rules was rescued.

The Speaker today, despite the reduction of his power, is not without authority. He presides at sessions of the House, puts questions to a vote, and reports votes. Further the Speaker establishes the order of business, rules on points of order, and is authorized to prevent delaying tactics. He appoints the Chairman of a Committee of the Whole House and appoints members both to select and conference committees. He chooses speakers *pro tem*. He refers bills and reports to committees, as well as bills and reports to the several calendars he deems appropriate. With the assistance of the parliamentarian, the Speaker interprets rules of the House, usually within the bounds of precedents established by past Speakers. He even holds a power of recognition, although severely circumscribed.

LEGISLATIVE PROGRAMMING

Nevertheless, the aimless scheduling of legislation persisted, as it had during the two years of the Eighty-ninth Congress.

Members were unable to plan working periods in their districts. Desperate at being held in Washington by an expectation that on some vague *mañana* an important bill would come to the floor for action, a large bipartisan majority came to favor amending the rules of the House to authorize a recess each August. A substantial majority within the Rules Committee, which had jurisdiction over recess legislation, favored the recess. Speaker McCormack awoke belatedly. He enlisted the services of Minority Leader Ford of Michigan. Between them they talked a majority of the committee into killing the recess proposition on the grounds it would hurt the image of Congress.

The legislative road was made even more difficult because Democratic leaders in both House and Senate, in a sense, disowned the Ninetieth Congress before it began. There were forecasts that the new Congress would be essentially one of "assimilating" and "remedying" major legislation passed in the previous, productive Eighty-ninth Congress. The leaders encouraged the members to mark time, and the record of the Ninetieth Congress reflects this. Those attending McCormack's customarily brief "press conference," preceding each day's meeting of the House, reported that, if he gave any response at all to questions relating to legislative problems, it consisted of "I'll play that one by ear" or "I'll cross that bridge when I get there." It was curious that the Speaker paid so little attention to the majority leader, Carl Albert of Oklahoma, a highly intelligent, hardworking, and skilled legislator and planner. If the Speaker bothered to listen to Albert's advice, it was obvious he ignored it.

The affair of Powell, coupled with that of Senator Thomas Dodd, had brought to the surface strong but latent public support for a written gauge of ethical standards in the Congress. The Senate had established an ethics committee, the Committee on Standards and Conduct. There was, quite properly, insistent demand for corresponding action in the House. Speaker McCormack obviously expected to shove the matter under the rug.

The personal integrity and personal honesty of Speaker McCormack is not in question. The issue simply did not appear relevant to him in a political and a general moral sense. McCormack represented a different age in American urban politics. The old-time urban member was a product of ethnically saturated politics; special favors, special influence, and the use of one's political power to forward one's personal affairs were all part of a politician's survival-and-advancement kit as he led himself and his abused and beleaguered Irish or Jewish or Italian fellows out of their ghettos and into the precincts of power. Such members took a rather casual attitude toward the larger aspects of a public official's behavior, such as conflicts of interest, collecting and spending of campaign funds, and the use of public funds for semiprivate or private purposes. It wasn't that any of these men were necessarily personally dishonest, but they were not their brother's keeper, either.

For reasons I do not understand, Colmer, now Rules Chairman, appointed me as chairman of a six-member subcommittee to develop a legislative solution to the ethics question. Private consultations were held with H. Allen Smith of California, senior Republican on Rules, who also served on the subcommittee. We worked out a resolution in the full subcommittee to establish a permanent Committee on Standards of Official Conduct. This title carried with it the clear understanding that concern should be focused on the conduct of a member in the course of performing his official duties and responsibilities. The personal conduct of a member was not to be within its jurisdiction unless it affected his official conduct or the reputation of the House. Of course, to implement the resolution more was needed than phrases urging virtue and rectitude. Therefore, the proposed new committee was directed to study and report to the House not only a code of conduct but also the means of enforcing such a code. There came a time in the evolution of this legislation when Speaker McCormack realized that ethics legislation would emerge from Rules and emerge as more than a piety. He came to realize too that if custom were followed, because I was chairman of the subcommittee which dealt with the matter, I would report the resolution from Rules and, by so doing, be the normal choice as Chairman of the Committee on Standards of Official Conduct. Soon after our resolutions, therefore, Chairman Colmer, in great embarrassment, advised me he had virtually been ordered to see to it that the resolution to establish the committee not be reported in my name. He was discreet, but the message's origin was clear. After all, as has been told, he owed his own chairmanship to McCormack.

To succeed in accomplishing anything useful, the chairman of such an ethics committee must have the confidence of the Speaker. I told Colmer I was not upset. I wasn't; what had happened was what I had expected to happen. In my previous book, *House Out of Order*, my assessment of McCormack's abilities had been less than enthusiastic. He had not liked it.

The resolution to establish the ethics committee was promptly passed out of Rules. It bore Colmer's name. The House unanimously passed it. The Speaker appointed a twelve-member committee which consisted of able, sincere, and honest members.

The Speaker's attitude toward the ethics problem carried over to the Monroney-Madden legislative reorganization bill. It passed the Senate in March, 1967, and came to the House. There, it was referred to the committee of original jurisdiction, Rules, and there it languished through the remainder of 1967 and into 1968. Behind the scenes, Speaker McCormack has exerted every effort to prevent enactment of any version of the bill designed to provide a limited measure of modernization of the antiquated machinery and antiquated ways of doing business in both House and Senate.

Attempts to move it to the floor failed. The Joint Congressional committee that fathered it was given an extension of life and then it was allowed to die. When a Republican member of Rules offered to move a resolution to continue the life of the committee into 1968, only a few Democrats, I among them, indicated support of the extension. Thus, authority for the joint committee expired on the last day of 1967. It is to be hoped that public pressure will revive it. If not, Republicans will certainly make it a legitimate partisan issue in the 1968 election.

There were other legislative problems that the Speaker would not or could not deal with. "Must" amendments to the antipoverty act became bogged down in Education and Labor.

Albert, who had taken a trouble-shooting assignment on this committee, moved in to save the bill from its enemies—and from its squabbling friends, some of whom misunderstood it. Millions of America's walking wounded were relying on the antipoverty program as a causeway across which they could move to self-sufficiency and independence. Albert managed to have the bill, battered and maimed, reported to the House.

Then we in Rules were informed that we must report a rule for the bill on a Thursday so that it could be adopted by the full House on Friday, the next day. There would be general debate on the following Monday and Tuesday, and the bill would be amended and passed that week. With some effort, Rules reported a rule, as Speaker McCormack wanted. The House approved it the following day. Members, changing plans, turned up the following Monday to discover that Speaker McCormack had also scheduled twelve largely inconsequential bills for that Monday, November 6. Further delays developed. The result was that the antipoverty bill was passed 283 to 129, a week later than originally indicated. When it did, funds were cut by 20 per cent.

The week's delay, and the overall lack of planning resulted in an undue reliance on accident to assure the votes to keep the cut from being deeper. When it is announced that a bill will be acted on during a certain time, the effective pressure groups favoring the legislation organize their efforts so as to achieve a peak of favorable votes on hand at a specific time. They make contacts by letter, telegram, telephone, and in person. Delay lessens the impact of this pressure. Members favoring the bill may well have canceled engagements they have made involving commitments to large groups of constituents. Not only are they embarrassed by the cancellation, but they are irritated when it turns out not to have been necessary. Hence, they become much less likely to cancel engagements the next time an important bill is "scheduled." All of these factors hurt the chances of important and controversial legislation.

In early August, President Johnson made an urgent request for a tax increase in the form of a 10 per cent surcharge on Federal income tax obligations. The proposal was referred to the committee of jurisdiction, Ways and Means, which, with the Speaker's permission, had fallen into the hands of its conservative faction led by its chairman, Mills. Exactly two months later, the Committee proceeded to table the bill by a vote of 20 to 5. In the process, Mills made another of his alliances with conservatives on the committee. They used the tax legislation, ardently desired by the President, as a blackjack to force him to curtail domestic growth programs, such as in the health and education sectors. Expenditures needed cutting, not in the essential health, education, and welfare programs, however, but in programs such as public works, the "pork barrel." Of course, expenditures in that sector are considered by conservatives of both parties as a foolproof springboard to continued reelection. As a cover, they scream economy in the direction of those programs that would permit all Americans to share in our country's bounty.

Republicans were permitted to gain a public relations victory in the form of an "economy drive" that had mean and petty features, such as barring Federal employees of the Office of Economic Opportunity, the antipoverty command, from a general pay raise. As a result of the misplaced economy drive, House Democrats held caucuses on a substantive issue, government spending, for the first time since the 1945–1946 Congress. Even in the unfamiliar situation, the Speaker should have been able to rally his divided party to defend the President and his programs. It would have required effective leadership from the Speaker, but there was none. Republicans snickered.

Finally one evening in late 1967, the pent-up rage and frustration of Democrats, and some Republicans, erupted to the point that Speaker McCormack nearly lost complete control of the House. The point when debate is started, interrupted, continued, or stopped is determined by the majority leadership, in this case McCormack. Often the leadership consults with the minority leader. The occasion was a foreign-aid appropriation bill. Having no constituency, this bill is guaranteed to attract the hostility of members who feel freer to vent it upon foreign aid than on any other issue. Debate on the appropriation was scheduled to be

completed on a Thursday night. In a sudden reversal, arrived at
by some reasoning process no one had been able to discern, the
Speaker determined to carry the discussion over into the next
day. Of course, many members had made Friday plans on the
basis of the previous commitment. Their patience buffeted
enough, an open revolt erupted. The House resembled the floor
of the New York Stock Exchange on a heavy selling day. Senior
members and employees of the House had never seen such a situation. Fortunately, some of those who were most critical of
Speaker McCormack's performance as Speaker were able to influence enough irate colleagues to restore order. The next day a
similar situation began to develop. This time it was possible to
take quick and effective action to prevent the House from reach-
ing the brink two days running.

   None of these failures to anticipate trouble would have happened in Rayburn's Speakership. His intelligence system, bol-
stered by his willingness to listen, almost always warned him in
time. Very few of the serious inconveniences to members and
disruptions of their and their constituent's plans would have
been permitted to occur under Rayburn. Rayburn knew it was
important not to make decisions either too quickly and then be
forced by circumstances to change them, or to change them
cavalierly and without explanation. Very rarely did he postpone
when it was in his power to keep to the schedule announced, and
it is unconceivable that Rayburn would risk losing control of the
House for a whim or a sudden change of mind. He would drive
the House to the limits of its endurance, when it was important
to the nation, but his sense of the House was so acute that he
could feel the subtle changes in atmosphere. He used to say to
me when I asked "How the devil did you know that was going
to happen, Mr. Sam.?" "Dick, if you can't feel things you can
neither see nor hear, you don't belong in this business." It can be
said fairly that Speaker McCormack couldn't understand the significance of things that he both saw and heard. By now Speaker
McCormack's incompetence was beyond dispute to most Democrats, to most Republicans (who prospered by it nevertheless),
and to most in the press gallery.

The first session of the Ninetieth Congress ended December 15, 1967, 340 days after it had begun; only twelve others had lasted longer. The authoritative *Congressional Quarterly* reported that the conservative coalition had won more victories than in any year since the weekly periodical began to measure its performance in 1957. Less than half of President Johnson's requests had been approved.

CONCLUSION TO CHAPTER 6

The second session was not much different. Its three major legislative accomplishments were primarily the result of events external to the House. Action on both the landmark open housing civil rights bill of 1968 and the much-delayed tax increase of the same year originated in the Senate. The former's successful passage in the House was greatly affected by the assassination of Martin Luther King. The price of passage in the House of the long overdue 10 per cent tax surcharge, was a spending limit which could only reduce the effectiveness of the programs of health, education, and welfare that were giving some hope to the agonized people of the urban ghettos.

Enactment of the bitterly controversial gun control law was the direct result of the assassination in June of Senator Robert Kennedy, whose violent death, coming so soon after that of Dr. King, galvanized a reluctant Congress into something more than token action.

But after the promises of the Eighty-ninth, the Ninetieth was a disappointment. Why?

First, the 1966 elections had restored real control of the House to the conservative coalition. Forty of the forty-seven House Democrats defeated in that November had been liberals. The simple arithmetic which was to prevail into the succeeding six years, 1969 through 1974, had its effect as well. Take a House with between 240 and 255 nominal Democrats, subtract between 60 and 100 Democrats who vote conservative, and in the absence of very skilled leadership the 218 votes needed for a majority fail to materialize. The workings of the unchecked seniority system added to the difficulties. A Mills of Arkansas, Chairman of Ways and Means, who voted with the conservative coalition in the first session of the Ninetieth Congress 74 per cent of the time on 54 roll calls, would not push President Johnson's request for an unpopular 10 per cent tax surcharge essential to stemming inflation. Nor would Mississippi's Colmer, Chairman of Rules, (with his 85 per cent coalition support record) expedite consideration of concurrence in the Senate's open housing amendments to a minor civil rights bill in the House. Colmer retired from the House at the end of the Ninety-second Congress.

But finally, it must be said quite frankly that Speaker McCormack simply did not have the necessary qualities to be an effective legislative leader of modern Democrats. Wedded to the past, he resisted all reform, internal and external. Even when he supported important programs such as civil rights and the tax increase, his adherence to rigid seniority made him support the placing of these bills' sworn enemies, Colmer and Mills, in the key Chairmanships where they could obstruct action on these same measures. Furthermore, he displayed again and again his lack of legislative skill. Behind-the-scenes discussion of his ineptitudes became a principal topic. In 1967 I publicly urged his retirement. He was to hang on through still another Congress after the Ninetieth, thus serving longer as Speaker than any man in history except Sam Rayburn of Texas.

But McCormack's failures of skill and understanding were playing an important role in the development of the new attitudes which were to bring about the very changes he resisted.

7

Transition in the House
1969–1973

John McCormack, the sometimes great poker player, stood firm in his last two years as Speaker, but change rolled over and around him. Aware that he would not change or help bring about change, modern Democrats devised new strategies. In situations where there was a remedy within the Democratic caucus, they fought for relief there. When the situation demanded alliance with modern Republicans, they drafted their strategy and tactics to enlist their help. It has not been a smooth road. Progress has been uneven with false starts, stops and new starts, and the journey, while well begun, is far from completed. But now there is increasing understanding that not only is change in the House necessary, but it is essential to the survival of our representative government.

In the Preface to my first book about the House (*House Out of Order*, Dutton, 1965) I said, "I believe it is possible to restore representative government to the people of the United States."

When I wrote the first draft of that book in the fall of 1962, I remember asking myself, "How long will it take?" How long for the ills of the Congress and representative government in the United States not only to be described but also to be analyzed? How long after analysis would recognition of those ills become general enough within and without our representative institutions so that action would be begun? And finally, how long after the beginning of remedial action would it be before representative government's health would be restored? The answer I gave myself in 1962 was, a long time, perhaps several generations.

Progress has been swifter than that, in large part because of events in the world outside the Congress which have affected it.

In 1963, scandal forced Bobby Baker's resignation as Secretary to the Senate Majority—the Democratic Majority, which during the Fifties had been led by his patron, Majority Leader Lyndon Johnson, who was Vice President by the time of Baker's resignation.

Representative Tom Johnson, Democrat of Maryland, was convicted under the conflict of interest law.

Then came the scandals of Adam Clayton Powell, black Democratic Representative from Harlem, and his unconstitutional exclusion from the House in early 1967.

And revelations of misdeeds caused Senator Tom Dodd, Democrat of Connecticut, to be censured by the United States Senate.

Both the House and the Senate then acted to establish Ethics Committees to provide and administer Codes of Conduct for their members. The standing Committee on Standards of Official Conduct in the House was the product of the work of a House Rules subcommittee which I chaired. First established in April, 1967, by 1969 its new regulations required all members of the House and their principal employees to disclose their sources of income, with certain limitations. Those provisions have been added to. More still needs to be done.

In 1967 I felt the quickening in the House, but recognized that further reform of the old ways was inhibited by a real, if largely false, belief that the present ways of the House were unalterable —that they had always been that way, never had been changed, and never would be changed.

That recognition led to the crash project which produced the first edition of this book urging the modification of the seniority system by the same caucus reforms as proposed in *House Out of Order*. I began the new book with a short history of the House of Representatives to demonstrate how often and drastically the

House had changed its methods of organization and operation over the less than 200 years of its existence.

Developing and enforcing ethical codes for members went forward slowly. Even more slowly—imperceptibly in fact to nearly everyone on the outside of the House and most people in it—patterns were being broken on the inside. In 1961 the first great legislative fight of the Kennedy Administration had been the packing of the House Committee on Rules. That achievement modified the seniority system by depriving its beneficiaries of absolute control of the traffic cop committee of the House. The workings of blind seniority would not be allowed to block the wishes of the House leadership on the new President's legislative program.

In 1965 the pattern was broken again. Two Democratic Congressmen, John Bell Williams of Mississippi and Albert Watson of South Carolina, who had supported Republican Barry Goldwater for President, were deprived of their seniority on their respective committees.

In 1966 and 1967 not only was Congressman Powell rightfully denied his chairmanship of the Committee on Education and Labor for his misdeeds in that position, but he was wrongfully denied his seat in the Congress itself.

Also, the accession of Congressman William Colmer of Mississippi to the position of Chairman of the House Rules Committee was challenged by a majority of the Democratic Study Group in a bitter fight which I led. While Colmer did become Chairman, he paid a great price. In order to assure his selection as Chairman, he agreed to give up most of the Chairman's personal power to obstruct liberal legislation, a power enjoyed and much used by his predecessor, Howard Smith of Virginia. Smith was defeated in the 1966 primary. The price Colmer paid was to agree that the Rules Committee have written rules of procedure and meet once a week. Thus the obstructive power of its Chairman was reduced by 90 per cent.

More and more the Democratic Study Group leaders, staff and members concerned themselves with internal procedures and their reform. In 1968 their Chairman, James O'Hara of Michigan, negotiated an agreement with Speaker McCormack requiring the Democratic caucus to have regular monthly meetings. The national Democrats, the modern Democrats of the D.S.G., were beginning to realize the potential of the power they might wield there. And, too, they were beginning to realize that they could work on common causes with like-minded Republican members, a minority whose reformist frustrations were even greater than their own.

At this time, too, the contest over the bitterly divisive war in Southeast Asia was moving off the streets and into the Congress. Doves on the outside as well as on the inside of Congress were learning that if they wanted record votes on End-the-War Amendments they must interest themselves in internal procedural change. In like fashion, consumer advocate Ralph Nader and his activist followers became involved in internal reform. The League of Women Voters and Common Cause had also joined those old-line organizations like the AFL-CIO and the Leadership Conference on Civil Rights, which had supported the earliest reform efforts in pushing for inside reform of the Congress, and for reorganization and modernization of its ancient ways.

Most important of all was the support of these groups for new laws providing for strict control and public accounting of all aspects of the financing of all federal election campaigns.

In 1970, finally, after years of effort the Sisk (B. F. Sisk, D.–Calif.) Subcommittee of the House Rules Committee, of which I was a member, produced a viable vehicle for the passage of the Legislative Reorganization Act of 1970—the first such act to become law since 1946. It provided for a whole series of modernizations in organization and procedure, including better research support, electronic voting, and the introduction of television and radio to House Committee proceedings. Its consideration led to the most far-reaching and significant of modern changes in House rules, the so-called record teller vote, an amendment adopted in the House which stipulates, for the first time in the history of the country, that each member's vote be recorded at the earliest stage of the amending process.

In May, 1970, John McCormack announced his retirement as Speaker at the end of that term. A year and a half before, Congressman Morris Udall of Arizona had courageously challenged McCormack's reelection as Speaker. While Udall did not get many votes, in much the same way as I had had few vocal supporters when I suggested in 1967 that McCormack retire at the end of that Congress, he made the point.

In early 1970 Congressman Jerome Waldie (D.–Calif.) had introduced a resolution in the Democratic caucus expressing lack of confidence in McCormack. For tactical reasons the resolution was tabled.

McCormack had discouraged the passage of most of the more important provisions of the Reorganization Act and in fact had not shown any willingness to encourage any action on the whole subject.

By contrast his Majority Leader and successor as Speaker, Carl Albert of Oklahoma, had been most helpful and encouraging to those seeking change, reform, and reorganization in the House. Albert actively supported the Reorganization Act and the record teller amendment.

In 1971, as he became Speaker, he played his cards very carefully. In the first caucuses of that Congress he supported modest changes in the seniority system, making those members proposed as committee chairmen by the Democratic Committee on Committees subject to a vote of acceptance or rejection by the full membership of the Democratic caucus if ten members challenged the nomination.

On the other hand, when the nomination of South Carolina's John McMillan as Chairman of the House District of Columbia Committee was challenged, Albert voted to continue him as Chairman and the attempt to unseat him failed 126 to 96.

Albert suffered a defeat which, while not of his making, he was powerless to prevent when a key vacancy on the Democratic side of the Committee on Ways and Means was filled by the reactionary, Nixon-supporting Joe D. Waggonner, Jr. of Louisiana, who defeated outgoing D.S.G. Chairman Donald Fraser of Minnesota. That defeat was doubly important because it was not only a lost opportunity to strengthen the national Democratic component on this key committee, with its legislative jurisdiction over Social Security, tax-writing, and foreign trade. It also weakened the national Democratic majority on the Democratic Committee on Committees, whose role in recommending all other Democratic committee members is second in importance to its legislative function.

Throughout 1971 and 1972 the new Speaker generally but cautiously encouraged the development of the Democratic caucus as a Democratic policy-making instrument. When a major issue such as the Federal Election Campaign Act of 1971 presented itself, he used his great influence to ensure its consideration and enactment. But during those two years Speaker Albert was consolidating the power in his new position. He was learning the several aspects of his new role just as the national Democrats were beginning to learn theirs. And his role, like theirs, was both complicated and subtle. The Speaker understood the various parts of his role and their different limitations better than did most of his national Democratic colleagues. He knew he was the only constitutional officer on Capitol Hill and that he was the Speaker of the whole House—Republicans and Democrats and Independents together. Speaker Albert knew that he was also the leader of a bitterly divided party—divided on the Vietnam war —divided on domestic policy issues—and struggled to reconcile those differing aspects of his role.

The D.S.G. members learned more slowly. They exploited successfully the opportunities of coalition legislative action with their like-minded Republican colleagues on the Reorganization Act and its amendments and on the Federal Election Campaign Act. But they were not sure how much power they could use, or exactly what limitations there were on their developing reform majority in the Democratic caucus and on the somewhat different membership of the antiwar majority in the same place. But they learned and they kept trying.

Change in the House had arrived.

More was to come.

But not yet enough.

8

To Restore
Representative Government

Late in 1972, as the Ninety-second Congress was struggling to adjourn for the November election, the House passed, but the Senate failed to accept, the spending limit for fiscal year 1973 (July 1, 1972 to June 30, 1973) of 250 billion dollars requested by President Nixon. When agreement was not reached on a version acceptable to both House and Senate, legislation was passed setting up a Joint House-Senate Committee to study the question of spending control and overall Congressional action on budgetary matters.

Soon after the election, a group of D.S.G. leaders and members began a series of meetings to devise and perfect strategy and tactics for further modifications of the seniority system and the rules and methods of organization in the committee system. Also under discussion was the question of establishing a new Democratic Steering and Policy Committee. During the Ninety-second Congress, D.S.G. had had its most aggressive and activist chairman, Phillip Burton of California. Burton's tremendous energy and overwhelming drive was balanced by the influence of an experienced and able staff, led by the veteran Richard Conlon. D.S.G. membership had increased, its service to its members had grown, and in sum it was feeling its muscle.

Although the Vietnam war was still a major issue in the first caucuses of the new Congress in early January, 1973, it had already wound down enough so that it did not dominate those sessions.

When the smoke of battle cleared several months later, seniority had been further modified. Now, each nominee for a committee chairmanship was subjected to a secret ballot vote of acceptance or rejection. None was rejected, but some received rather large negative votes.

Committee organization and procedures had been modified substantially in an effort to obtain greater legislative responsibility and opportunity for newer members. Also, rules were passed seeking to assure less secrecy in the proceedings of all committees and a modification in the use of closed or gag rules. The Speaker, Carl Albert, the Majority Leader, Thomas P. (Tip) O'Neill, and the Caucus Chairman, Olin E. (Tiger) Teague of Texas, were added to the fifteen Democratic members of the Ways and Means Committee to form an enlarged Democratic Committee on Committees, and a new Democratic Steering and Policy Committee was established.

All these proceedings were important, but other significant actions were taking place in different arenas at the same time. Soon after the election, Speaker Albert, as a matter of highest priority, saw to it that the new members of the crucial Rules Committee would be people who usually supported the Democratic majority's legislative program and could be relied on to be loyal to him. When it became clear that the new Majority Leader, O'Neill, a long-time member of Rules, would leave that Committee, there were three vacancies to fill, for Chairman Colmer had retired and William R. Anderson of Tennessee had not been reelected. After a long and bitter, but largely hidden struggle, the Speaker got what he wanted. Morgan Murphy of Illinois, Gillis Long of Louisiana, and Clem McSpadden, a new member from the Speaker's own state of Oklahoma, were elected to fill those vacancies.

Also established at the Speaker's request, with the full cooperation of Minority Leader Gerald Ford, was a bipartisan Select Committee on Committees to study and to recommend reorganization of the jurisdiction and operation of "the little legislatures" of the House, its committees. I was selected as Chairman of that committee. My opposite number as Vice Chairman is my friend, co-worker and also the senior Republican on the Rules Committee, Dave Martin of Nebraska.

Not long after the establishment of the Select Committee, the Joint Study Committee on Budget Control made an earlier-than-expected report recommending the formation of a standing Joint Committee on the Budget.

In the meantime President Nixon impounded billions of dollars in funds for a variety of programs for which Congress had appropriated money. In some cases the effect of the President's impoundment action actually sought to abolish programs created by the Congress. Individuals and committees in the House and the Senate proposed various anti-impoundment bills.

There were increasingly obvious and numerous clashes between the Congress and the Executive over these matters. Although all American troops were withdrawn and American POWs returned from Vietnam early in 1973, the cease-fire in Southeast Asia was by no means completely effective.

Continued American bombing in Cambodia deprived the President of his last effective support in the Congress for longer direct American military involvement in Southeast Asia. Even before the first polls showed that American public opinion opposed the continuation of the bombing in Cambodia, the brand-new Democratic Steering and Policy Committee, by an overwhelming vote, recommended passage of an antibombing resolution in the House. This soon followed and the ultimate result was the Executive-Congressional compromise of late June, 1973, which finally approved ending American military involvement in that tragic and bloody region.

But by that time the urgent necessity of restoring representative government by revitalizing the Congress, and in particular the House, was made shockingly and unmistakably clear by the revelations of Watergate. That a sitting President's friends and intimate associates could plot and carry out schemes to subvert the political process of this country for partisan purposes came as a shock equal to the sudden glare of the atomic era to all Americans, voter and nonvoter, Republican, Democrat, and Independent alike.

No series of events could more completely prove the absolute necessity of reforming and modernizing the methods of operation of the House.

There has been change in the last few years.

There will be more change in this Congress.

But will it be enough?

Will the Congress as a whole meet the challenge of having a responsible budgetary process? It must if the American economy is to prosper, because our ability to maximize employment and minimize inflation depends in large measure on the soundness of the Federal budgetary process.

Will the bipartisan Select Committee I chair be able to devise and to pass through the House the changes in jurisdiction, organization, and operation of the committees of the House which will enable us to anticipate and thus to prevent the riots of the cities of yesterday, the energy crisis of today and the Vietnams or even worse of tomorrow?

Will the new Democratic Steering and Policy Committee, the new control of the critical Rules Committee give the elected leaders of the Democratic party the instruments to build an effective legislative team so that the choice between party policies will be made clear to the American people?

Will the reforms within the Republican party as well as the Democratic party of the House enable the combined leadership of the House, the Alberts and the Fords of today and of the future, to work together to strengthen the people's branch—the House—the last place where each individual American, each minor interest, can expect not to be ignored?

New tools, new techniques of all sorts are needed.

But I still believe, as I have for so long, that an essential element still lacking amidst all the change taking place, is a more observable, responsible, and accountable power placed in the hands of the leadership of the seemingly perpetual majority party in the House, the Democrats.

Aside from an emergency, the House has effectively functioned only when there was a harmony between the purposes of the party and the means to achieve these purposes. Such a situation prevailed during the Speakerships of Clay, Reed, and Cannon and during the dual administration of Speaker Clark and Majority Leader Underwood.

There is no suggestion that there be a return to "King Caucus" or "Czar Speaker." It would be undesirable to impose the kind of party discipline which has been the rule in the modern British Parliament, whose members are now struggling to break their bondage. Dissent must not be stifled in the Democratic party. No member shall be subject to greater coercion than now exists. This country is too large and diverse to attempt to homogenize either party. Surely there is no reason, however, why a distillation, impervious to gross abuses, of the best in the historical caucus and the best in the historical Speakership cannot be made.

By 1908, the power of the Speakership had developed autocratic traits. Members were held back from genuine disagreement out of fear that they would lose their desired committee assignments and fair treatment for their bills. It does not seem dangerous to me now, however, to restore a modified grant of power to the Speaker. Each Democratic member would then bear increased responsibility, and accountability, for shaping the nature and design of his party's leadership. No member should be able to evade responsibility to his constituents by explaining his party's legislative failures on the grounds of the method of committee assignments or seniority.

The titular Democratic leader of the House, be he Speaker or Minority Leader, should become the operating head of the legislative apparatus. There his power would be observable and responsible and, therefore, accountable.

According to the prevailing situation, the House Democratic caucus, on the eve of the opening of each new Congress, select its leadership. When the Democratic party is in the majority, its candidate for Speaker, by rule of numbers, is in effect elected when he is first nominated in party caucus. The "election" of Speaker between nominees of both parties in a floor contest is a sham, of course. Conversely, if the Democrats are the minority party, their candidate for Speaker is defeated on the floor and becomes the floor leader or *Minority Leader* of the party.

According to custom, Democratic members of the Committee on Ways and Means from the previous Congress are assured re-election to the Committee in the new Congress. If there are vacancies by death or retirement or defeat, they are filled by majority vote in the caucus. These Democratic members, plus now the Speaker, the Majority Leader, and the Caucus Chairman, in turn acting as the Committee on Committees, select other Democrats to sit on the other standing committees. But these Democrats, *i.e.*, committee members, too, by seniority, are virtually assured re-appointment on the same committees on which they sat in the last Congress, unless they themselves request reassignment. These committee assignments are then submitted to the full House for ratification, a *pro forma* act, as in the case of the Speakership "contest."

These procedures should be revised so that:

1. The member selected in caucus for Speaker (or Minority Leader as the case may be) shall have the sole power to nominate the following:

   a) All the Democratic members of the Committee on Ways and Means and its Chairman (or ranking minority member, as the case may be).

   b) All the Democratic members of Rules and its Chairman (or ranking minority member as the case may be).

2. After these nominations are made in caucus, a vote will be taken to confirm such nominees by majority vote. No nomination may be made from the floor. In the event that the majority rejects one or more of the nominees, the party leader will submit as many nominations as are necessary to fill the assignments.

3. The members approved for appointment to Ways and Means will continue to act as the Committee on Committees with the three party leaders. At a subsequent caucus, they will submit their nominations for seats on the other committees. Approval will be by majority vote. If one or more nominations are rejected in the caucus, the Committee on Committees will submit fresh nominees until all vacancies are filled.

4. The top leader, be he the Speaker or Minority Leader, will now nominate the chairman or ranking minority member for each standing committee. If one or more are rejected, as in the other proceedings, he will continue to make nominations until all necessary appointments are approved.

A new rule should be adopted by the House to assign to each party in its caucus (Democrats) or conference (Republicans) the ultimate power to assign members to committees. This would formally recognize what is now practice.

The change would modify the rule of seniority. Length of service, realistically, would remain a prime factor in distributing assignments. The implied disciplinary factor in the new procedure, however, would make the obstructionist wary of persisting in his conduct.

The power to nominate members of Ways and Means and Rules and to select committee chairmen would restore a needed measure of authority to the Speakership. It would also reintroduce an element of accountability. No longer could a Speaker blame the District of Columbia Committee for not passing out a local suffrage bill or Ways and Means for not reporting out a tax or Medicare bill. The Speaker would be obliged to answer as to why he did not change the membership of the Committee on Committees or change committee chairmen, or both, so as to achieve party objectives.

The revision also contains a built-in hedge against abuse by an autocratic Speaker. His power would be offset by the right of a majority in caucus to reject his nominations to committees and to chairmanships. In turn, the caucus is held in check because it cannot make nominations from the floor.

The revision does not interfere with the right of a member to vote his conscience. There would be no change in the requirement that a two-thirds vote is required to bind members on issues. Even then, a member is not bound to such a caucus decision if he announces to the caucus at the time that he believes the proposal to be contrary to the Constitution or that he has already committed himself in contrary fashion to his constituents.

The purpose in the revisions, therefore, is to make assignments to committees representative of the position of a majority of the Democrats in the House. It couples this equity with other advantages: the leadership and rank-and-file members are made accountable and responsible. The majority of the Democratic party has every reason to demand that its legislative proposals be discussed, debated, and voted on by the full House without undue delay or without the obstructionism that prevents voting on these major issues.

There is no implication here that the Democrats be a "rubber stamp" for a Democratic president. It would be expected that the two would be on better than speaking terms. There is no reason, however, that the House Democrats in caucus could not review a President's legislative program, particularly with a view to assigning priorities to individual items. Reform of the House and the removal of its ineffective leaders and of the chairmen hostile to their own party platform have been too long delayed.

Is it to be denied that the pressures on our cities and on our schools and the effluence of our polluted environment would be less aggravated if the House had been properly organized during the last thirty years? Properly organized, the House's Howard Smiths could not have arbitrarily killed off school aid and housing and civil rights in the 1940s, 1950s, and early 1960s? Or if Mills had not been allowed to sit on Medicare until 1965? Is it not possible that Congress would be a more respected body today, if it, not the Supreme Court, had outlawed malapportioned Congressional districts and a disastrously discriminatory school system?

Is the Congress to continue as the least responsible organ of Government, acting, if at all, ten and twenty and thirty years late? Is the essential well-being of the nation dependent on a political landslide every generation? Or will the nation improve itself by means of other institutions and, thereby, push the Congress to the outskirts of American society?

Education, social justice, and a healthy environment are measures of a decent, prosperous society. A majority of the Democratic party in the House has permitted its minority Tories to obstruct, damage, and deflate those fundamental strengths. Alien ideologies hold parliamentary institutions in contempt. Representative assemblies are seen as reflecting oppressive forces of capitalism. Emerging nations can be persuaded that parliamentary institutions are a sham and elections a mere reshuffling of political hierarchies. In still another sense, then, it is important to the United States that Congress be responsible, effective, and responsive.

A comparable state of affairs would not be tolerated in the kitchens, faculty rooms, or boardrooms of America. It is tolerated in the United States House of Representatives, however. It is, of course, not a case of "white hats" versus "black hats." In Congress, men of sincerity, purpose, and ability contest among themselves for social purposes. We of a moderately liberal view should not, however, insist that we handcuff ourselves during the battles. Battles are difficult enough without unwarranted restraints.

This book was designed to instruct, not to please. It is written, however, with awareness of the tricky thickets of politics wherein ambushes are laid.

In a remarkable series of two articles in the British periodical *Encounter* in 1967, Henry Fairlie wrote:

> Politics is not a prize-giving or a garden fête. It is the attempt to reconcile the all too discordant appetites, wills, interests and aspirations of men—whether men in the mass, in society . . . or [as] individual men in the closets of power—in no more than the hope that any decision will be at least in the direction of the people's good. It is dirty work in the engine room.

It is untidy, too. Progress is often ephemeral, frustrating, deceptive. One legislative solution generates another problem. If the ends of politics and political parties seem certain in this book, I realize the means are often uncertain. What is asked is a fair shake and fair shares for the majority of the House Democratic party. If my judgments seem harsh, I fully realize that the tasks are difficult and poorly defined and our constituencies often hazardous.

> Politicians, then [wrote Fairlie], begin with recalcitrant material; resources which are limited; human wills which are unpredictable and human emotions which are more so. . . . He cannot remove obstinate human wills; he cannot destroy inter-

ests which he finds inconvenient. . . . He is a potter who cannot choose his own clay, a painter who cannot mix his own paints, a composer who must score for a brass band what he had perhaps intended for a string quartet. That is the measure of his art.

The first task of a politician, therefore, is to try to reconcile the multiplicity of conflicting interests and wills, which exist in any free society.

The difficulties should not be overdrawn, however.

The House can be made to work. The House must be made to work. It is now clear that what is at stake is the survival of the very process by which we govern ourselves. Our government of divided powers obviously cannot survive if the most representative of its branches cannot maintain its place and its share of the powers. Unless the Congress works better it will be abandoned by the people. Should that happen, it is inevitable that the people will lose their freedom to some form of Executive Government. That cannot be allowed to happen.

An essential to survival of the representative process in America lies in organizing the power of the Democratic party in the House of Representatives so that it is observable, responsible, and accountable. The place to do that is in the caucus of Democrats preceding the opening of the next Congress in January of 1975.

Appendix

ON THE FLOOR OF THE HOUSE

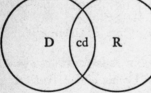

R + cd = A working Republican majority
on the floor of the House.

IN DEMOCRATIC CAUCUS

D − cd = A working Democratic
majority in the caucus.

Legend
D - moderate to liberal Democrats
R - Republicans
cd - conservative Democrats

Bibliography

Adams, Sherman. *Firsthand Report: The Story of the Eisenhower Administration*. New York, Harper & Brothers, 1961.

Agar, Herbert. *The Price of Power*. Chicago, University of Chicago Press, 1957.

Alexander, De Alva Stanwood. *History and Procedures of the House of Representatives*. Boston and New York, Houghton Mifflin Company, 1916.

Allen, Frederick Lewis. *The Big Change: America Transforms Itself: 1900–1950*. New York, Harper & Brothers, 1952.

Allen, Robert S., and William V. Shannon. *The Truman Merry-Go-Round*. New York, The Vanguard Press, Inc., 1950.

Arnett, Alex Mathews. *Claude Kitchin and the Wilson War Policies*. Boston, Little, Brown & Company, 1937.

Bailey, Stephen Kemp. *Congress Makes a Law*. New York, Columbia University Press, 1950.

Bates, Ernest Sutherland. *Story of Congress*. New York, Harper & Brothers, 1936.

Beard, Charles A. *American Government and Politics*. New York, The Macmillan Company, 1925.

Bentham, Jeremy. *Theory of Legislation*. London, Oxford University Press, 1914.

Berstein, B. J., and A. J. Matuson. *Truman Administration: A documentary history*. New York, Harper & Row, 1966.

Blaine, J. G. *Twenty Years of Congress, from Lincoln to Garfield*. 2 Vols. Norwich, Henry Bill Publishing Company, 1884–1886.

Bloom, Sol. *The Autobiography of Sol Bloom*. New York, G. P. Putnam's Sons, 1948.

Brogan, D. W. *Government of the People, A Study in the American Political System*. New York, Harper & Brothers, 1943.

Brown, George Rothwell. *The Leadership of Congress*. Indianapolis, The Bobbs-Merrill Company, Inc., 1922.

Brown, George Rothwell. *The Speaker of the House: The Romantic Story of John N. Garner*. New York, Brewer, Warren & Putnam, 1932.

Brown, Stuart Gerry. *The American Presidency*. New York, The Macmillan Company, 1966.

Bryce, James. *American Commonwealth*. 2 Vols. New York, The Macmillan Company, 1921–1922.

Buckley, William F. *The Committee and Its Critics*. New York, G. P. Putnam's Sons, 1962.

Burnham, James. *Congress and the American Tradition*. Chicago, Henry Regnery Company, 1965.

Burns, James MacGregor. *Congress on Trial*. New York, Harper & Brothers, 1949.

Burns, James. *The Deadlock of Democracy*. Englewood Cliffs, N.J., Prentice-Hall, Inc., 1963.

Cannon, Clarence. *Cannon's Procedure in the House of Representatives*. Washington, D.C., Government Printing Office, 1944.

Carroll, Holbert N. *The House of Representatives and Foreign Affairs*. Pittsburgh, University of Pittsburgh Press, 1958.

Cater, Douglass, *Power in Washington*. New York, Random House, Inc., 1964.

Celler, Emanuel. *You Never Leave Brooklyn*. New York, The John Day Company, Inc., 1953.

Chevalier, Michael. *Society, Manners and Politics in the United States*. Garden City, Anchor Books, Doubleday & Company, Inc., 1961.

Chiu, Chang-wei. *The Speaker of the House of Representatives since 1896*. New York, Columbia University Press, 1928.

Clark, Champ. *My Quarter Century of American Politics*. New York, Harper & Brothers, 1920.

Clay, Henry. *Life and Speeches of Henry Clay*. 2 Vols. New York, Greeley & McElrath, 1843.

Coolidge, Calvin. *The Autobiography of Calvin Coolidge*. New York, Cosmopolitan Book Corp., 1929.

Croly, Herbert. *Progressive Democracy*. New York, The Macmillan Company, 1915.

Cox, James M. *Journey Through My Years*. New York, Simon and Schuster, Inc., 1946.

De Chambrun, Clara Longworth. *The Making of Nicholas Longworth*. New York, Ray Long & Richard R. Smith, Inc., 1933.

Dorough, C. Dwight. *Mr. Sam*. New York, Random House, Inc., 1962.

Dos Passos, John. *Mr. Wilson's War.* New York, Doubleday & Company, Inc., 1966.

Faulkner, Harold U. *From Versailles to the New Deal, A Chronicle of the Harding-Coolidge-Hoover Era.* New Haven, Yale University Press, 1950.

Fenno, Richard, Jr. *The President's Cabinet.* Cambridge, Mass., Harvard University Press, 1959.

Follett, Mary P. *The Speaker of the House of Representatives.* New York, Longmans, Green & Co., Inc., 1896.

Fuess, Claude M. *Calvin Coolidge: The Man from Vermont.* Boston, Little, Brown & Company, 1940.

Fuller, Hubert Bruce. *Speakers of the House.* Boston, Little, Brown & Company, 1909.

Galloway, George B. *Congress at the Crossroads.* New York, Thomas Y. Crowell Company, 1946.

Galloway, George B. *History of the House of Representatives.* New York, Thomas Y. Crowell Company, 1961.

Galloway, George B. *The Legislative Process in Congress.* New York, Thomas Y. Crowell Company, 1953.

Goldman, Eric F. *The Crucial Decade: America, 1945–1955.* New York, Alfred A. Knopf, Inc., 1956.

Gross, Bertram. *The Legislative Struggle.* New York, McGraw-Hill Book Company, Inc., 1953.

Gwinn, William Rea. *Uncle Joe Cannon, Archfoe of Insurgency.* New York, Bookman Associates, 1957.

Harlow, Ralph V. *The History of Legislative Methods in the Period before 1825.* New Haven, Yale University Press, 1917.

Hasbrouck, Paul Dewitt. *Party Government in the House of Representatives.* New York, The Macmillan Company, 1927.

Hechler, Kenneth W. *Insurgency, Personalities and Politics of the Taft Era.* New York, Columbia University Press, 1940.

Hehmeyer, Alexander. *Time for Change; a proposal for a second constitutional convention.* New York and Toronto, Farrar & Rinehart, Inc., 1943.

Hinds, Asher C. *Precedents of the House of Representatives.* 8 Vols. Washington, D.C., Government Printing Office, 1907.

Hofstader, Richard. *The American Political Tradition.* New York, Alfred Knopf, Inc., 1948.

House Republican Task Force. *We Propose: A Modern Congress.* New York, McGraw-Hill Book Company, Inc., 1966.

Hull, Cordell. *The Memoirs of Cordell Hull.* 2 Vols. New York, The Macmillan Company, 1948.

Ickes, Harold. *The Secret Diary of Harold Ickes: The First 100 Days —1933–36.* New York, Simon and Schuster, Inc., 1953.

James, Marquis. *Mr. Garner of Texas*. Indianapolis, The Bobbs-Merrill Company, Inc., 1939.

Jefferson's Manual. Washington, D.C. Government Printing Office, 1967.

Judah, Charles, and George W. Smith. *The Unchosen*. New York, Coward-McCann, Inc., 1962.

La Follette, Robert M. *Autobiography*. Madison, Wis., The Robert M. La Follette Company, 1913.

Kaplan, Sheldon. *Eightieth Congress and the United Nations*. Washington, D.C., Government Printing Office, 1948.

Laski, H. J. *A Grammar of Politics*. New Haven, Yale University Press; London, George Allen & Unwin, Ltd., 1925.

Lief, Alfred. *Democracy's Norris, the Biography of a Lonely Crusade*. New York, Stackpole Sons, 1939.

Link, Arthur S. *Wilson: The Road to the White House*. Princeton, N.J., Princeton University Press, 1947.

Lodge, Henry Cabot. *Democracy of the Constitution*. New York, Charles Scribner's Sons, 1915.

Longworth, Alice Roosevelt. *Crowded Hours*. New York, Charles Scribner's Sons, 1933.

Lowitt, Richard. *George W. Norris: The Making of a Progressive, 1861–1912*. Syracuse, N.Y., Syracuse University Press, 1963.

Lubell, Samuel. *The Future of American Politics*. 2d Edition, revised. Garden City, N.Y., Anchor Books, Doubleday & Company, Inc., 1956.

Luce, Robert. *Congress: An Explanation*. Cambridge, Mass., Harvard University Press, 1926.

Luce, Robert. *Legislative Procedure*. Science of Legislation Series, Vol. I. Boston, Houghton Mifflin Company, 1922.

Luce, Robert. *Legislative Assemblies*. Science of Legislation Series, Vol. II. Boston, Houghton Mifflin Company, 1924.

McCoy, Donald R. *Calvin Coolidge, the Quiet President*. New York, The Macmillan Company, 1967.

MacNeil, Neil. *Forge of Democracy*. New York, David McKay Company, Inc., 1963.

Martin, Joe, and Robert J. Donovan. *My First Fifty Years in Politics*. New York, McGraw-Hill Book Company, Inc., 1960.

Mayhill, George Roger. *Speaker Cannon under the Roosevelt Administration, 1903–1907*. Abstract of a doctoral thesis in history. Urbana, Ill., University of Illinois, 1942.

Mellon, Andrew M. *Taxation: The People's Business*. New York, The Macmillan Company, 1924.

Mill, John Stuart. *Considerations on Representative Government*.

People's Edition. London, Longmans, Green & Co., Ltd., 1876.

Miller, Clem. *Member of the House*. New York, Charles Scribner's Sons, 1962.

Moley, Raymond. *After Seven Years*. New York, Harper & Brothers, 1939.

Morison, Samuel E., and H. S. Commager. *The Growth of the American Republic*. New York, Oxford University Press, 1942.

Myers, William S., and Walter H. Newton. *The Hoover Administration: A Document Narrative*. New York, Charles Scribner's Sons, 1936.

Nash, Walter C. *Sam Rayburn, the Congressman of the Fourth District of Texas*. Master's thesis. Commerce, East Texas State Teachers College, 1950.

Nelson, John M. (M.C.) "The Necessity for Parliamentary Reform in the House of Representatives." Reprint of speech delivered Oct. 14, 1908, before City Club of Chicago.

Neustadt, Richard E. *Presidential Power: The Politics of Leadership*. New York, John Wiley & Sons, Inc., 1960.

Nevins, Allan. *Diary of John Quincy Adams*. New York, Longmans, Green & Co., Inc., 1928.

Nixon, Richard M. *Six Crises*. Garden City, N.Y., Doubleday & Company, Inc., 1962.

Norris, George W. *Fighting Liberal: The Autobiography of George Norris*. New York, The Macmillan Company, 1945.

Patterson, James. *Congressional Conservatism and the New Deal*. Lexington, Ky., University of Kentucky Press, 1967.

Pepper, George Wharton. *Family Quarrels: The President-The Senate-The House*. New York, Baker, Voorhis & Co., 1931.

Poore, Ben Perley. *Perley's Reminiscences of Sixty Years in the National Metropolis*. 2 Vols. Philadelphia, Hubbard Bros., 1886.

Pringle, Henry F. *The Life and Times of Wm. Howard Taft*. New York, Farrar & Rinehart, Inc., 1939.

Riddick, Floyd M. *The United States Congress, Organization and Procedure*. Manassas, Va., Capitol Pub., Inc., 1949.

Riddle, Donald W. *Congressman Abraham Lincoln*. Urbana, Ill., University of Illinois Press, 1957.

Robinson, James A. *House Rules Committee*. Indianapolis, The Bobbs-Merrill Company, Inc., 1963.

Robinson, William A. *Thomas B. Reed, Parliamentarian*. New York, Dodd, Mead & Company, Inc., 1930.

Rossiter, Clinton. *Parties and Politics in America*. Ithaca, N.Y., Cornell University Press, 1964.

The Rules of the House of Representatives. Washington, D.C. Government Printing Office, 1967.

Schlesinger, Arthur M., Jr. *The Age of Jackson.* Boston, Little, Brown & Company, 1945.

Schlesinger, Arthur M., Jr. *The Coming of the New Deal.* Boston, Houghton Mifflin Company, 1959.

Schlesinger, Arthur M., Jr. *The Crisis of the Old Order, 1919–1933.* Boston, Houghton Mifflin Company, 1957.

Sherwood, Robert E. *Roosevelt and Hopkins—An Intimate Portrait.* 2 Vols. New York, Harper & Brothers, 1950.

Stoddard, Henry L. *As I Knew Them.* New York and London, Harper & Brothers, 1927.

Stone, Melville E. *Fifty Years a Journalist.* Garden City, N.Y., Doubleday, Page & Company, 1921.

Taussig, Frederick W. *The Tariff History of the United States.* New York, G. P. Putnam's Sons, 1923.

Taylor, Edward T. *History of Committee on Appropriations.* House Document No. 299, 77th Congress, 1st Session, 1941.

Taylor, Eric. *House of Commons at Work.* Baltimore, Penguin Books, Inc., 1961.

Thompson, Charles Willis. *Party Leaders of the Time.* New York, G. W. Dillingham Company, 1906.

Timmons, Bascom N. *Garner of Texas.* New York, Harper & Brothers, 1948.

Tocqueville de, Alexis. *Democracy in America.* 2 Vols. New York, Alfred A. Knopf, Inc., 1945.

Truman, David B. *The Congressional Party, A Case Study.* New York, John Wiley & Sons, Inc., 1959.

Tuchman, Barbara, W. *The Proud Tower.* New York, The Macmillan Company, 1966.

Underwood, Oscar W. *Drifting Sands of Party Politics.* New York, Century Company, 1931.

Vandenberg, Arthur H., Jr. *The Private Papers of Senator Vandenberg.* Boston, Houghton Mifflin Company, 1952.

Voorhis, Jerry. *Confessions of a Congressman.* Garden City, N.Y., Doubleday & Company, Inc., 1947.

Walker, Harvey. *The Legislative Process, Lawmaking in the United States.* New York, The Ronald Press Company, 1948.

Wallas, Graham. *Human Nature in Politics.* London, Constable & Co., Ltd., 1920.

Walworth, Arthur C. *Woodrow Wilson.* 2d Edition. Boston, Houghton Mifflin Company, 1965.

Watson, James E. *As I Knew Them.* Indianapolis, The Bobbs-Merrill Company, Inc., 1936.

Webb, Sidney and Beatrice. *A Constitution for the Socialist Commonwealth of Great Britain.* London, Longmans, Green & Co., Ltd., 1920.

Webb, W. L. *Champ Clark.* New York, Neal Publishing Co., 1912.

Wecter, Dixon. *The Age of the Great Depression.* A History of American Life, Vol. 13. New York, The Macmillan Company, 1948.

Westphal, Albert C. F. *The House Committee on Foreign Affairs.* New York, Columbia University Press, 1942.

White, Theodore H. *The Making of a President, 1960.* New York, Atheneum Press, 1961.

White, William Allen. *A Puritan in Babylon: The Story of Calvin Coolidge.* New York, The Macmillan Company, 1938.

White, William S. *Citadel: The Story of the United States Senate.* New York, Harper & Brothers, 1957.

Wilbur, R. L. and A. M. Hyde. *The Hoover Policies.* New York, Charles Scribner's Sons, 1937.

Wilson, Woodrow. *Congressional Government.* Boston, Houghton Mifflin Company, 1885.

Wolfe, Harold. *Herbert Hoover: Public Servant and Leader of the Loyal Opposition.* New York, Exposition Press, 1956.

Young, James Sterling. *The Washington Community, 1800-1828.* New York, New York University Press, 1966.

Zinn, Howard. *LaGuardia in Congress.* Ithaca, N.Y., Cornell University Press, 1959.

PERIODICALS AND MISCELLANEOUS SOURCES

American Mercury. Vol. 19, January-April 1930.

American Political Science Review. Vol. 44, September-December, 1950.

American Scholar. September, 1966.

Annals of American Academy of Political Science. September, 1953.

Atkinson, C. R., and C. A. Beard. "The Syndication of the Speakership." *Political Science Quarterly* 26:381-414, September, 1911.

Calendars and History of Legislation of House of Representatives. Final Editions at end of each Session.

Catlin, G. E. G. "The Doctrine of Power and Party Conflict." *American Political Science Review* 19:718-34, November, 1925.

Chamber of Commerce of the United States. *Resumé of the 80th Congress, First Session.*

Cooper, Joseph. "Committee Theory and Practice in Congress." Unpublished doctoral dissertation. Harvard University, 1960.

Fairlie, Henry. "Life of Politics." *Encounter* Vol. 28, 25–38, January, 1967.

———. "Lives of Politicians." *Encounter* Vol. 29, 18–37, August, 1967.

Green, W. R. (Chairman of Ways and Means). "How Congress Works." *Saturday Evening Post* 199: No. 24, p. 31, December 11, 1926.

Hinds, Asher C. "The Speaker of the House of Representatives." *American Political Science Review* 3:155ff., May, 1909.

Hoar, G. F. (Senator). "The Conduct of Business in Congress." *North American Review* 128:111–134, February, 1879.

Huntington, Samuel P. "Revised Theory of American Party Politics." *American Political Science Association Review.* Vol. 44, No. 3, 669–677, September, 1950.

Kitchin, Claude. Memorial Address. Sixty-eighth Congress, 2d Session. Washington, D.C., U.S. Government Printing Office, 1925.

New England Magazine. March–August 1904, N.S. 30. March–August 1890, N.S. 2.

Norris, George W. (member of Congress). "The Secret of His Power: A History of the Insurgent Movement in the House of Representatives." *LaFollette's Magazine,* January 8, 1910.

North American Review. July–December, 1890.

Outlook, The. Vol. 96, September–December, 1910.

Pollack, J. K. "The Seniority Rule in Congress." *North American Review* 222:235–45, December, 1925.

Polsby, Nelson W. "Institutionalization of the U.S. House of Representatives." A paper. 1966.

Reed, T. R. "Two Congresses Contrasted." *North American Review* 155:227–36, August, 1892.

United States Congress. *House Reports.* Vol. 9, 1956.

U.S. News & World Report. "An Interview with Sam Rayburn." October 13, 1950.

Western Political Quarterly. Vol. 12, 1959.

NEWSPAPERS

The Boston Globe
The Chicago Tribune
The Dallas Morning News
The New York Herald
The New York Times
The Washington Post

Index